Bride's Quilt (pages 163–171).

A

The magnificent pieced quilt at left is Sunburst I (pages 63–64), one of the three Sunburst patterns featured—each of a different genre. Below is an appliqué quilt, Thistle (pages 100–104), which appears to be a translation of one of the popular crewel patterns of the time.

Heirloom Quilts You Can Make

Maggie Malone

 Sterling Publishing Co. Inc. New York

Library of Congress Cataloging in Publication Data

Malone, Maggie, 1942-
   Heirloom quilts you can make.

   Includes index.
   1. Quilting.   I. Title.
TT835.M348   1984   746.9′7′0973   83-24363
ISBN 0-8069-5508-2
ISBN 0-8069-7838-4 (pbk.)

Edited and Designed by Barbara Busch

Second Printing, 1985

Contents

Introduction

Quilting is traditionally a thrift craft, a method of using up odds and ends of leftover fabric as well as salvageable pieces of worn or outgrown clothing. At a time when, even among the upper classes, women tended to be poorly educated, they took those odds and ends of fabric and created quilts of breathtaking beauty, which show a design talent, imagination and creativity that our best trained artists can envy.

Whenever I see one of those quilts, my fingers itch to make one just like it, or at least use it as a starting point for my own quilt. Unfortunately, my reference books don't include patterns of the quilts shown. Mr. Burton Hobson of Sterling Publishing was receptive to the idea of a pattern book of antique quilts, but I was somewhat dubious when he suggested that I limit the quilts chosen to those made prior to 1850. I didn't think there were enough still in existence to fill a book. You can imagine my surprise and delight when I discovered the marvellous collections our museums have.

I spent six months in travelling, researching and studying collections available in museums across the United States, as well as those in the possession of historical societies and antique dealers. Many of these collections were begun around the turn of the century, before American folk art was yet appreciated as an art form. We owe a debt of gratitude to those foresighted early collectors who helped preserve our quilting heritage.

Most museums have special shows at which they display their quilt collections because they lack the space to display a large number of quilts at all times. One exception to this is the Shelburne Museum in Vermont. They have over six hundred quilts in their collection, two hundred of which are on display at all times.

The fabrics in antique quilts are very fragile and the larger museums have special storage vaults that help preserve the quilt and minimize further deterioration of the fabric. If you are planning to travel to any museum to see its collection, it's a good idea to write in advance and set up an appointment.

The Smithsonian Institution in Washington, D.C. has a large collection of quilts as well as other needlework, including samplers, embroidery, crochet and weaving. Most of their collection has been photographed and you can buy slides or photographs of any of these works for a very reasonable fee (this also applies to most of the other large museums).

The DAR Museum, also in Washington, D.C., has a very nice collection of quilts. They have a slide program available on quilting for presentation to small groups for a modest fee of $7.50 a month (as of 1983). The presentation contains 61 slides, depicting just about every type of quilting, along with a brief text sheet explaining each slide.

Large and small collections can be found across the United States. The Denver Art Museum has over 300 quilts. Other museums with sizeable collections are the Newark Museum in New Jersey; the Brooklyn Museum, The Museum of American Folk Art and The Metropolitan Museum of Art in New York City; The Henry Ford Museum in Dearborn, Michigan; The Kentucky History Museum and the Arizona Heritage Center in Tucson. I apologize for any omissions, but these are the ones that immediately come to mind.

In your search for quilts, don't overlook your local historical society. Many of them have a surprising number of quilts in their collections, and even if the quilts are in storage, the societies are usually very generous in making them available to the public (provided, of course, that you make an appointment).

My most pleasant and memorable experiences were with the personnel of historical societies. They were warm, friendly people who went out of their way to be helpful, not because I am a writer who would include some of their quilts in my book, but because it is their general policy. Lois Dater, a curator at the Stamford Historical Society in Stamford, Connecticut, told me of a lady from New Hampshire who had seen a picture of one of their quilts and wanted to reproduce it. She wasn't able to draft a complete pattern from the picture, so the quilt was made available to her so that she could draft a pattern from the original.

My visit to the Geauga County Historical Society's Century Village in Burton, Ohio was one of the highlights of my research trips. The Village is a collection of 20 buildings from the early days of settlement in the Western Reserve. All the personnel are volunteers who devote their time and talents to the restoration and preservation process. The day we visited it, our guide was Judith Sheridan, a member of the Board of Trustees. Mrs. Sheridan exemplifies the type of volunteers they have available. In addition to involving herself in the business affairs of the Village, she is very knowledgeable in the field of antiques, has acquired many pieces for Century Village and helps in the restoration of the pieces as well as in the finishing of the buildings open to the public. She did a beautiful job stencilling a room in one of the restored houses. The day we visited, she was also scheduled to teach a group of children basket weaving.

Since she wasn't sure where the quilts were stored, we got a brief tour through five buildings. Weaving was being featured at the time, and each interior incorporated several weavings as part of the decor. We finally located the storeroom in the attic of one of the restored houses. As we climbed the dusty stairs, I saw stacks and stacks of boxes and trunks brimming over with every type of needlework imaginable. I only had glimpses of this gold mine as we passed through in search of the trunks which contained the quilts. Oh, how I wished I had the time to go through all those other boxes.

Mrs. Sheridan spent several hours with us going through the collection, helping me select and date the quilts chosen.

From the hundreds of quilts I examined, I had to choose less than fifty for inclusion in the final book. The appeal of a pattern is a highly personal matter, and of course, my own likes and dislikes made the final choices. I have tried to select a broad range of designs and techniques. The overriding consideration was space, so that only a few very involved patterns could be included. For example, in the section on Album quilts, I was able to select only a few blocks from the Baltimore quilts shown because they are so intricate that you could fill a book with only two quilts. In a few instances, I show more than one version of the same pattern so you can see how different quiltmakers took a design and made it uniquely their own.

I would like to take this opportunity to thank the museums and their personnel for their help and interest. I would also like to thank my husband, Larry R. London, who travelled with me and served as photographer when museum photos were not available.

Some Basics About Quilting

SELECTING FABRICS

Just about every type of fabric imaginable has been used for quiltmaking. In the 1700's, the highly prized Indian chintzes were the favorite fabric of quiltmakers. However, these fabrics were expensive, and, therefore, used only for "best" quilts. Every little scrap was utilized in some way. Utility tops were often made from wool with linsey-woolsey backings. As a testament to the durability of wool, many examples have survived to the present and can be seen in museums around the country.

Velvets, velveteens, silks and satins have been used at different times, but the fragility of these fabrics limits their use to special quilts that will not see hard wear.

The favored fabric for quiltmaking, however, is 100% cotton. Its smooth, soft finish allows the needle to glide through the quilt easily during both the piecing and quilting processes. But cotton is not always easy to come by and even when it is available, your choice may be limited as to colors and prints. My personal preference is for the cotton/polyester blends. They are always available, come in a wide range of colors and prints, and work up beautifully. Over the years, my experience has been that they wear well, don't shrink and don't fade. And in spite of all the horror stories and advice to the contrary, I never preshrink fabric. On this point, I would not think of advising you not to preshrink; I am just stating that I never have. I may be sorry someday, but so far so good.

Quilting is known primarily as a scrap craft and worn-out clothing has often been used for this purpose. In recent years, even blue jeans and T-shirts have been used for making special memory quilts for children. When using worn clothing, however, be sure to use only those portions that are not worn. You're going to put a lot of work into your quilt and any borderline pieces of cloth will wear out before the rest of the quilt.

Buying fabric for a quilt can get expensive, so when you come across sales be sure to buy as much fabric as you can. Discount stores generally have lower prices than your local fabric shop. Check around for remnant stores. These stores sell first-quality goods that have been discontinued by the manufacturer or overstocked. In those areas near manufacturers, you frequently can find outlet stores that have fantastic prices on fabric. One of my favorite sources for fabric is sheets. They are periodically on sale at considerable savings and the white and pastel colors are great for background fabric.

TEMPLATES

Your template is your most important tool in making a quilt. It must be accurate to ensure that the fabric pieces go together properly. My first step is always to make a full-size drawing of the block, using the pattern pieces given, to be sure that they are correct. This is quicker than making a sample block. I can make any corrections necessary on the drawing before making my templates.

Templates can be made from heavy cardboard backed with sandpaper to prevent slippage or from plastic that is backed with sandpaper. The plastic is a better material since it doesn't wear down with use.

To make a template, trace the pattern piece onto white typing paper. Glue the paper to your template material and cut it out. When adding the seam allowance, you have two choices. Once you have drawn the pattern onto the white paper, you can add the seam allowance before you cut out the template. The template will then include the seam allowance, and when cutting, you just cut on the line drawn. The second method is to make your template the exact size of the finished pattern piece. Trace around it on the fabric, spacing the patterns far enough apart to allow for a seam allowance when cutting. Your cut piece will show the seamline, giving you a guide for sewing.

Marking the Quilt Top

For many patterns, quilting along each side of the seamline will bring out the pattern to best advantage. In this case, no marking is necessary. For straight lines, you can use dressmaker's carbon and a tracing wheel, or even a carpenter's chalk line. For the chalk line, have someone hold one end of the line, and pull it across the top. Hold your end down tightly and shape the line. The nice thing about both of these methods is that they wash out easily. In fact, the chalk may disappear too easily, flaking off before the quilting is completed.

For more intricate designs, use a template and a soft lead pencil. Better yet, try a dressmaker's pencil. It always washes out.

Assembling the Quilt

Lay the top wrong-side-up on a large, flat surface. I've found the floor to be the most convenient place. Spread the batting over the top and smooth it out.

Seam the backing fabric together to the width of the quilt top, plus one inch or two inches all around. This extra allowance is especially important when doing machine quilting. The extra margin allows for any shifting of the fabric as you sew.

Hand Quilting. Baste the three layers together diagonally from corner to corner, then three or four rows up and down the quilt and crosswise. The quilt is now ready to be placed in the frame.

The quilting stitch is a small running stitch, 10 to 15 stitches to the inch. Pull the thread through so that the end is in the batting. Take a small backstitch, bringing the needle to the top.

Push the needle through to the back, bring it up a short distance away, and repeat, following your quilting lines.

Machine Quilting. First, do not baste the layers of the quilt together. My experience has been that the fabric tends to pile up on the basting stitches, causing puckers and ripples. By cutting the fabric slightly larger for the back, I can smooth the top in front of the presser foot, taking out any wrinkles as I sew.

Second, loosen the pressure on the presser foot. This helps cut down on shifting and pushing of the fabric, which is the major problem in machine quilting.

A large table on which to sew is an absolute must. It helps keep the quilt flat, cutting down on the amount of shifting you will experience. Position your machine at one end of the table so you can spread the quilt out.

Slide the edge of the quilt under the presser foot and roll it up to the center. The center section is the most difficult because so much fabric is rolled under the machine. As you move out towards the edges, it gets easier. Following the quilting line from the center, stitch to the outer edge of the quilt, smoothing the fabric as you go. Do two or three rows in this direction, then turn the quilt and go in the opposite direction. This alternating technique helps keep the quilt smooth and flat.

If your top is of a simple design that requires only straight-line stitching, you can start at one end of the quilt and work to the other end. In this case, the backing fabric should be longer on the end towards which you are sewing so that any shift in the fabric is covered by the backing when finished. Always start sewing at the same end.

By the Block

This is an easy way to quilt, either by hand or machine, because you are working with only one block at a time. For intricate designs, this method is by far the best, since the block is easy to manipulate under the needle.

Cut the filler the size of the finished block, and if using the sewing machine, cut the backing one inch larger than the block. Otherwise, cut it the same size. Lay the three layers together and quilt in the design, being sure that you do not quilt beyond the seamline into the seam allowance.

To Assemble the Blocks. Turn back the seam allowance of the backing and push the filler out of the way. Lay the quilted blocks with the right sides together and stitch the seams, being sure not to catch in the backing or the filler. Continue adding blocks until the first row is complete, then repeat for each succeeding row. Join the rows in the same manner.

Finishing the Back. Smooth the batting down and trim off any excess. It should meet in the middle of the seam. Smooth one side of the backing down. Turn under the seam allowance on the other seam and lay over the first one. Stitch with a slipstitch.

A really nice finish for the back is to place lattice strips over the seams and stitch in place.

PIECING THE QUILT

Your second most important tool in making a quilt is your iron. When each seam is finished, press it before joining to another seam. The seam allowance is usually pressed to one side. When joining two seams together, press one seam to the left and the other seam to the right. The two pieces will slide right into the seamline making a perfect match.

I do all piecing on the sewing machine. As an example, I will run all of some units through the machine in a long strip, then take the strip to the ironing board to press and cut apart. Since I use a sewing machine, I generally press the seams open rather than to one side.

SETTING THE TOP

The final step in assembling the quilt top is the setting. The simplest method is to alternate plain and pieced blocks. With this setting you only have to piece half as many blocks and you have more space for decorative quilting.

Many designs require that the blocks be set solid to bring out the pattern. Often, a secondary pattern emerges to give added interest to the overall design.

The use of lattice strips to separate the blocks is another popular setting method, especially if the pattern has been executed in scrap fabrics. The lattice strips pull the design together into a coherent whole. And again, you don't need to piece as many blocks because the lattice strips add to the size of the quilt with little additional work.

Many blocks are designed to be set on the diagonal, but you should also try some of your favorite patterns set diagonally. The change of perspective will give you an entirely different quilt.

Lattice strips are also effective on a diagonally set quilt. They can either blend in by being the same color as the background blocks or you can set the design off by using color in the strips. The long lines of solid color enhance and accentuate a diagonal design.

QUILTING

Quilting is the finishing touch to your patchwork top. The primary purpose of the quilting stitches is to hold the three layers of the quilt together, but it has evolved into a highly decorative design element.

A quilt is a sandwich of three layers: the pieced top, the filler, and the backing.

Fillers or Batts

Cotton Batts. This is a cotton material in batt form. It must be closely quilted, with no more than an inch between the quilting lines because the batt will shift and bunch up when washed. It gives a rather flat appearance to the finished quilting.

Bonded Polyester Batts. This is a polyester material which has been treated to hold the fibres together. It is easy to work with since the layers of the batt will not shred or tear, giving a smooth, uniform surface. The finished quilt has a higher loft and the quilting stitches stand out in relief. It need not be quilted as closely as cotton batts; two to four inches is usually sufficient.

Unbonded Batts.   These batts give a very soft, fluffy appearance to the finished quilt. Like the bonded batts, they are easy to work with during the sewing step, but care must be taken when spreading the batt on the top or it will shred, leaving thick and thin spots. You will have to pull off pieces from the thick spots or along the edges to fill in the thin spots. It, too, can be quilted two to four inches apart.

Lining or Backing Fabrics

Your choice is varied as to what you use to back your quilts; yard goods seamed to the width required, flannel, sheets or lightweight blankets are all suitable. You might even try a reversible quilt, piecing both the top and the backing.

Given in memory of Louise Warten Hagan, William James Hagan, Jr. and William James Hagan, III by Mrs. William James Hagan, III. Courtesy Museum of Art, Birmingham, Alabama.

Medallion Quilts

The central medallion style was developed in Europe over a period of several hundred years. During the fifteenth century the practice of embroidering designs onto a ground, cutting them out and appliquéing them onto a larger, more expensive cloth was very popular. This form of needlework was used for bedhangings, covers and draperies up until the seventeenth century when England began importing cotton fabrics from India. The Indian cottons were brilliant and colorfast, a great improvement over European fabrics, which did not stand up well for any period of time.

The Indian fabrics initially had a small market, due largely to their dark red backgrounds. To capture a larger market, in 1662, the East India Company sent English embroidery patterns to be painted on white backgrounds. These English designs were interpreted with an Eastern influence, which made them exotic and highly desirable to the English.

These fabrics were used for everything from carpets to clothing, and became so popular that domestic producers of wool and silk raised an uproar which caused the sale of imported India cottons and chintzes to be forbidden in 1701. The prohibition didn't stop the importation or sale of fabrics from India, and in 1721 another act was passed, which prohibited the use or wear of any calico or cotton materials from India. This act did slow the importation of the cotton fabrics, which, in turn, caused women to hoard and use up every scrap of fabric they had.

Small designs were cut from the scraps and appliquéd to larger pieces of cloth in imitation of the earlier embroidery work. From a distance, it had the look of the earlier embroidered pieces, with only a fraction of the labor involved. As the cloth became scarcer, small pieces were joined to other small pieces to form one large piece, or they were placed in a symmetrical pattern and used as borders around a central panel. The earliest surviving example of such a pieced quilt was made in 1708 and is now in the Victoria and Albert Museum in England.

The colonists who came to the New World brought the tastes and fashions of the Old World with them. The upper classes still followed the dictates of English taste in their clothing and home furnishings. Although plain quilted pieces and even some patchwork—as we know it—was made, the medallion was still the preferred design and remained popular into the early nineteenth century.

The Sally Hobbs quilt on the preceding page is an excellent example of the medallion style. This quilt was made in 1790 by Martha (Sally) Hobbs. She was born in August 1770, the daughter of William Hubbard Hobbs of Merryoaks Plantation, Brunswick County, Virginia. She later married a man named Lucas and moved to Athens, Alabama, where she died in 1850.

The central theme is the Tree of Life, appliquéd to a ribbed white cotton background with cutout motifs taken from copperplate and possibly woodblock-printed fabric. A blue figured, cotton stripe material is used for the bands and scrolls. The cutouts are stitched with a fine buttonhole stitch with additional embroidery to enhance the design. Fine blind-stitching joins the scrollwork to the border.

Certain patterns occur again and again in medallion quilts with the Flying Geese pattern seemingly the favorite of earlier quiltmakers. You can see it in the Framed Medallion quilt and the Peale Medallion quilt, as well as in the example from the Brooklyn Museum of Art on the facing page.

This elaborate piece contains nine borders, framing a central pictorial of a basket of fruit. The quiltmaker used a wider variety of borders than is shown in the other two quilts mentioned, ranging from *broderie perse*, to pieced borders, to simple alternating strips. Note that starting with the inner Sawtooth border, the corners of each border are finished with a different block.

I've included this quilt as an idea quilt, and no pattern is given, but it would be fairly simple to make up the pattern from the others given in the book.

After the eighteenth century, American and English quilt styles diverged; the English still prefer the medallion style even today, while the Americans went on to refine the block style that we know so well.

The medallion quilt has enjoyed an increased popularity in the last few years, spurred by the work of Jenny Beyers. As you will see from the quilts that follow, this is an excellent method for making a scrap quilt as well as a sampler. The borders lend themselves beautifully to a variety of different fabrics and blocks that become a coherent, even elegant, statement of the quiltmaker's art.

Courtesy of the Brooklyn Museum of Arts and Science

National Museum of American History, Smithsonian Institution

Framed Medallion

This medallion quilt, from the Smithsonian Institution's National Museum of American History, was made by Rachel Burr Corwin of Middle Hope, New York, around 1825. The dominant color is navy blue with a small white pindot, with the remainder done in varying shades of brown. A number of patterns have been worked into the quilt starting with an Album block in the center, alternating with a plain navy block. The first border is Flying Geese, followed by

two rows of an eight-point star design. The third border is a simple X-block, then two rows of a nine-patch with a final zigzag border. The original quilt measures 114″ × 117″.

The patterns given here will make a quilt 102″ × 114″. I have modified the quilt so that all the rows will be symmetrical. In the original quilt, each of the outer corners is different, and some of the inner borders wind up with a half-block here and there.

FABRIC REQUIREMENTS

A	1 yard	B	¼ yard	C	½ yard
D	¼ yard	E	½ yard	F	¾ yard
G	Scraps	H	Scraps	I	1 yard
J	1 yard	K	1 yard Light	L	3 yards
M	Scraps		1 yard Dark	N	1¼ yards Dark
O	¼ yard				1¼ yards Light

Center of Medallion

Need 24 plain blocks (Part A) and 24 pieced

A 24

ADD SEAM ALLOWANCE

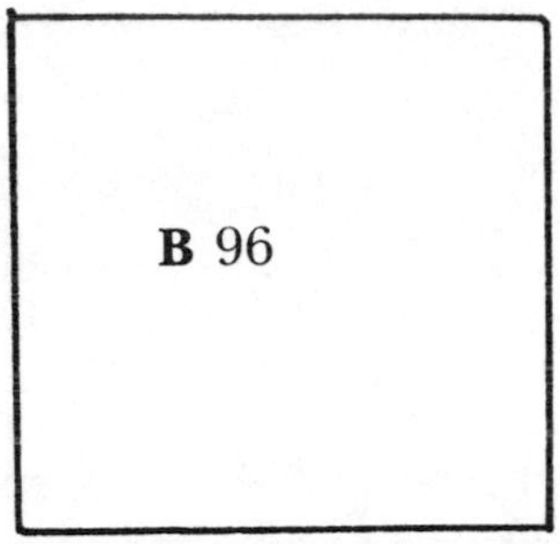

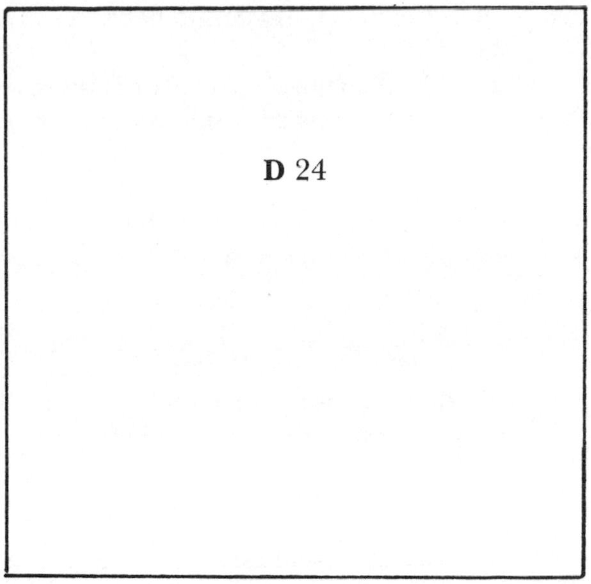

B 96

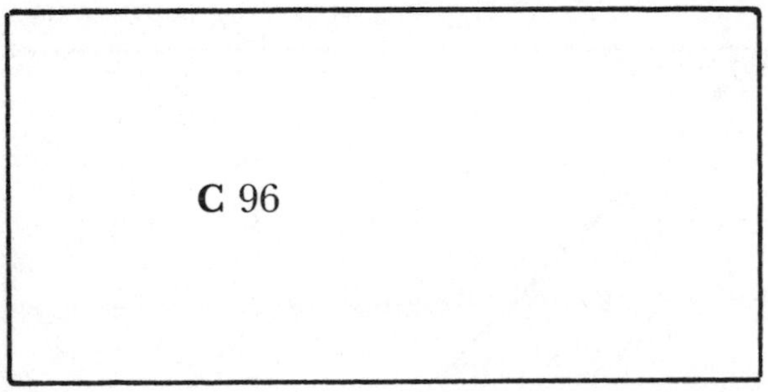

D 24

C 96

ADD SEAM ALLOWANCES

**Piecing diagram for
pieced blocks**

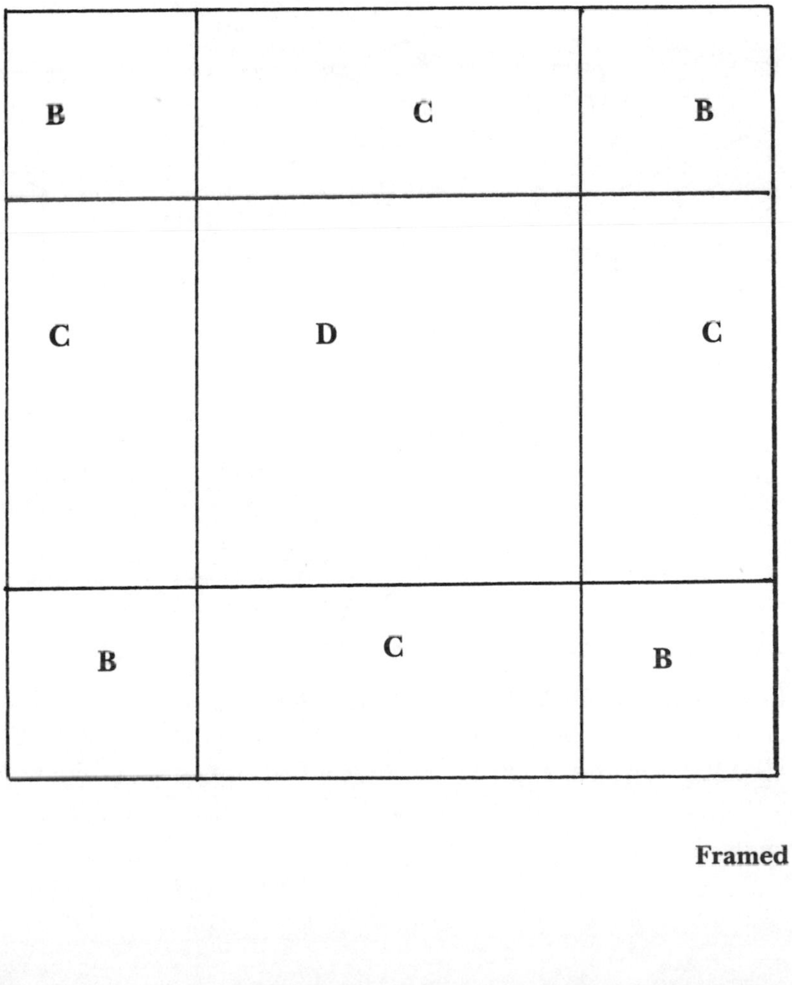

B	C	B
C	D	C
B	C	B

Border 1—Flying Geese

Two strips 36 units for long sides
Two strips 24 units for short sides

ADD SEAM ALLOWANCE

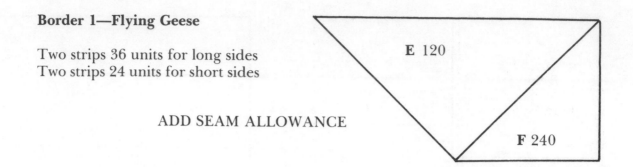

E 120

F 240

Border 2—Star Pattern (see next page for piecing diagram for corners)

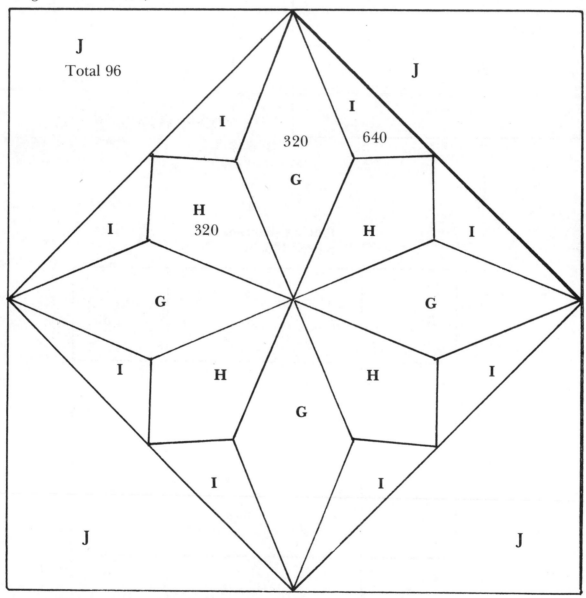

J

Total 96

Row 1: Two strips 11 blocks long for long sides; two strips 8 blocks long for short sides

Row 2: Two strips 12 blocks long for long sides; two strips 8 blocks long for short sides

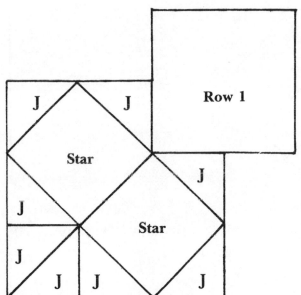

Piecing diagram for corner of second row of Border 2

Border 3

Full-size pattern and piecing diagram

22 blocks long for short sides
28 blocks long for long sides

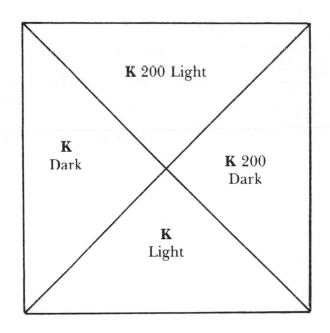

ADD SEAM ALLOWANCE

Border 4—Nine-patch block set on the diagonal

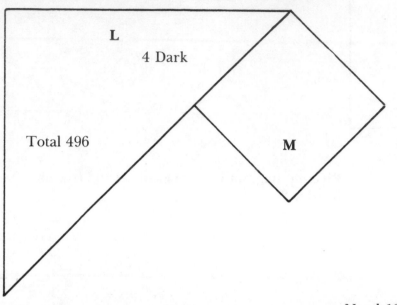

L

4 Dark

Total 496

M

ADD SEAM ALLOWANCE

Need 124 blocks
5 Light Part M per block, total 120
4 Dark Part M per block, total 496

Need 124 blocks set in two rows
Where the blocks join will form the dark square
Two rows 28 blocks long, two rows 22 blocks long

Border 5

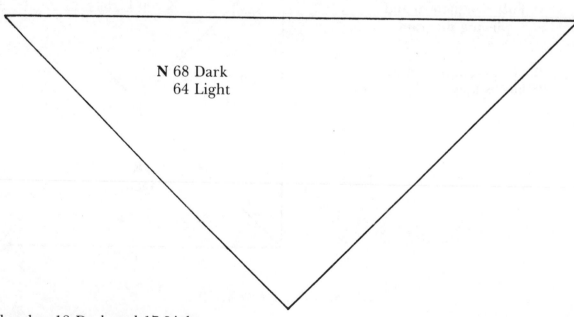

N 68 Dark
64 Light

Long side takes 18 Dark and 17 Light
Short side takes 16 Dark and 15 Light

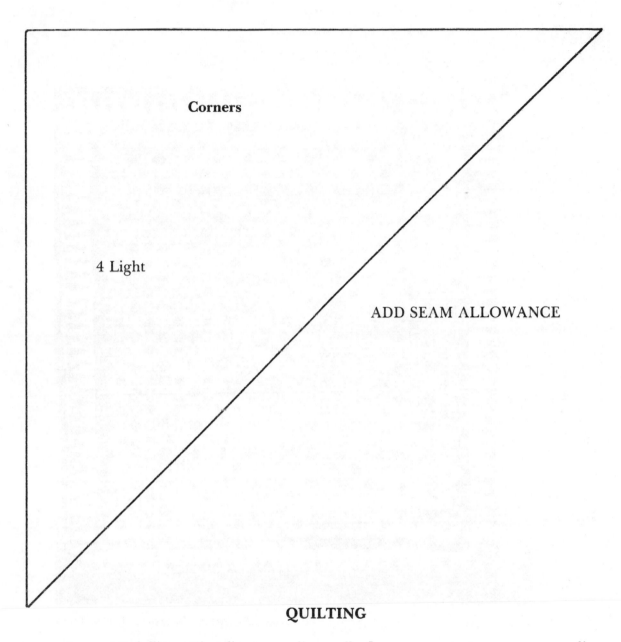

Corners

4 Light

ADD SEAM ALLOWANCE

QUILTING

Inner Medallion: First line runs diagonally from corner to corner, succeeding rows form a chevron to the center of the block.

Flying Geese: Outline quilting.

Star Border: Outline quilting, with two rows following the zigzag pattern.

X-Border: Outline quilting.

Nine-patch Border: Quilting runs through the center of the diagonal block. Chevron to the center of the block.

Outer Zigzag Border: Three rows following the shape of the piece.

Courtesy of Darwin Bearsley, Akron, Ohio

Ohio Star Medallion

The Ohio Star pattern is one of the most versatile patterns there is, and this quilt is an outstanding example of its versatility. The corners of the block have been cut on the diagonal to form an octagonal block. When the blocks are set together you can see at least three different patterns.

A private dealer owns this quilt, and the only background he had on it was that it comes from either New York or Pennsylvania and dates from 1820–1830.

It is a scrap quilt, but the maker used mostly browns for the print pieces and white to tie it together. Finished quilt is 89½" by 102".

BLOCK (152 needed)

A	4 White	608
	4 Print	608
B	1 Scrap	152
C	4 Scrap	608
	4 White	608

MEDALLION

20″ square
2″ wide print border—two strips 20″ long
two strips 24″ long

D	8 Print, same as border
E	8 Print, same as border
F	4 Print, same as border
G	4 Print, same as border
H	16 Print

FABRIC REQUIREMENTS

5½ yards White
4⅓ yards Print
Assorted Scrap Fabrics

ADD SEAM ALLOWANCE

Piecing diagram

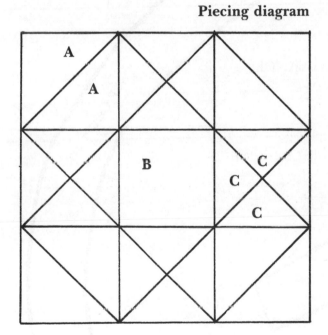

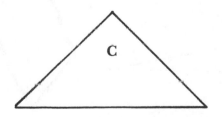

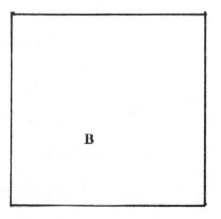

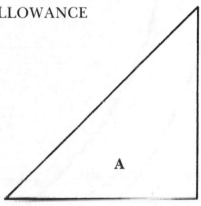

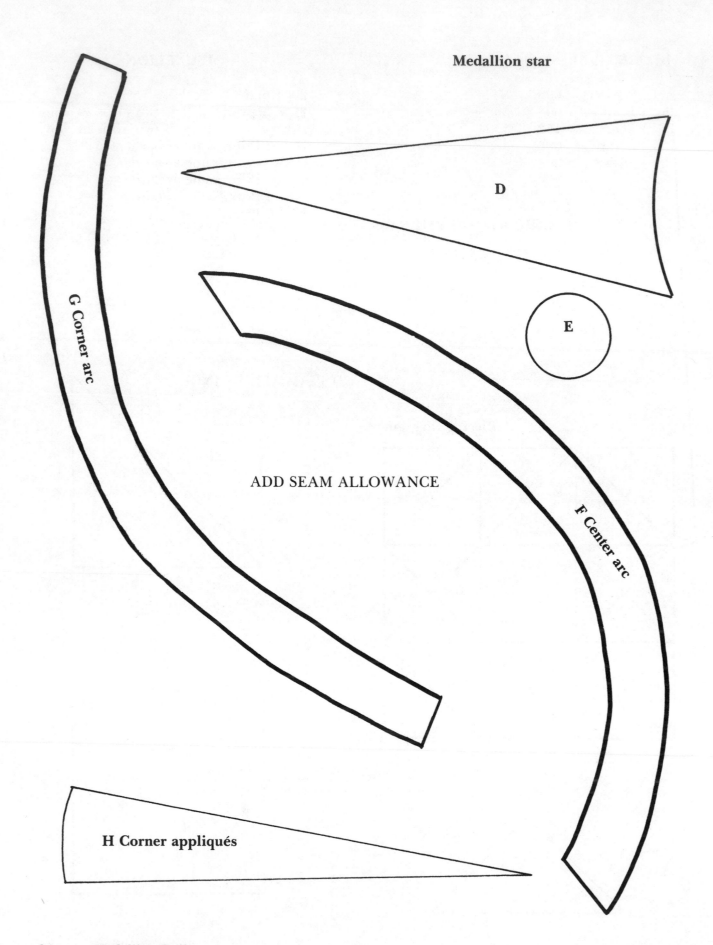

Medallion star

G Corner arc

D

E

ADD SEAM ALLOWANCE

F Center arc

H Corner appliqués

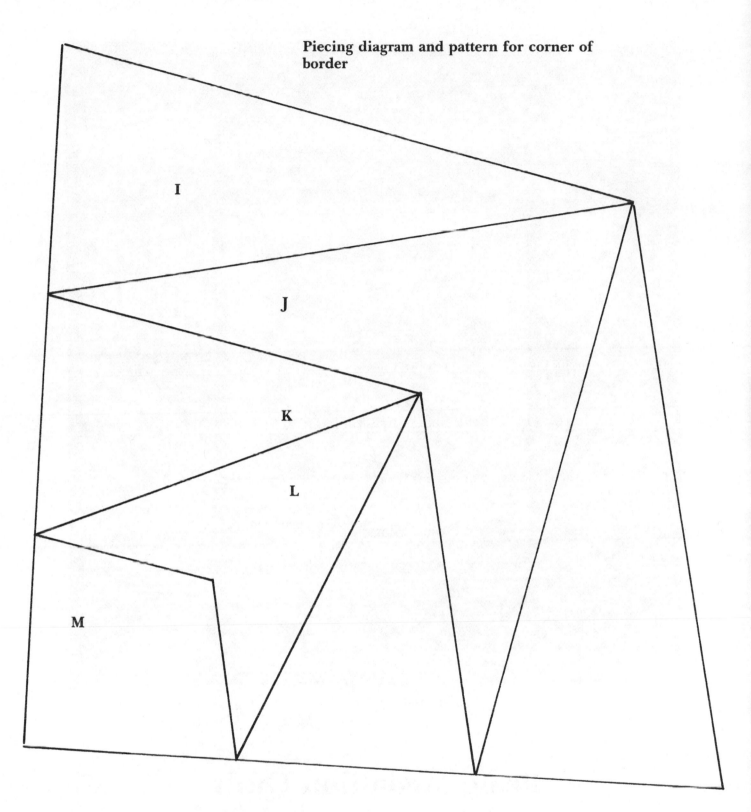

Piecing diagram and pattern for corner of border

I

J

K

L

M

ADD SEAM ALLOWANCE

From the Philadelphia Museum of Art, given by Mrs. Horace Wells Sellers, photographed by Philadelphia Museum of Art

Peale Medallion Quilt

The medallion quilt has long been a favorite design for quiltmakers and lends itself to infinite variation. This version, from the Philadelphia Museum of Art, was made by Sophinisba Peale around 1850. The quilt is made of printed cottons. Alternate pieced and plain borders frame the central Star of Bethlehem.

Most medallion quilts were square, or with

only a slight variation in the dimensions, which was probably due to the stretching that took place over the years. The original quilt measures 115¼″ × 113″. I've scaled the pattern down somewhat so that the pattern given will make up into a quilt 90″ × 90″.

The center square measures 29″, with the star made up of seven rows of scrap fabrics. I have omitted the small square and triangle that are set into the center units and given dimensions for the pieces to complete the square.

FABRIC REQUIREMENTS

Print for center and plain borders: 2¾ yards

D	40, ¾ yard		I	240, 1¼ yards
E	80, 1 yard		J	192 total, assorted fabrics for 8-point stars
F	4, ½ yard		K	96, ¾ yard
G	4, ½ yard		L	96, ¾ yard
H	60, assorted fabrics		M	96, 2 yards

For the ½″ border around the star blocks, you need 1 yard of fabric, or a decorative ribbon could be used, which would require 32 yards of ½″ ribbon.

Center star

A

B—triangle, straight sides 9½″
C—7 ¾″ corner square

2″ border around center star
two strips 29″ long, two strips 33″ long

Flying Geese border

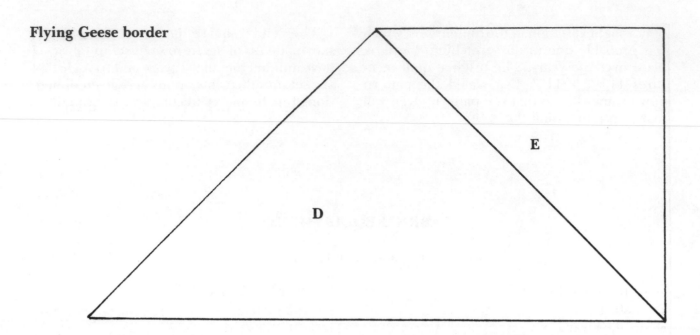

ADD SEAM ALLOWANCES

½″ wide border around eight-point star square

**Outer border
eight-point star**

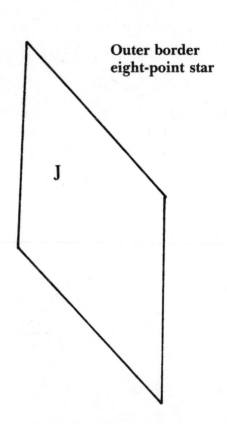

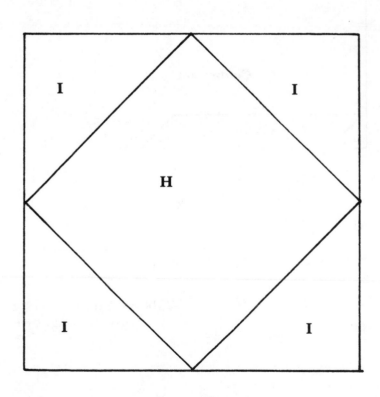

2″ Border, two strips 56″ long, two strips
60″ long

F—Center block for Flying Geese border

G—6″ Corner block

ADD SEAM ALLOWANCES

2″ Border, two strips 33″ long; two strips 49″ long

The outer border has been broken down into a 12″ square with the eight-point star set on the diagonal

Triangle for border star

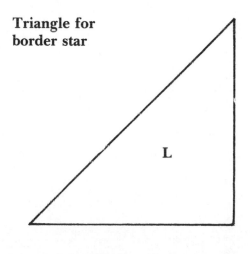

L

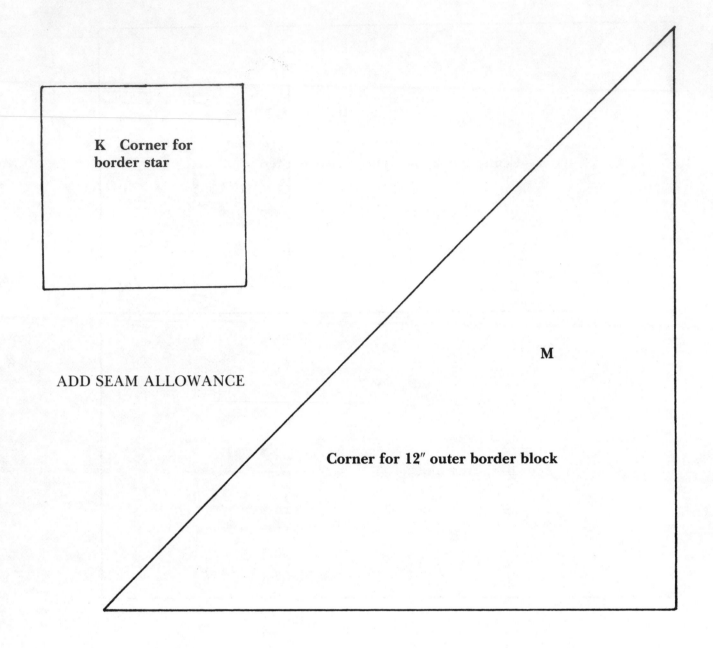

K   Corner for border star

ADD SEAM ALLOWANCE

Corner for 12″ outer border block

M

Final border 3″ wide, two strips 84″ long, two strips 90″ long, plus seam allowance

Oak Leaf and Reel Medallion

Unlike most medallion quilts, which use a variety of patterns for the borders, this one uses only one pattern to set off the Eagle centerpiece. It is also unusual in that the design for the frame is appliquéd rather than pieced. The maker's initials, CAC, and the date, 1853, are worked in embroidery above and below the eagle to become an integral part of the design. It can be seen in color in the section between pages 32 and 33.

PIECES NEEDED

12 16½″ squares
16 8½″ × 16½″ half-blocks

4 corner blocks,

A	1	Red	12
½A	1	Red	16
B	4	Red	96
C	4	Green	80

CENTER PANEL   35½″ × 35½″ square

D	24	Red
E	1	Red
	1	Right wing
	1	Left wing
F	1	Green
G	1	Red
H	1	Red
I	8	Green
	8	Red

FABRIC REQUIREMENTS

7 yards White
2 yards Red
2⅓ yards Green

QUILT SIZE   85″ × 85″, 16″ blocks set with 1″ lattice strips

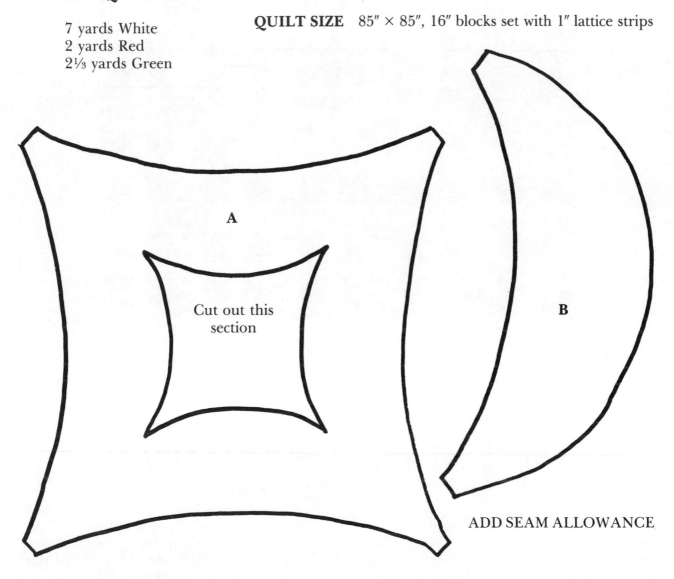

A

Cut out this
section

B

ADD SEAM ALLOWANCE

QUILTING   The oak leaf is·used as the quilting motif.

These are three examples of the increasingly popular medallion quilt. At left is the cheerful Oak Leaf and Reel Medallion (pages 31–37). The quilter's initials and the date are embroidered into the design. Below left is Ohio Star Medallion (pages 22–25). Below right is Framed Medallion (pages 15–21), which uses a number of patterns.

C

The vivid colors of these two quilts give them a startlingly modern look. Above is the Pennsylvania Dutch appliquéd Snowflake (pages 105–107). At left is the Amish strip quilt, Bars (page 123).

D

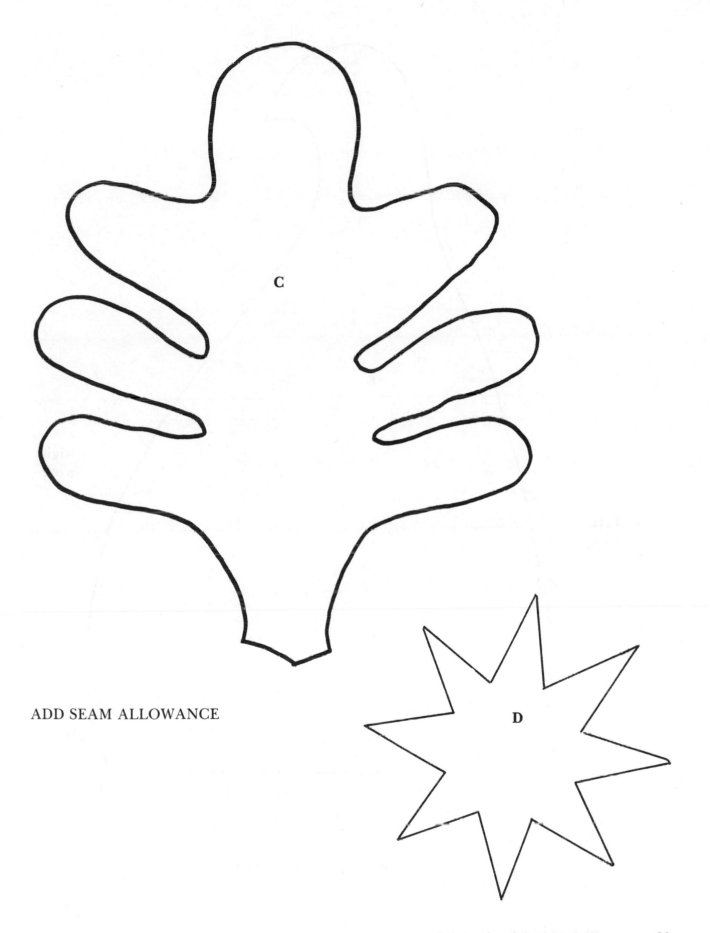

ADD SEAM ALLOWANCE

C

D

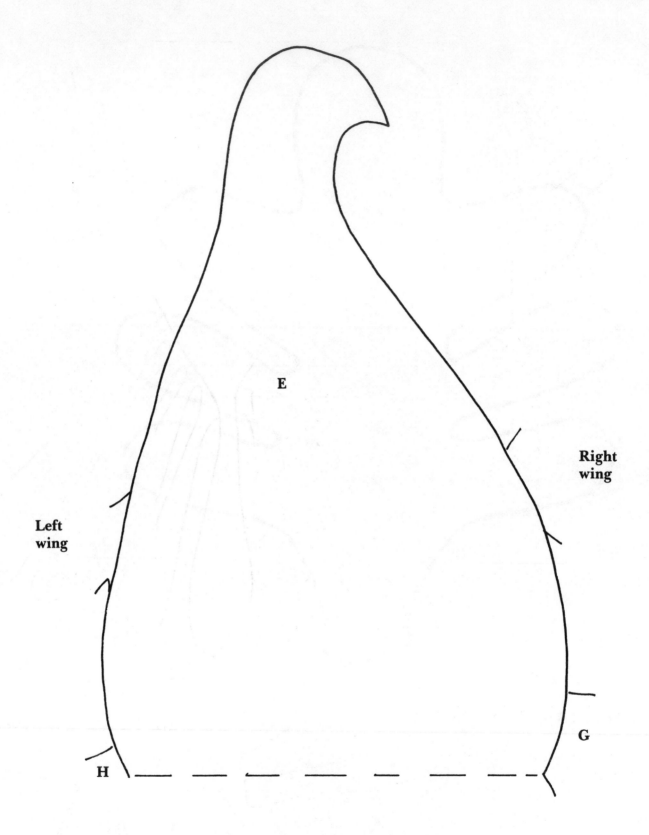

E

Right
wing

Left
wing

H

G

ADD SEAM ALLOWANCE

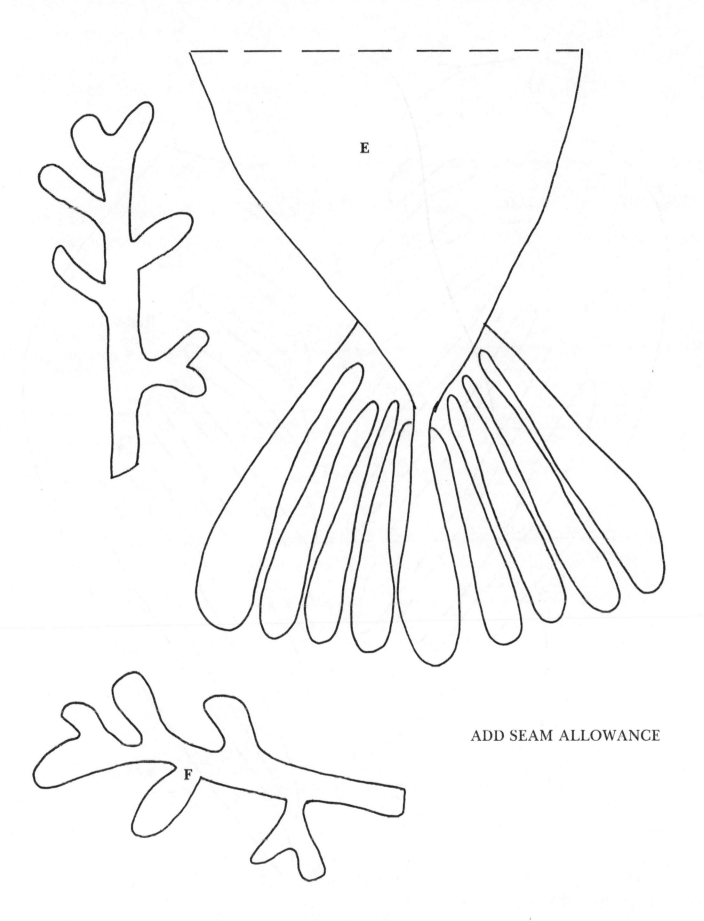

E

ADD SEAM ALLOWANCE

F

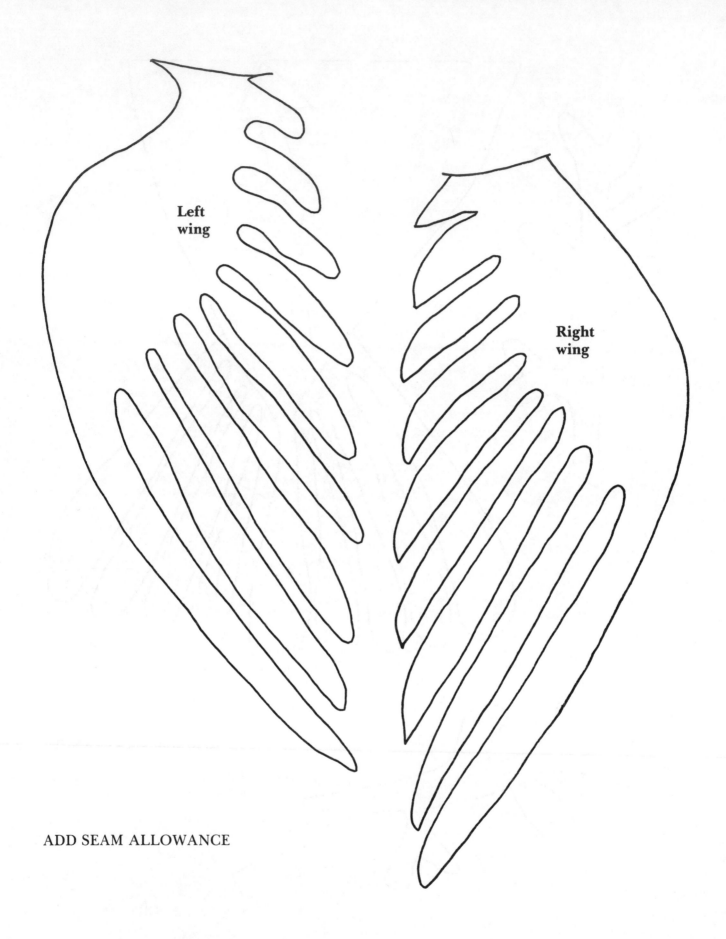

Left
wing

Right
wing

ADD SEAM ALLOWANCE

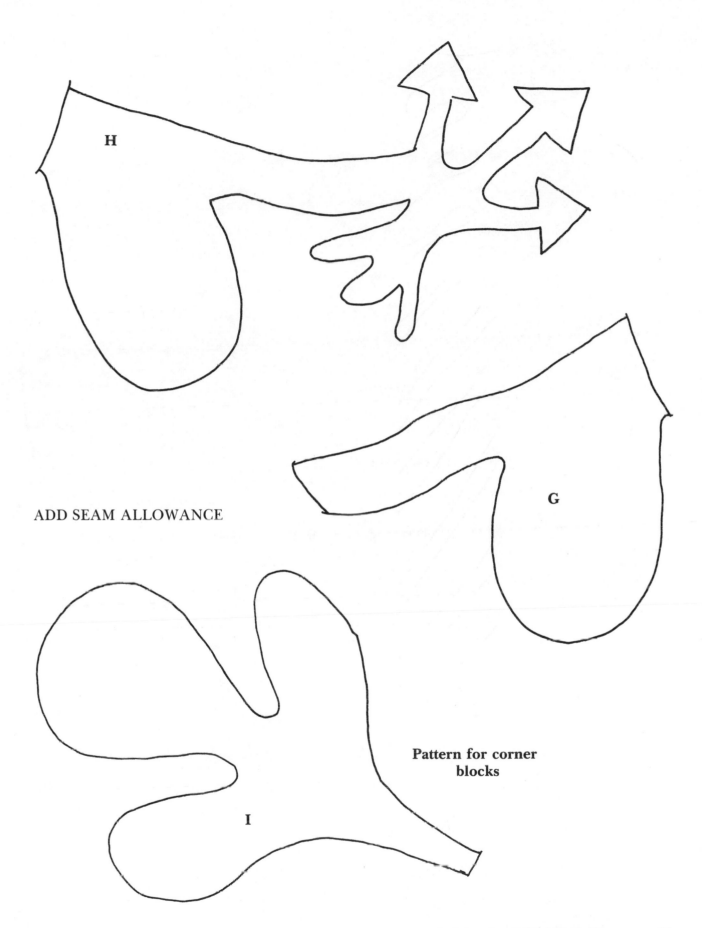

H

ADD SEAM ALLOWANCE

G

Pattern for corner blocks

I

Oak Leaf and Reel Medallion   37

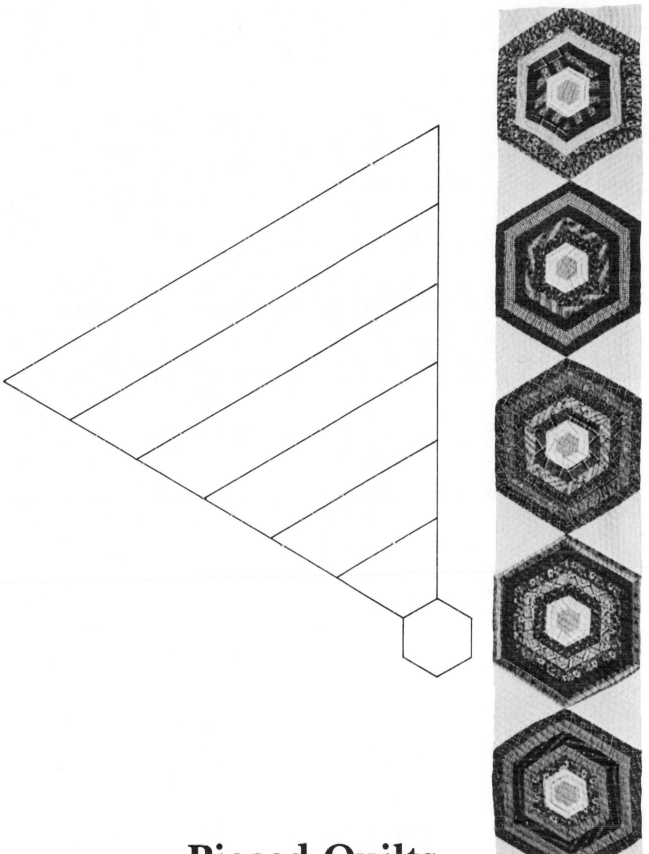

Pieced Quilts

When the English colonists first landed on American shores they brought the tradition of quilting with them. Tucked away in their baggage were quilted bedcovers made at home.

Many of the colonists who came to America were of the nobility, or after their arrival had managed to amass fortunes—either as landowners or as traders. Until the Revolution, Europe continued as the arbiter of taste and fashion, which the colonists were eager to follow. Trade was brisk between Europe and America, and among the items imported were bedcovers, quilts and the fabrics with which to make them.

During this early period, many types of quilts were made. Whole cloth quilts were fast to make to meet the needs of the cold winters. Wealthier ladies along the eastern seaboard made quilts in the fashion of England, which was the medallion or appliqué style. A thrifty housewife would use odd pieces or strips of cloth to stretch her small cache of fabric enough to make a quilt. In addition, old quilts would wear out and need patching.

From the hands of the thrifty housewife evolved the truly American quilt form, the pieced block quilt. The pieced block type of quilt includes both those blocks that are entirely pieced from small bits of fabric and the more intricate appliqué designs. For many of the early colonists, fabric was scarce and expensive, so they utilized what they had, using small pieces to make blocks, that were later set together to make an everyday, utility quilt. As settlers moved west, there was always a gap between need and availability of materials, so that quiltmaking was reinforced as a necessity.

Ideas and pattern names came from every conceivable source; everyday items inspired such quilt patterns as Cotton Reels, Disk, Coffee Cups, Sugar Loaf, Schoolhouse and Broken Dishes. From the farm came such names as Churn Dash, Turkey Tracks, Duck and Ducklings, Hens and Chickens and Farmer's Daughter. The trek westward has been immortalized in such names as Indian Trails, Kansas Dugout, and Rocky Road to Kansas (or California); political events in such names as Mrs. Taft's Choice, Madison Block, Martha Washington Star, Coxey's Camp, Clay's Choice and Free Trade Block. And since religion played such an important role in their lives, Bible stories, too, were interpreted in quilt blocks with such names as David and Goliath, Joseph's Coat, Children of Israel and Tree Everlasting.

The pieced quilt has something for every level of expertise as patterns run the gamut from simple four-patch designs to intricate patterns, which may contain sixty or more pieces in a block, or to the very elaborate appliqué patterns.

From the Schoolhouse Collection, Canton, Ohio

Bear's Paw Variation

This quilt comes from a private collection and dates from about 1855. The red, white and green combination makes a very striking quilt.

The quilt measures 94½″ × 94½″ with the blocks set on the diagonal. The block size is 13½″ square.

PIECES PER BLOCK			PER QUILT
A	5	Red	80
	8	White	128
B	16	Red	256
	16	White	256
C	4	Red	64
D	8	Green	128
	4	White	64

16 pieced blocks, 9 plain blocks, 12 half-plain blocks, 4 quarter-plain blocks

Piece the borders to the following dimensions:

2 Red 3½″ × 77″
2 Red 3½″ × 83″
2 White 6½″ × 83″   Binding is red
2 White 6½″ × 95″

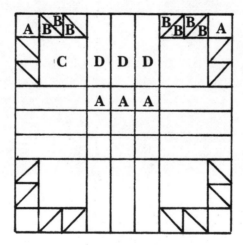

QUILTING   The pieced blocks are quilted in straight lines running up and down the block. The plain blocks are quilted in a circular Robbing-Peter-to-Pay-Paul pattern. The borders are quilted in diagonal straight lines.

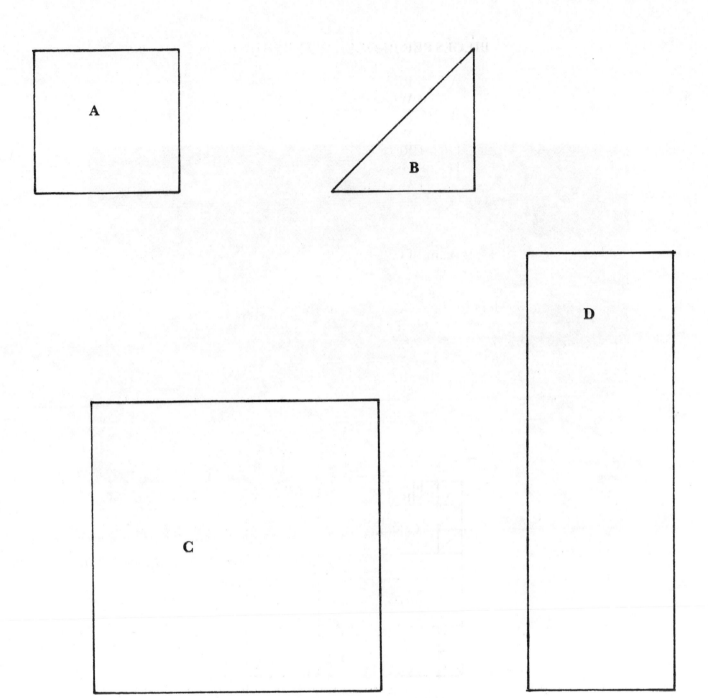

ADD SEAM ALLOWANCE

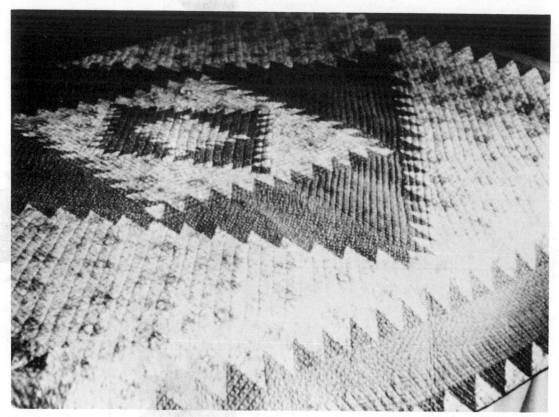

Courtesy of the Geauga County Historical Society, Burton, Ohio

Delectable Mountains

This quilt is on display at the George Bouthon House in Century Village, which is run by the Geauga County Historical Society. The room is furnished with antique pieces from the early days in Geauga County but this quilt is the most outstanding item in the room. It dates to around 1840. It is a good-sized quilt, measuring 90″ × 90″. The original was made up in a blue polka dot and a small floral of pink and grey or cream.

FABRIC REQUIREMENTS

6 yards Blue
5 yards Cream

PIECES REQUIRED

A	1 Cream	G	4 Cream triangles 11 ⅝″ on the straight sides
B	20 Blue	H	104 Blue
	20 Cream		104 Cream
C	4 Cream	I	4 Blue triangles 19½″ on the straight sides
D	4 Blue	J	2 Blue
E	32 Blue		4 Cream
	32 Cream	K	4 Cream triangles 33″ on the straight sides
F	6 Cream		
	2 Blue		

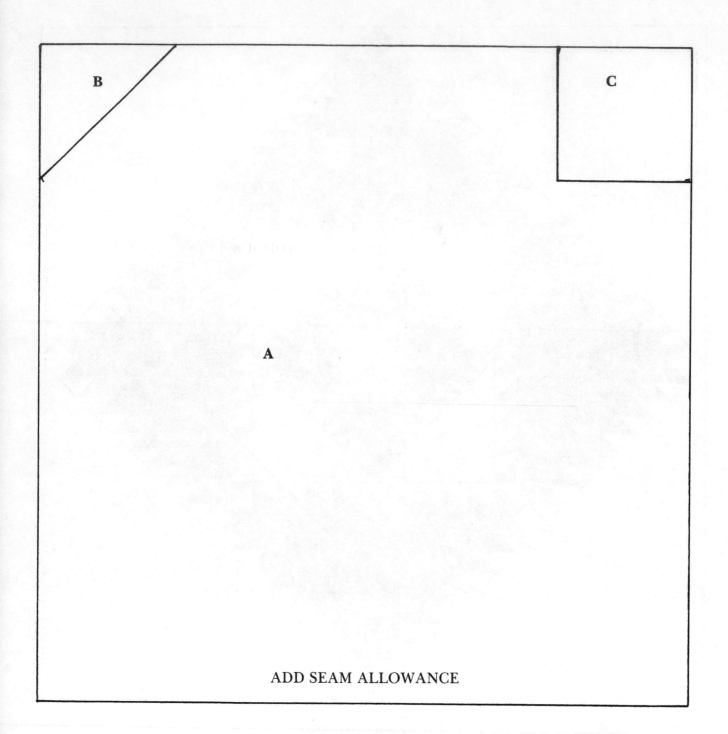

B

C

A

ADD SEAM ALLOWANCE

QUILTING Straight-line quilting on the diagonal

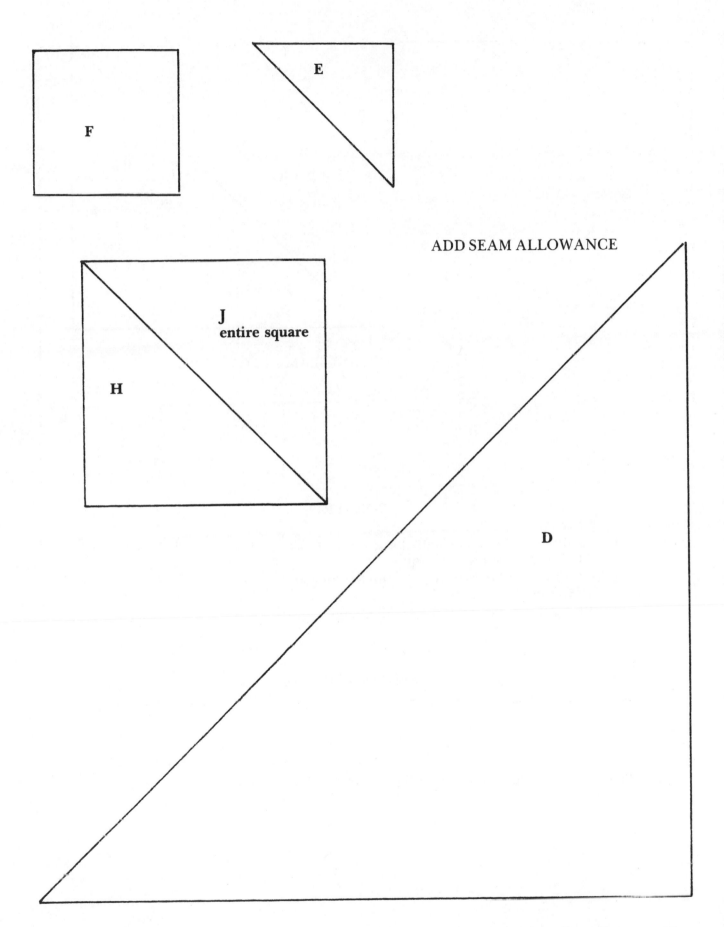

F

E

ADD SEAM ALLOWANCE

J
entire square

H

D

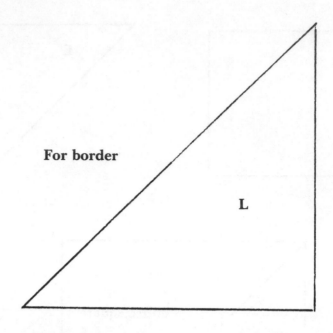

For border

L

ADD SEAM ALLOWANCE

BORDER

L 44 Blue   Inner Sawtooth, piece two strips 22 squares long and seam to two
   44 Cream   sides of the quilt
L 48 Blue   Piece two strips 24 squares long and seam to the remaining sides
   48 Cream
Blue strip: Two strips 6½″ × 72½″ and two strips 6½″ × 84½″

L 56 Blue   Outer Sawtooth, piece two strips 28 squares long and attach to two
   56 Cream   sides
L 60 Blue   Piece two strips 30 squares long and seam to remaining edges
   60 Cream

Courtesy of the Stamford Historical Society, Stamford, Connecticut

Robbing Peter to Pay Paul

This is another pattern that has proven its popularity over the years. This version from the Stamford Historical Society was made between 1840 and 1850. In this example, the blocks are set side by side, but the quilter changed the colors of the two outer rows to form a border. The center of the quilt is made of a blue and a tan cotton print. For the outer rows the tan print was used with a red, green and brown print, which has faded over the years so that you get the impression of a dark gold print. This was quilted with a diagonal crosshatch.

Besides being a very lovely quilt, it is a thrifty one. The cutaways from the main piece of one color are applied to the main piece of the contrasting color, hence, no scraps.

This pattern includes seam allowances. Cut along the dashed lines.

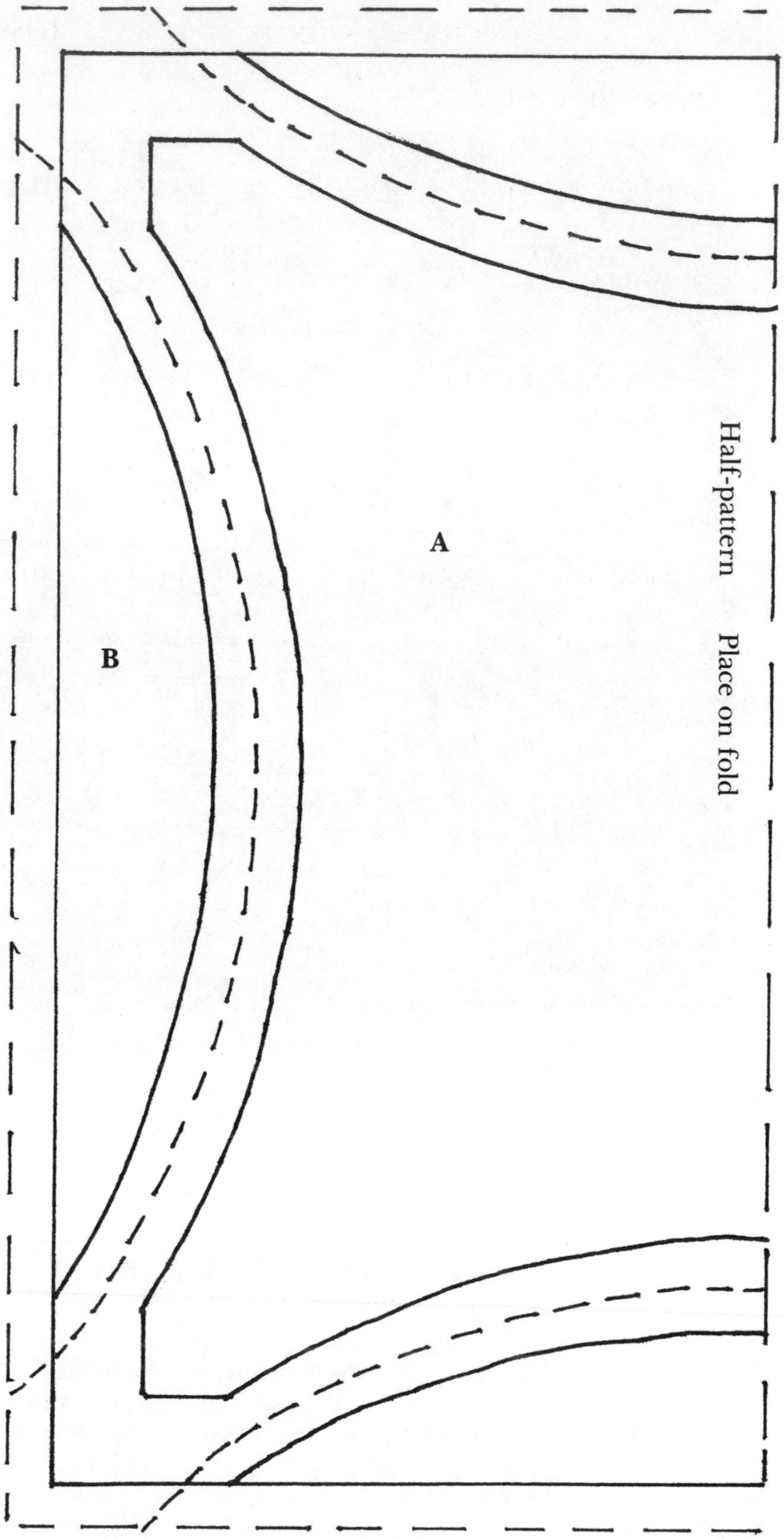

A

B

Half-pattern   Place on fold

BLOCKS SET SIDE BY SIDE, 12 ACROSS, 14 DOWN

QUILT SIZE 84″ × 98″

COLOR COMBINATION 1 FOR CENTER OF QUILT

A 32 Dark   B 128 Dark
   32 Light   128 Light

COLOR COMBINATION 2 FOR TWO OUTER ROWS

A 32 Dark   B 128 Dark
   32 Light   128 Light

FABRIC REQUIREMENTS

1¾ yards Dark Print #1
1¾ yards Light Print #1
1¾ yards Dark Print #2
1¾ yards Light Print #2

This is a very difficult pattern to piece because of the bias edges of the curved sections. If you use the sewing machine you might want to try using very lightweight, iron-on interfacing on the wrong side of the fabric. This will help stabilize the cut edges.

From the Smithsonian Institution

Feathered Star and Garden Maze

The Feathered Star pattern is one of those that lend themselves to many variations and interpretations. This most unusual quilt combines the Feathered Star with the Garden Maze pattern to create one that is truly unique. The original quilt was made by Rachel Burr Corwin of Orange County, New York, in 1829.

The Feathered Star is made from scrap fabrics, but many of the "feathers" are red, which lends continuity to the design. The Garden Maze is done in one color, which is repeated in the border. The original quilt was only 66″ wide, so I would assume it was for the equivalent of our twin-size bed. The pattern provided makes up into a quilt 72″ by 84″. You might want to enlarge it a little by making three full blocks across rather than the two and a half. I think it would also give a little better balance to the top to have identical corners and edges.

To make it as shown, you will need ten full-star blocks, nine half-star blocks, and two quarter-star blocks.

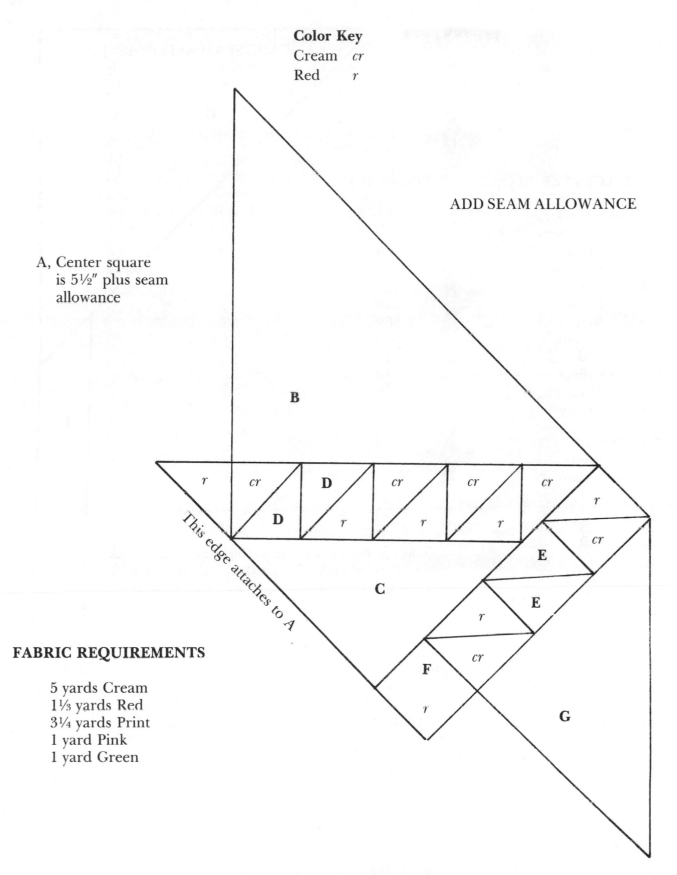

ADD SEAM ALLOWANCE

A, Center square
   is 5½″ plus seam
   allowance

B

r *cr* **D** *cr* *cr* *cr* *r*

D *r* *r* *r* *cr*

This edge attaches to A

C **E**

E

r

cr

F

r **G**

FABRIC REQUIREMENTS

5 yards Cream
1⅓ yards Red
3¼ yards Print
1 yard Pink
1 yard Green

Pattern and piecing diagram for Feathered Star

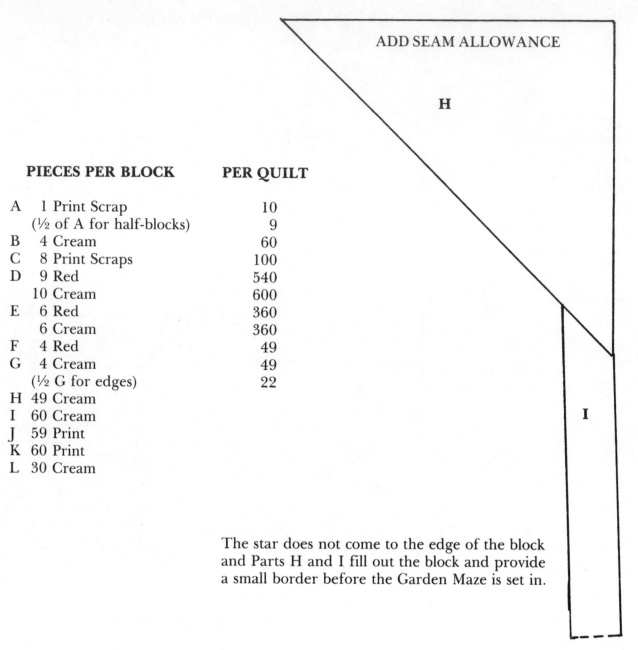

ADD SEAM ALLOWANCE

H

PIECES PER BLOCK	PER QUILT
A 1 Print Scrap	10
(½ of A for half-blocks)	9
B 4 Cream	60
C 8 Print Scraps	100
D 9 Red	540
10 Cream	600
E 6 Red	360
6 Cream	360
F 4 Red	49
G 4 Cream	49
(½ G for edges)	22
H 49 Cream	
I 60 Cream	
J 59 Print	
K 60 Print	
L 30 Cream	

I

The star does not come to the edge of the block and Parts H and I fill out the block and provide a small border before the Garden Maze is set in.

Half-pattern place on fold

QUILTING The stars are quilted along all seams, and the centers are done in straight lines, up and down and crosswise, but they do not cross to form squares. The plain spaces around the stars are done in various small floral designs. The quilting pattern for the space between the Garden Maze is marked on the pattern.

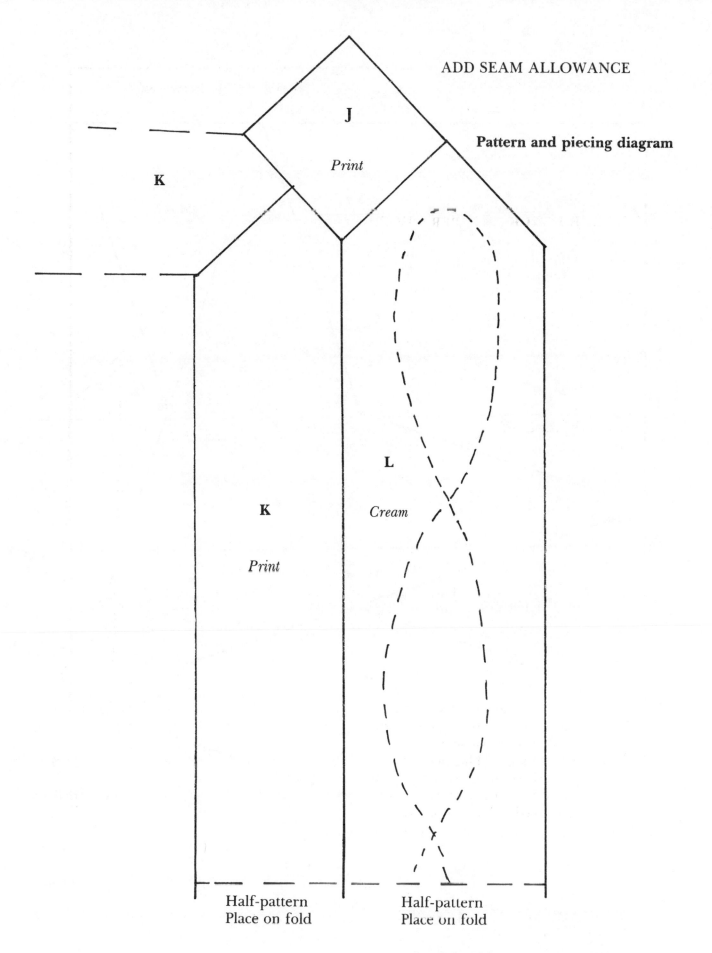

ADD SEAM ALLOWANCE

Pattern and piecing diagram

J
Print

K

K
Print

L
Cream

Half-pattern
Place on fold

Half-pattern
Place on fold

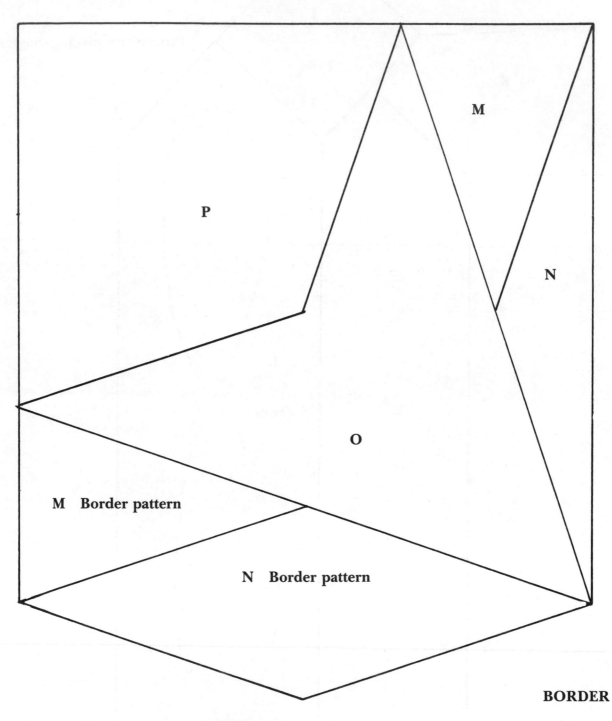

Pattern for border and piecing diagram for corners

ADD SEAM ALLOWANCE

BORDER

M	132	Pink
	132	Green
	72	Pink
N	132	Print
O	4	
P	4	

Courtesy of Darwin Bearsley, Akron, Ohio

Sawtooth with Variable Star Border

This unusual Sawtooth pattern creates a positive, negative effect when set together. You have both a colored Sawtooth and a white Sawtooth. The Variable Star border makes a richly patterned border for a simple quilt.

This quilt comes from New York State and dates to about 1830. It is a rather large quilt measuring 112½″ × 112½″.

FABRIC REQUIREMENTS

8 yards White
Assorted scraps

NUMBER OF BLOCKS 100

A	1 White	100
B	8 Print	800
	6 White	600
C	1 White	100

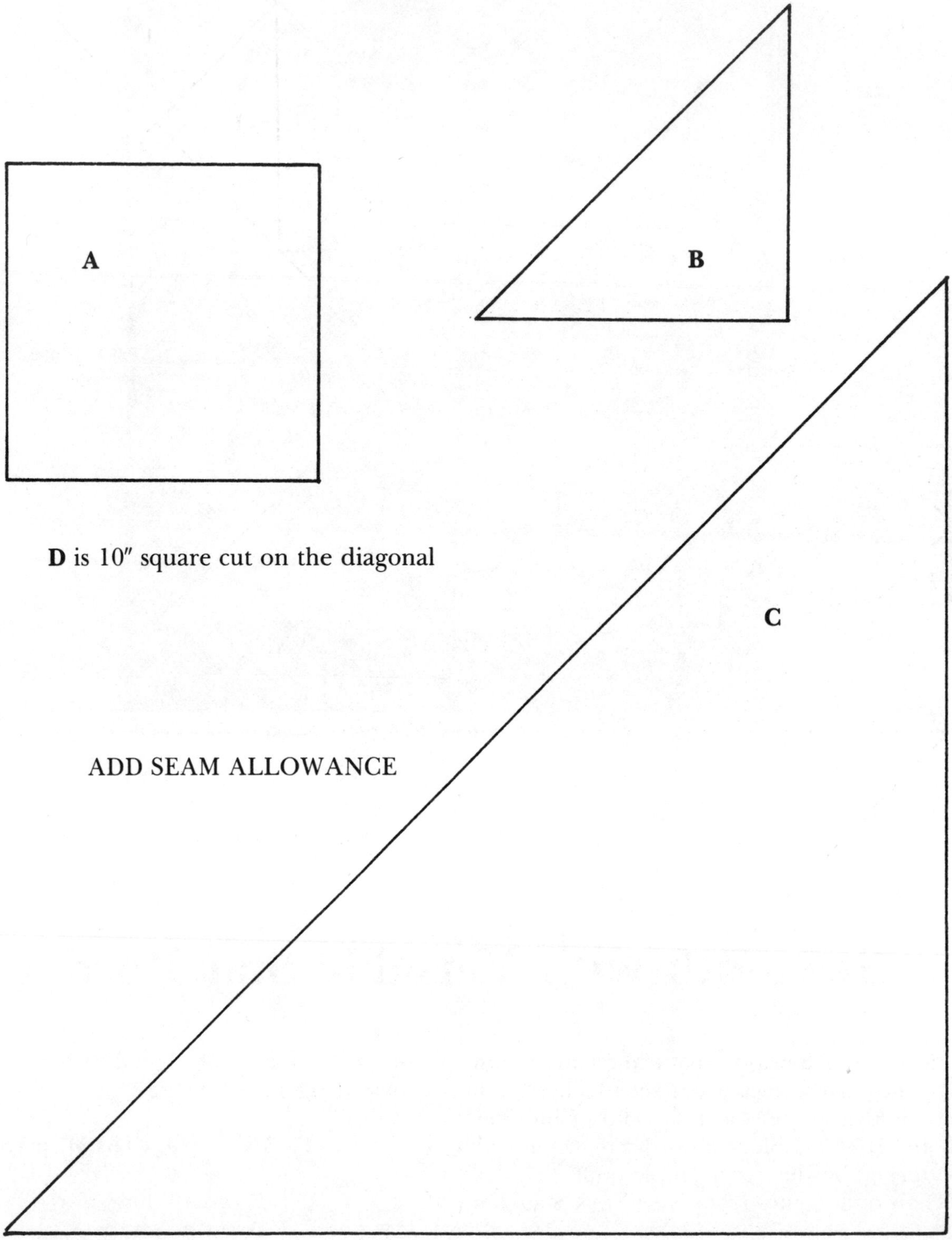

A

B

D is 10″ square cut on the diagonal

ADD SEAM ALLOWANCE

C

BORDER   NUMBER OF BLOCKS   60

E	1 Scrap	60
F	8 Scrap	480
G	4 White	240
H	4 White	240
I	Print	118
J	8 Print	8

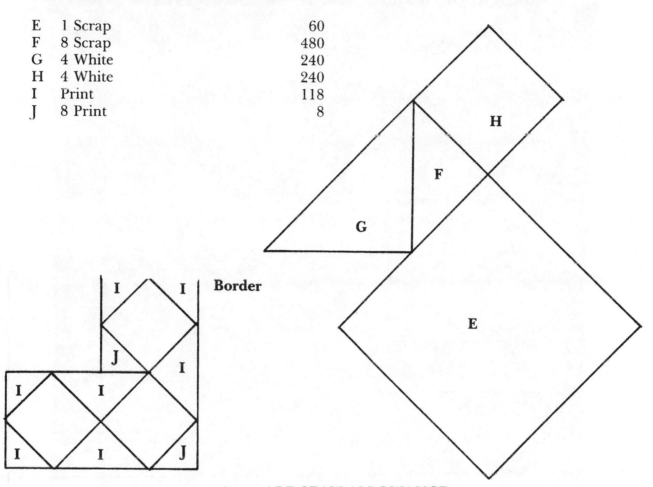

Border

ADD SEAM ALLOWANCE

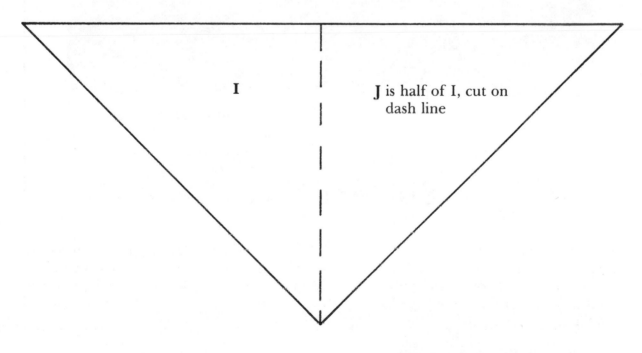

I

J is half of I, cut on dash line

Courtesy of the Kentucky Historical Society

Spider's Web

This quilt dates to the mid-1800's and was made by Margaret O'Sullivan Langford of Spencer County, Kentucky. It is now in the possession of the Kentucky Historical Society.

The quilt is on the small side, measuring 66″ × 77″. It's a marvellous quilt for using up scraps. The original has red print centers, and is made up, using browns, reds, and greys. The two-inch border is a blue print, finished with a red binding.

PIECES PER BLOCK   (All scrap fabrics)

A	1 Red	H	50 White
B	6		
C	6		
D	6		
E	6		
F	6		
G	6		

ADD SEAM ALLOWANCE

A

B

C

D

E

F

G

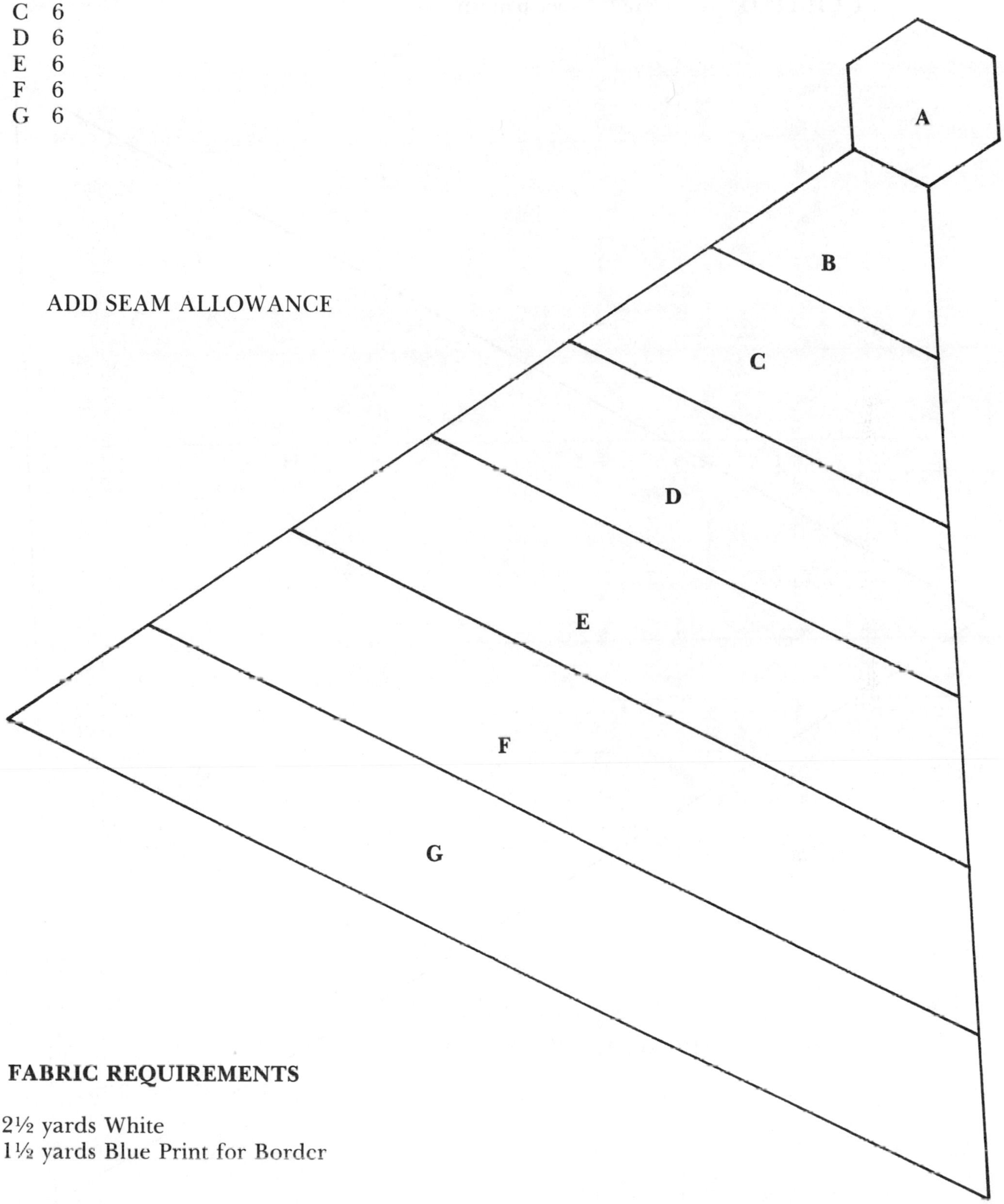

FABRIC REQUIREMENTS

2½ yards White
1½ yards Blue Print for Border

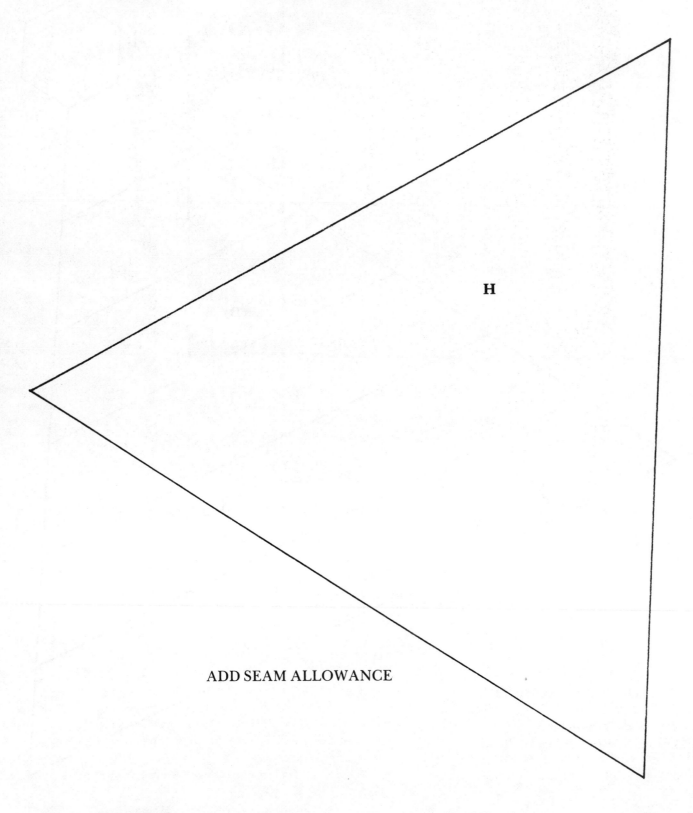

ADD SEAM ALLOWANCE

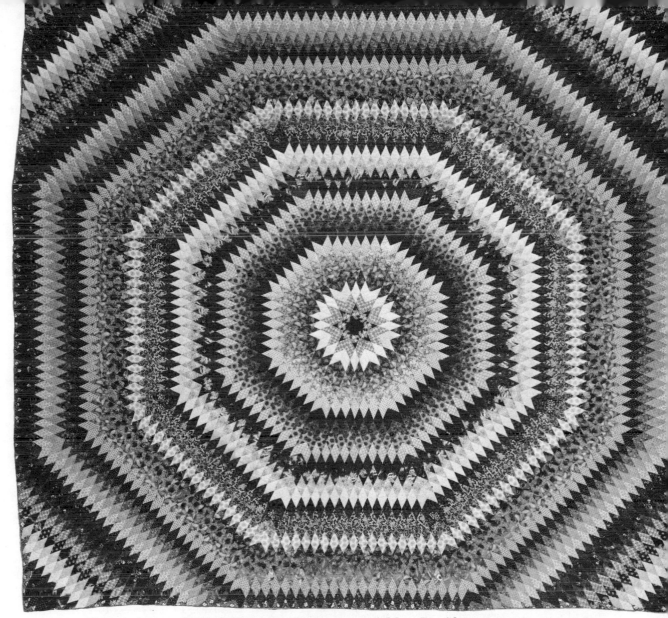

Given by Mrs. Lewis Barton and Mrs. David Barton, photographed by Philadelphia Museum of Art

Sunburst I

This magnificent quilt, owned by the Philadelphia Museum of Art, was made by Rebecca Scattergood Savery in 1839. It is a difficult quilt to piece, requiring great precision in cutting and piecing so that the quilt lies flat. A strong artistic sense is shown in the selection of color and fabric for the quilt. All the fabric is printed cotton chintz arranged in rows to accent the design. Another of Mrs. Savery's quilts of this pattern can be seen at the Museum of American Folk Art in New York City.

The pattern seems to have been popular from 1835 to 1850. With the exception of one made in 1870, all the ones I have seen date to this period.

This is a large quilt, measuring 119½″ × 115″.

Mrs. Savery did not use borders on her quilts, but merely squared off the corners and bound the edges. Other examples have been finished with borders ranging from the very simple, such as the one from the DAR Museum, to very elaborate treatments.

The quilt contains twenty-six complete rows of diamonds, and eight partial rows to square the quilt. Below is a breakdown of the rows, listing the number of diamonds for each row along with the fabric required:

Row 1	(8) ⅛ yard	Row 2	(16) ⅛ yard	Row 3	(24) ¼ yard
Row 4	(32) ¼ yard	Row 5	(40) ⅜ yard	Row 6	(48) ⅓ yard
Row 7	(56) ½ yard	Row 8	(64) ½ yard	Row 9	(72) ½ yard
Row 10	(80) 1 yard	Row 11	(88) 1 yard	Row 12	(96) ⅔ yard
Row 13	(104) ¾ yard	Row 14	(112) ⅞ yard	Row 15	(120) 1 yard
Row 16	(128) 1 yard	Row 17	(136) 1 yard	Row 18	(144) 1 yard
Row 19	(152) 1⅛ yards	Row 20	(160) 1¼ yards	Row 21	(168) 1¼ yards
Row 22	(176) 1¼ yards	Row 23	(184) 1⅜ yards	Row 24	(192) 1⅓ yards
Row 25	(200) 1½ yards	Row 26	(208) 1½ yards		

At this point you begin squaring off the quilt by adding diamonds only to the corners. Partial diamonds will be needed to make a straight edge along the top, bottom and sides. A different fabric is used for the partial diamonds along the edges, and you will need approximately 1½ yards.

Row 27	25 for each corner	(100) ¾ yard
Row 28	23 for each corner	(92) ⅔ yard
Row 29	20 for each corner	(80) ⅔ yard
Row 30	17 for each corner	(68) ½ yard
Row 31	14 for each corner	(56) ½ yard
Row 32	11 for each corner	(44) ⅓ yard
Row 33	8 for each corner	(32) ¼ yard
Row 34	5 for each corner	(20) ¼ yard

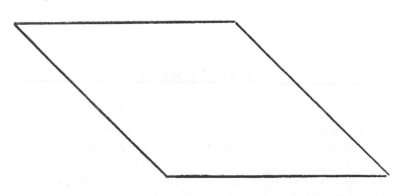

ADD SEAM ALLOWANCE

Here are three popular patchwork designs that lend themselves to a variety of interpretations. Above left is Feathered Star and Garden Maze (pages 52–56). This unusual version was made in 1829. Above right is a Star of Bethlehem (pages 79–80). The dark colors used for the background gives this quilt an almost Amish look. At right is an interesting variation of a New York Beauty (pages 74–78), which was made in Akron, Ohio, around 1850.

At left is an example of the album quilt. Floral and Eagle (pages 172−195) contains some very elaborate appliqué work that you might consider doing in reverse appliqué.

This lovely version of the popular Robbing Peter to Pay Paul (pages 49−51) was made between 1840 and 1850. The quilter changed the colors of the two outer rows so as to form a border. Here the tan print of the center was used with a red, green and brown print, which over the years has faded so that you get the impression of a dark gold print.

From the Smithsonian Institution

Hexagon Star

This lovely quilt was made by Mary Modie of Independence, Missouri between 1825 and 1830. Fine wool fabrics make up the stars with a rose and grape motif embroidered in wool yarns on the diamonds. The grape border is also embroidered in wool yarns.

FABRIC REQUIREMENTS

5⅔ yards Green (includes border)
½ yard Red
⅛ yard Yellow
4⅔ yards Cream

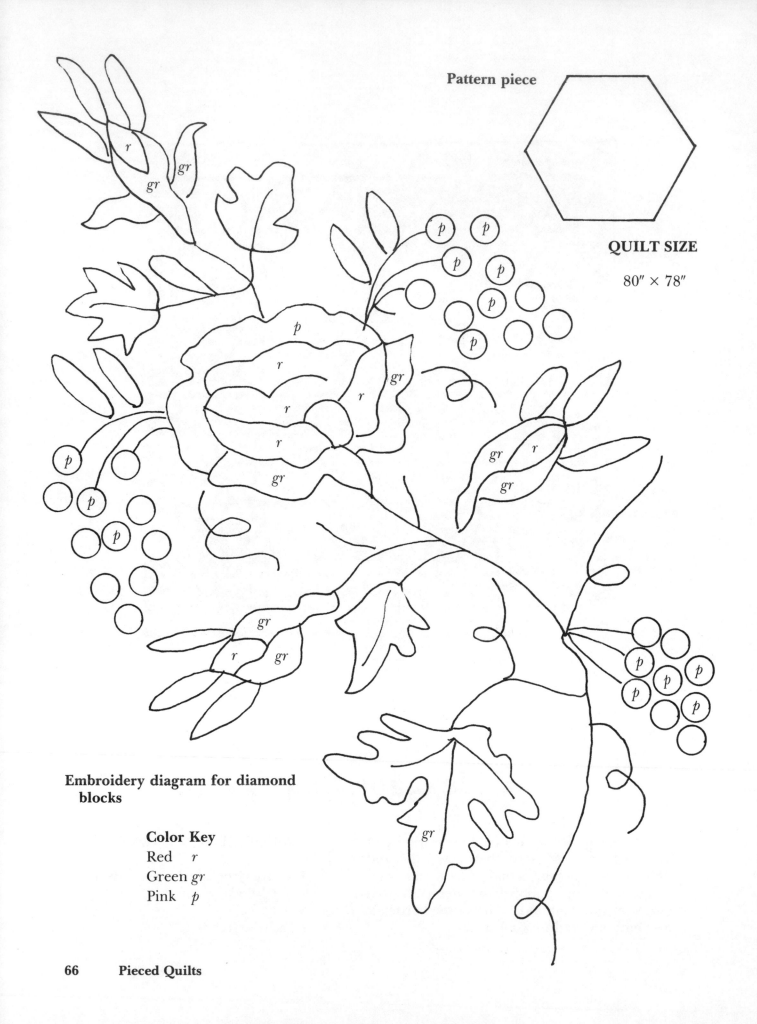

Pattern piece

QUILT SIZE

80″ × 78″

Embroidery diagram for diamond blocks

Color Key
Red   *r*
Green *gr*
Pink *p*

The border is 8″ wide, plus seam allowance.

All embroidery is done in satin stitch. If you are using wool fabric, use crewel embroidery yarns. For cotton fabric, use regular embroidery floss—three strands.

Embroidery diagram for border

The colors used are red, moss green, yellow and a dusty rose for the pink.

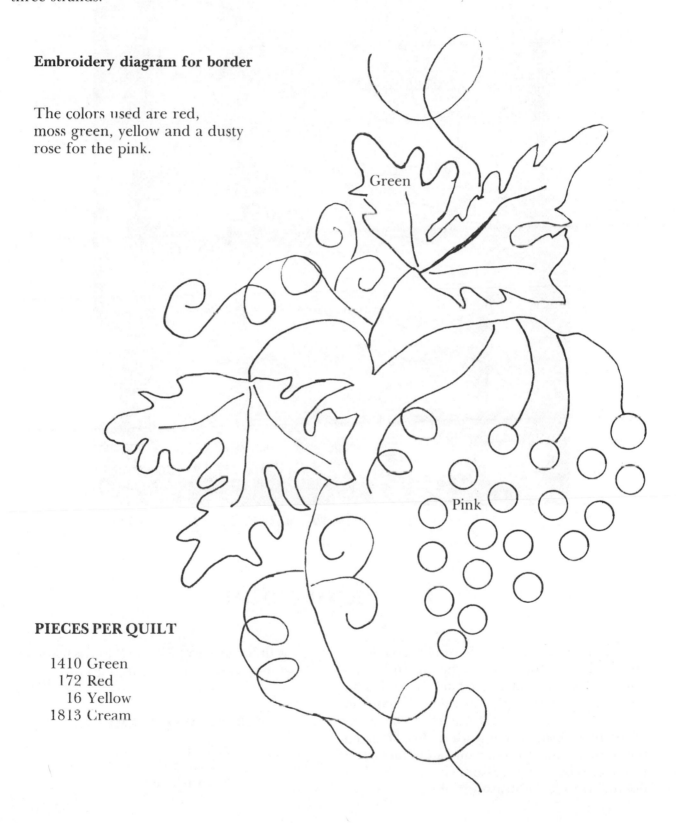

PIECES PER QUILT

1410 Green
172 Red
16 Yellow
1813 Cream

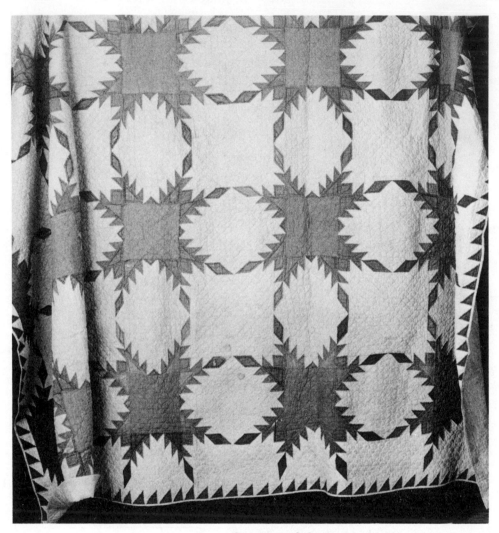

Courtesy of the Kentucky Historical Society

Twinkling Star

This quilt is from the Kentucky Historical Society, and unfortunately, the only information available is that it predates 1860. It's an interesting pattern, with something of an Indian flavor. The original quilt was made up in an olive green print, red and white. I've changed the color scheme to red, white and blue, but it would also be very handsome in any combination of strongly contrasting colors.

The quilt measures 85″ × 85″ and is made up of two blocks set with a plain block.

FABRIC REQUIREMENTS

6 yards White
2¼ yards Red
1 yard Blue

Piecing Diagram

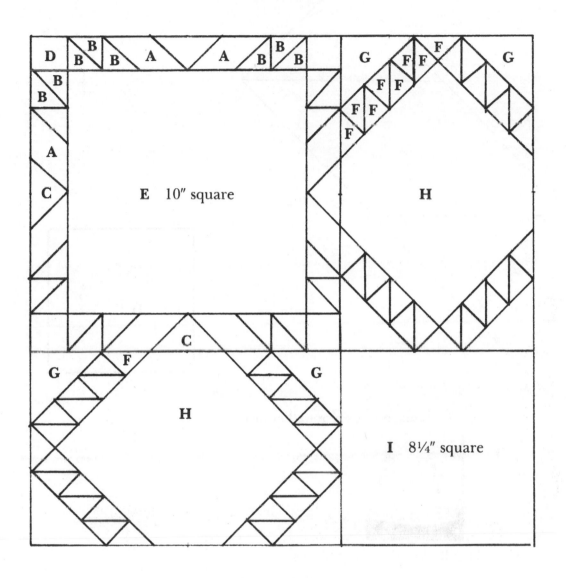

PIECES NEEDED

BLOCK 1 You need nine full blocks, twelve half-blocks and four quarter-blocks.

A	8 Red	136
B	16 White	256
	8 Red	136
C	4 White	64
D	4 Red	64
E	9 10″ squares plus seam allowance	

White 12   ½ squares, 5″ × 10″, plus seam allowance
        4   ¼ squares, 5″ × 5″, plus seam allowance

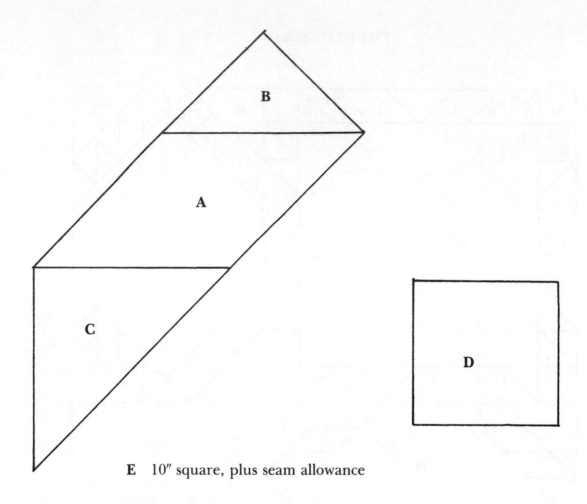

E 10″ square, plus seam allowance

BLOCK 2 24 full-blocks, 16 half-blocks

F	16 White	640
	14 Red	560
G	4 Red	128
H	1 White	24
	½ of H, White	16
I	16 Blue 8¼″ squares, plus seam allowance	

I 8¼″ square, plus seam
   allowance

QUILTING   A very small, allover clamshell, with outline quilting around the design areas.

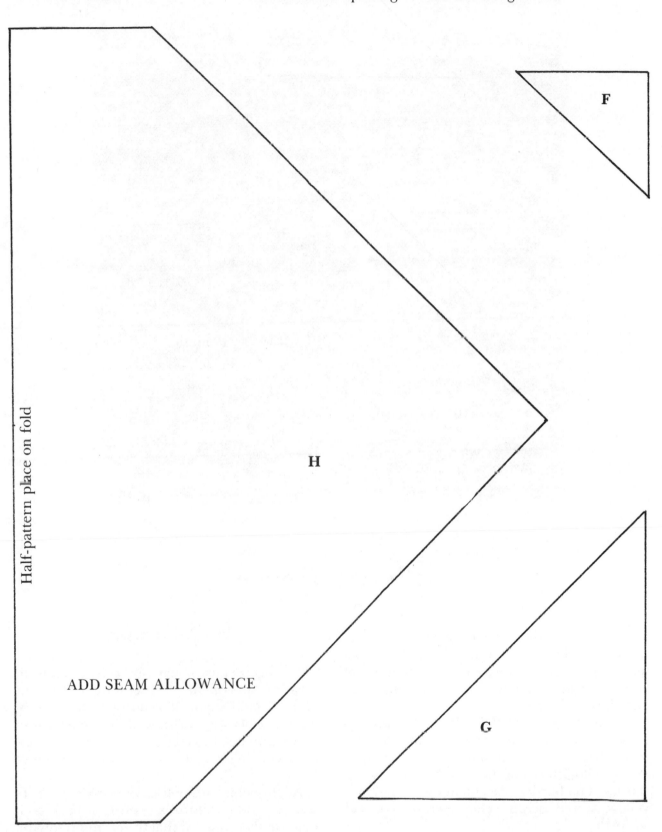

F

Half-pattern place on fold

H

ADD SEAM ALLOWANCE

G

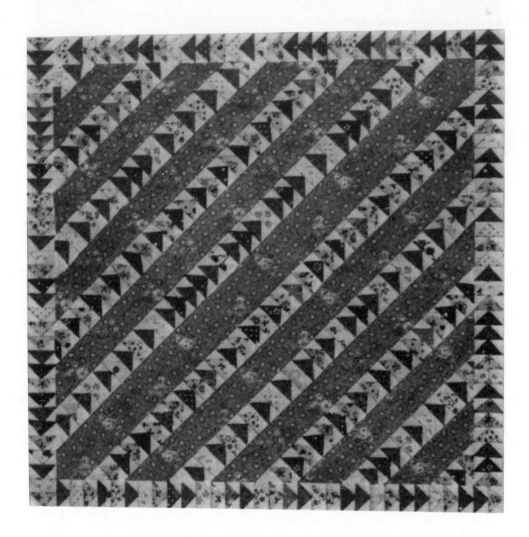

Flying Geese

This quilt is an adaptation of one made in New England in 1840. The unusual feature of this quilt is that the Flying Geese run diagonally across the quilt rather than in the usual up-and-down pattern.

The quilt measures 99″ × 99″ and is a scrap pattern. A red print and a yellow print alternate in the diagonal strips, and within each strip the red or yellow print alternates with various scrap fabrics. The border placement of the red and yellow is: red, scrap, yellow, scrap, red, and so forth.

INSTRUCTIONS

Piece together two strips of Flying Geese to measure approximately 116″ long. Cut center strip 9″ (add seam allowance) wide by 128″ long. I've allowed an extra 2″ in the length so there is no need to add a seam allowance. Sew the Flying Geese strips to each side of the center strip.

At this point, establish your corner. A T-square will be helpful so you can mark both edges and be assured that the corner is square.

Turn the strips on the diagonal and measure in 1″ on each end. Mark with a pencil. This will be the seamline.

All other plain strips are 6″ wide. Continue adding strips in the following order:

> two plain strips 6″ wide by 104″ long
> two pieced strips 89″ long
> two plain strips 6″ wide by 77″ long
> two pieced strips 65″ long
> two plain strips 6″ wide by 53″ long
> two pieced strips 41″ long
> two plain strips 6″ wide by 29″ long
> two pieced strips 14″ long

Spread the top out flat. From the corners you previously marked, measure in 1″ all around the top and mark. You should have an 87″ square. Using the seamline, measure out ½″ for seam allowance (or ¼″, see note above).

Cut off any excess fabric outside this second line.

For the border, piece two strips 87″ long (plus seam allowance) and two strips 99″ long (plus seam allowance). Attach to sides of top.

QUILTING Quilt along each seam of the pieced strips. Straight-line quilting was used in the plain strips.

By scaling this design down to one-third size, it would made a marvellous center for a medallion quilt. Add a large, plain border or use several different borders to bring it to full size. Study some of the medallion quilts, such as the Star of Bethlehem, for ideas. If you decide to scale it down, your finished square will be 33″. The center strips will be 3″ wide by 41″ long. All other strips are 2″ wide. Below is a pattern for the Flying Geese.

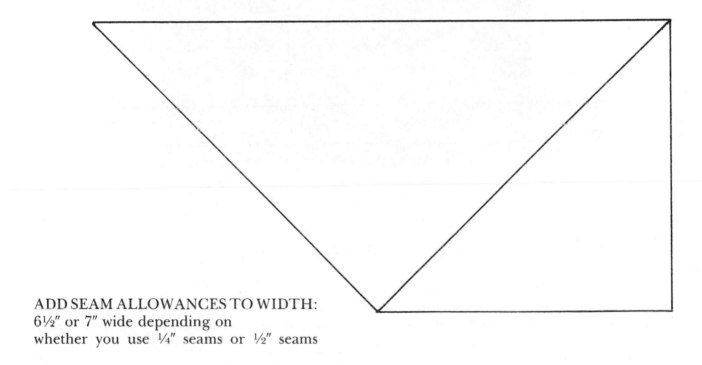

ADD SEAM ALLOWANCES TO WIDTH:
6½″ or 7″ wide depending on
whether you use ¼″ seams or ½″ seams

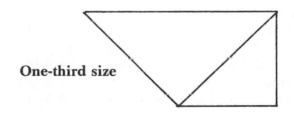

One-third size

From the Schoolhouse Collection, Canton, Ohio

New York Beauty

This lovely quilt came to my attention by way of a collector so I don't have a great deal of information on its origins other than it was made in Akron, Ohio around 1850. I was told that the quilt is a New York Beauty variation, but to me it looks more like a Flying Geese variation set in an unusual arrangement.

The fabric is blue with a small white design. The setting for the quilt is by the row rather than by the block since the pieced strips frame two centers. Another unusual feature about the setting of this quilt is the illusion that the white block at the intersection of each pieced strip alternates between a plain square and a solid Churn Dash.

QUILTING The pieced strips are quilted along each seam. In the large white triangles, the quilting follows the shape of the triangle in straight rows from base to tip. All other areas are quilted in straight lines on the diagonal.

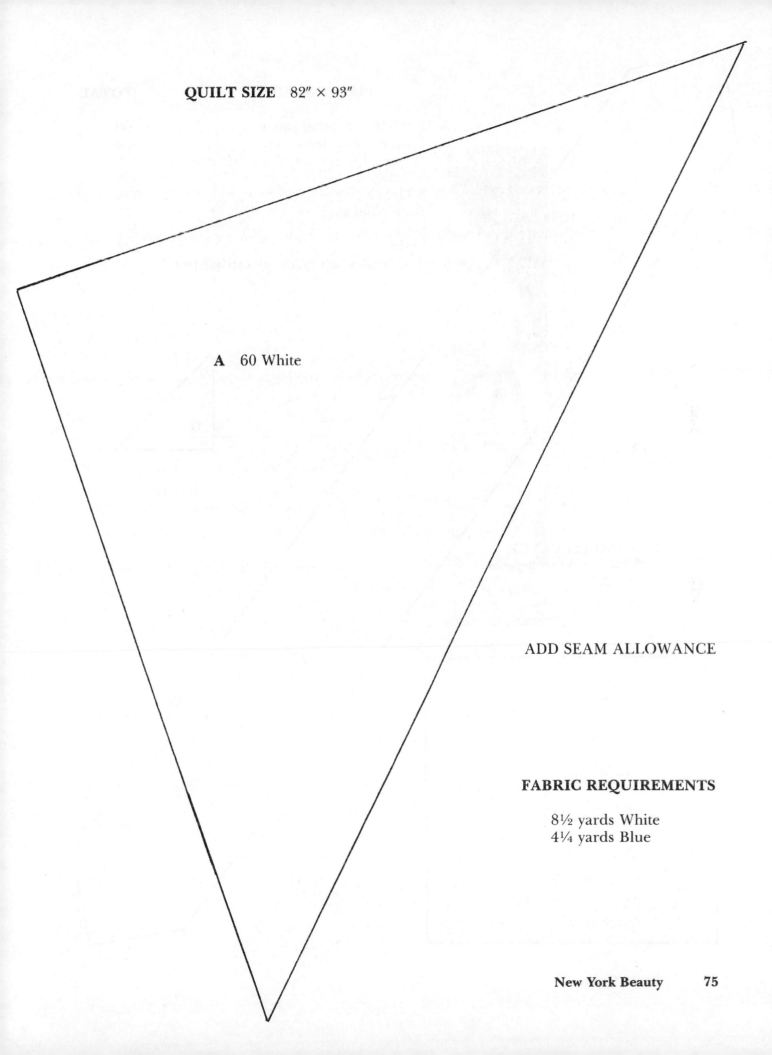

QUILT SIZE 82″ × 93″

A 60 White

ADD SEAM ALLOWANCE

FABRIC REQUIREMENTS

8½ yards White
4¼ yards Blue

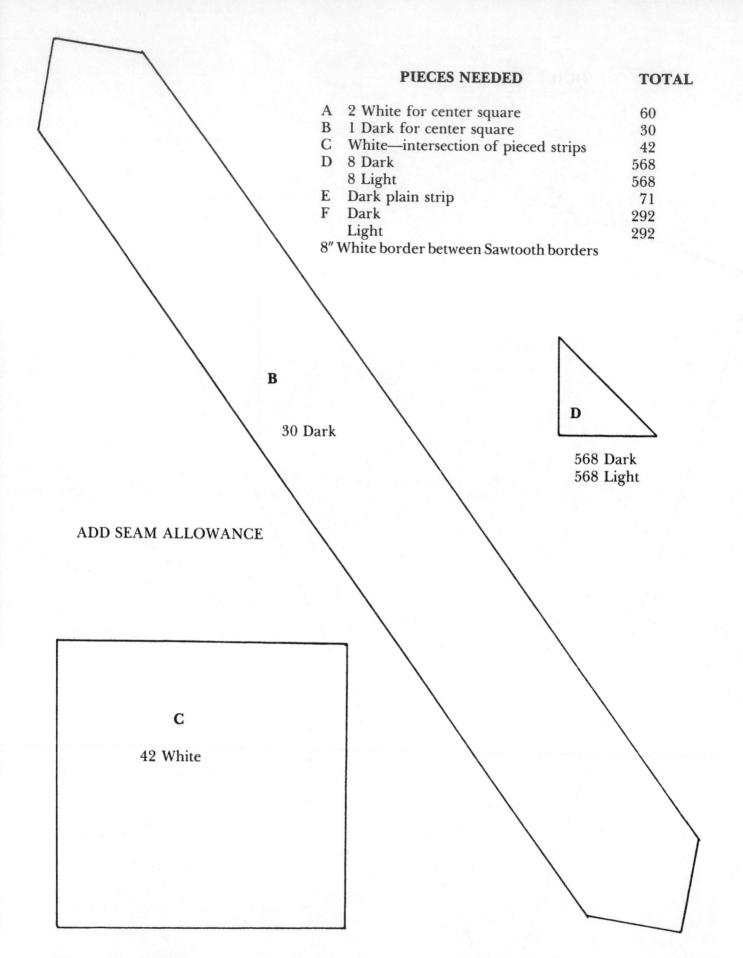

PIECES NEEDED   **TOTAL**

A	2 White for center square	60
B	1 Dark for center square	30
C	White—intersection of pieced strips	42
D	8 Dark	568
	8 Light	568
E	Dark plain strip	71
F	Dark	292
	Light	292

8″ White border between Sawtooth borders

B

30 Dark

D

568 Dark
568 Light

ADD SEAM ALLOWANCE

C

42 White

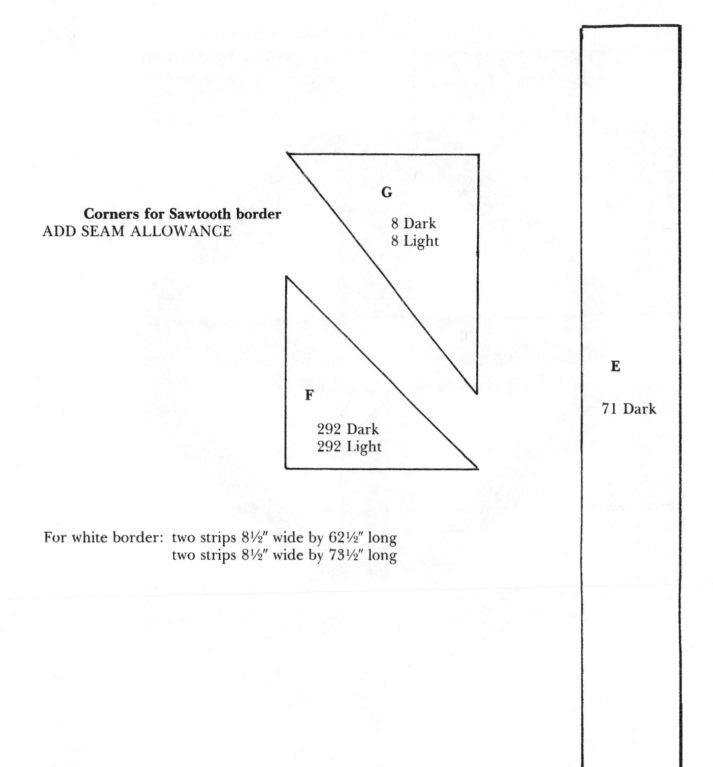

Corners for Sawtooth border
ADD SEAM ALLOWANCE

G
8 Dark
8 Light

F
292 Dark
292 Light

E
71 Dark

For white border: two strips 8½″ wide by 62½″ long
two strips 8½″ wide by 73½″ long

Outer Border   Repeat as for inner border making 39 units for top and bottom strips and 44 units for side strips. Add G-corners to side strips.

Diagram for corners of Sawtooth borders

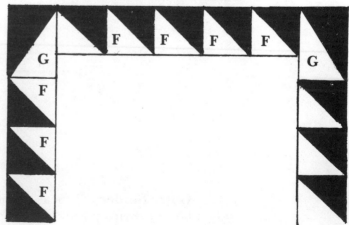

Inner Border Top and bottom, piece 58 light and dark F. Join to form strips 29 units long.

Sides Piece 68 light and dark F. Make two strips equal to 34 units, piece four light and dark G units. Attach one to each end of the 34-square strip. Sew to sides of quilt.

From the DAR Museum, Washington, D.C.

Star of Bethlehem

The Star of Bethlehem pattern is a favorite among experienced quiltmakers. This example from the DAR Museum is unusual in two respects. First, the color scheme, which gives it an almost Amish look due to the dark colors used for the background. (It can be seen in full color in the section between pages 64 and 65.) The second unusual feature is the diamond border. Most quilts using this pattern have some form of appliqué or a smaller design in the four corners and are finished off with a simple binding without a border.

This is a rather small quilt, measuring 60" × 60". There are 13 rows using part A, in the following order:

Row 1	8 Dark Blue	Row 7	56 Green
Row 2	16 Yellow	Row 8	48 Red
Row 3	24 White	Row 9	40 Gold
Row 4	32 Yellow	Row 10	32 Yellow
Row 5	40 Gold	Row 11	24 Dark Blue
Row 6	48 Red	Row 12	16 Yellow
		Row 13	8 White

4 Dark Blue 14" squares for corners
4 Dark Blue triangles 14" on straight sides
5" wide Dark Blue outer border

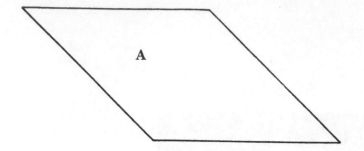

A

FABRIC REQUIREMENTS

4 yards Dark Blue
1 yard Yellow
¼ yard White
⅔ yard Gold
1 yard Red
½ yard Green

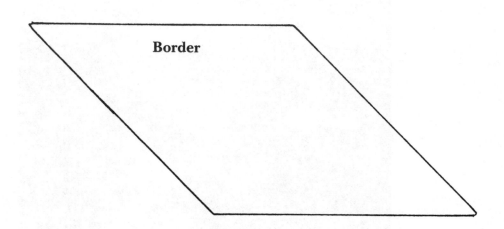

Border

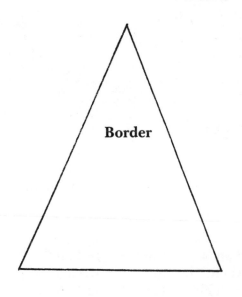

Border

Piece each point of the diamond, then assemble into the star. Add corner squares and center triangles to square the quilt.

Using the diamond pattern marked "For Border" piece a strip to fit each side. Finish with a 5″ dark blue border.

ADD SEAM ALLOWANCE

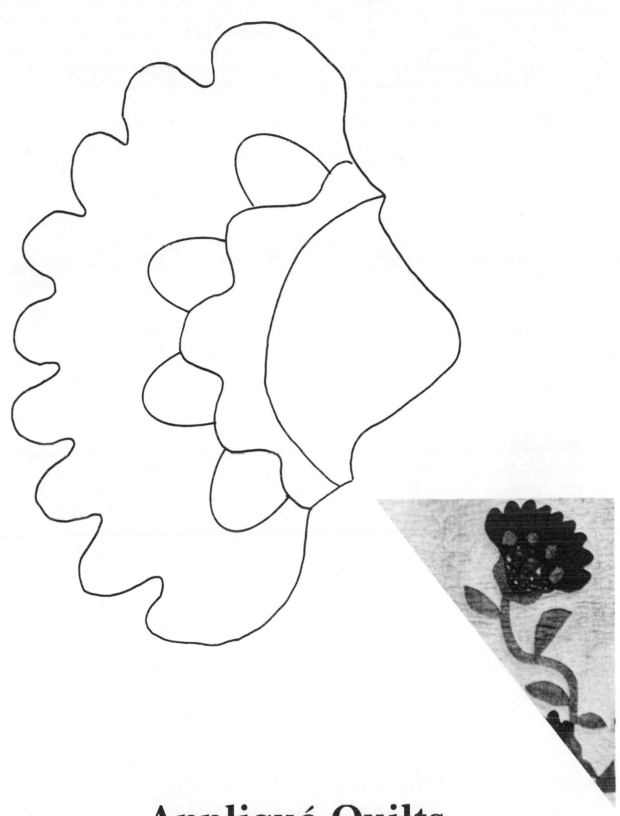

Appliqué Quilts

Appliqué, like piecework, developed through thrift. In the fifteenth century it was popular to embroider designs on one fabric, cut them out and applying them on to more expensive fabric.

Later, when printed fabric became scarce, bits and pieces were hoarded, and in imitation of embroidered work were appliquéd to larger pieces of cloth. Soon, further economy was practiced by joining small pieces to other small pieces to form one design which would be appliquéd. Much of the early appliqué is an imitation of other frequently more costly work. And you will find examples of appliqué in several of the other sections of this book.

From the Massillon Museum, Massillon, Ohio

Eagles

The eagle has always been a popular motif among quiltmakers and the pattern for this version from the Massillon Museum, Massillon, Ohio, was used extensively from Vermont to Ohio during the early 1800's. Several quilts of this design have weathered the years in almost mint condition. This one, made in 1850, apparently was never used as the pencil lines used for the quilting are still visible. The pattern can be seen in full color on the cover of the book and shown here in black and white.

The four eagles are each appliquéd to a 36" square of white fabric. The head and tail are in a plain beige, the body gold and the wings a bright red. Each eagle has three stars around the tail area, with an additional four stars appliquéd to the seams around the center wheel. The wheel, consisting of a yellow center star, a beige ring and a red ring is appliquéd after the four squares have been joined.

The quilting on the wings is a single running stitch to accent the shape of the wing. The body is quilted with a diamond design, and the tail has stitching, running from top to bottom to give dimension. Each star has a small circle quilted in the center. The 9½″ border is quilted with a large cable pattern.

Another version of this pattern finished the quilt off with a three-row sawtooth border.

QUILT SIZE 91″ × 91″

FABRIC REQUIREMENTS

6½ yards White   1½ yards Beige
1 yard Gold   1½ yards Red

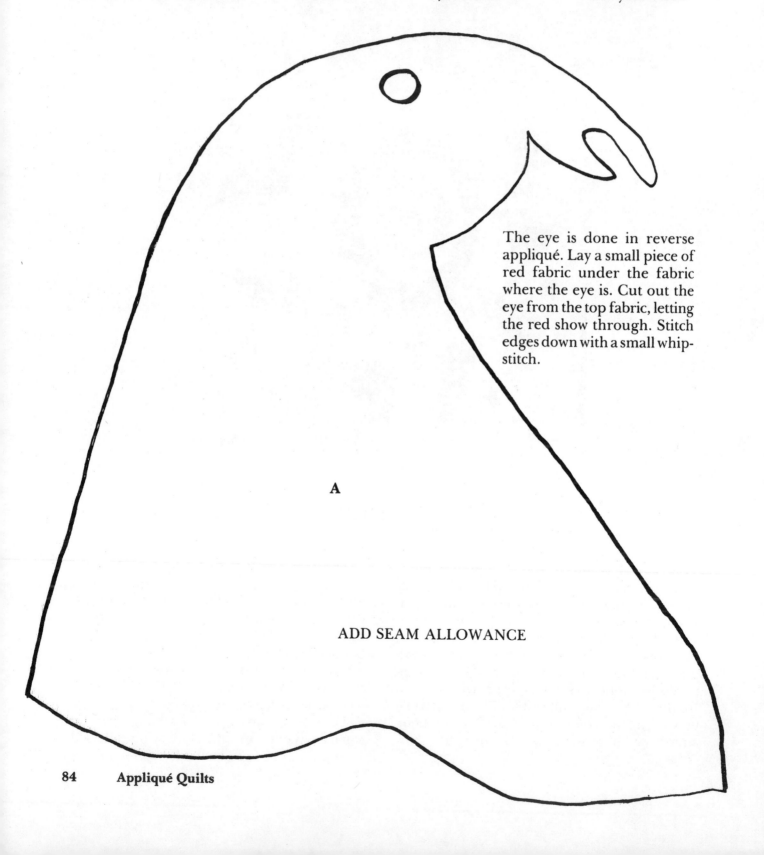

The eye is done in reverse appliqué. Lay a small piece of red fabric under the fabric where the eye is. Cut out the eye from the top fabric, letting the red show through. Stitch edges down with a small whip-stitch.

A

ADD SEAM ALLOWANCE

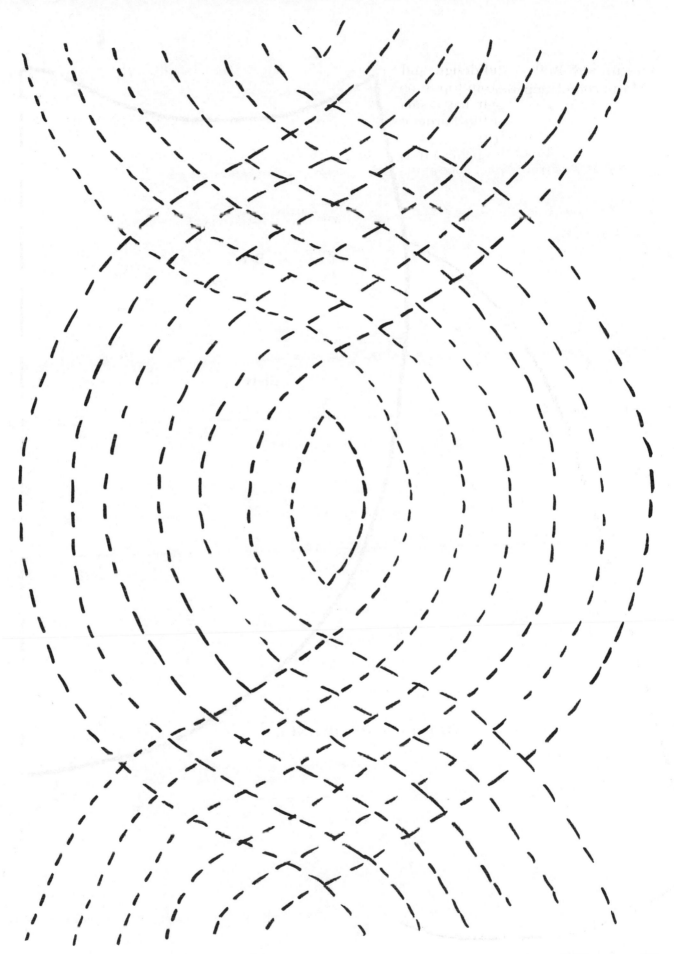

Line up with B-2
to form complete pattern

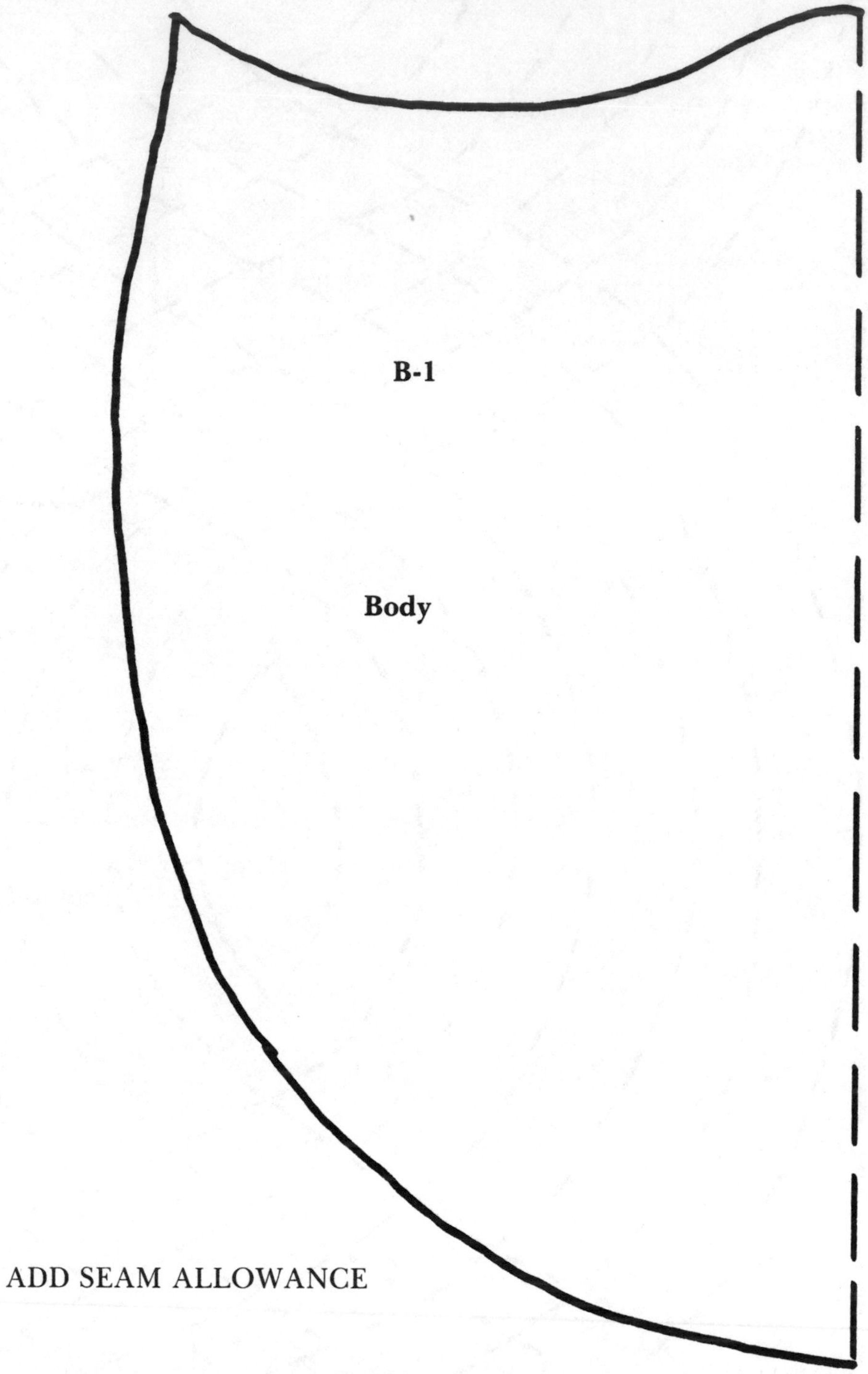

B-1

Body

ADD SEAM ALLOWANCE

ADD SEAM ALLOWANCE

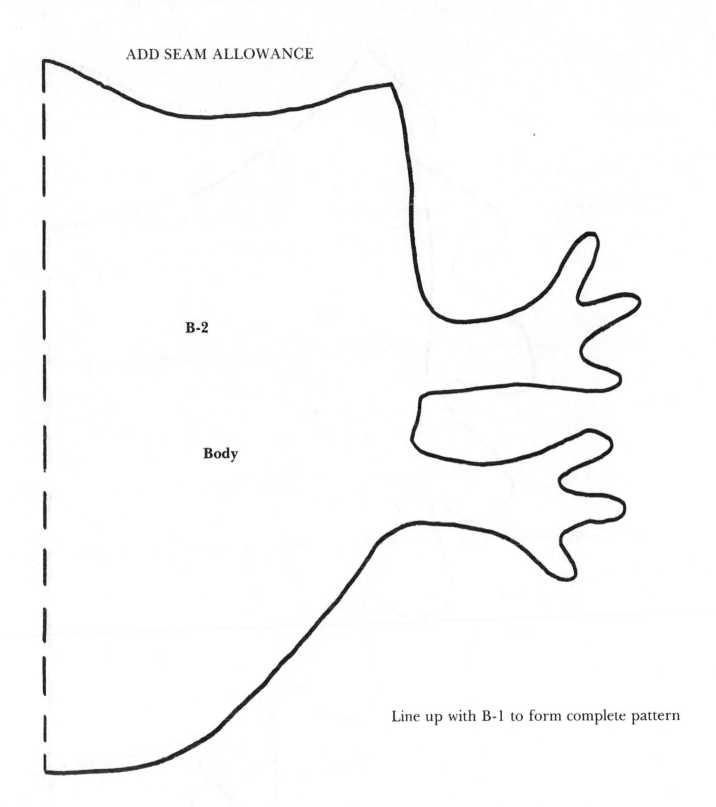

B-2

Body

Line up with B-1 to form complete pattern

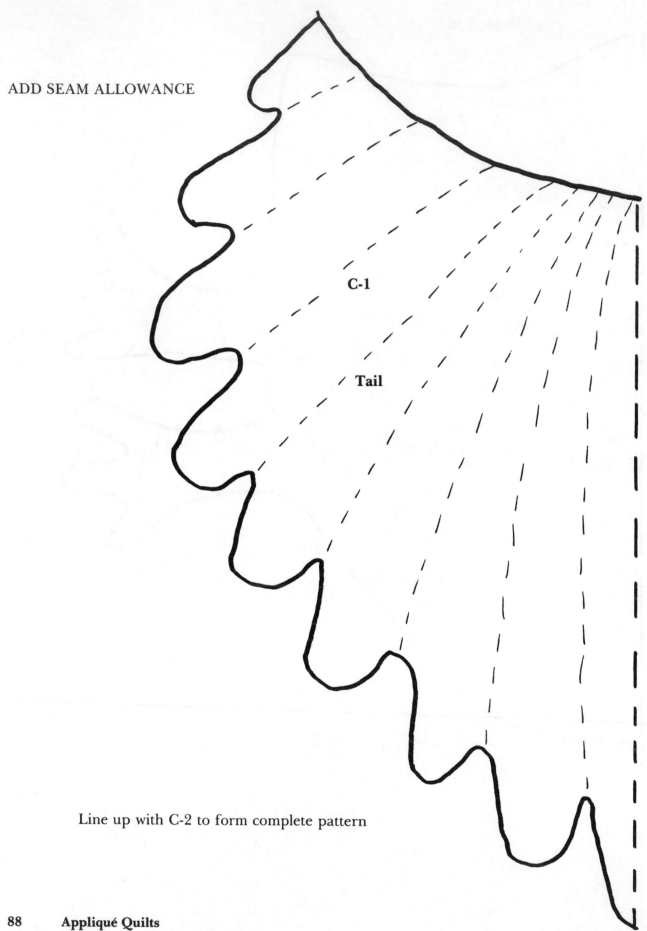

ADD SEAM ALLOWANCE

C-1

Tail

Line up with C-2 to form complete pattern

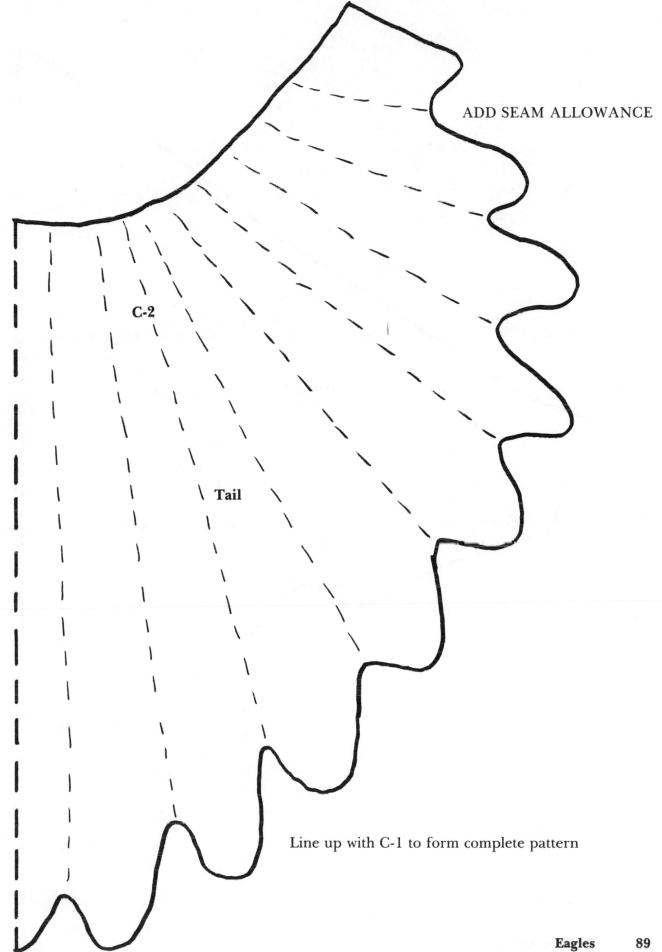

ADD SEAM ALLOWANCE

C-2

Tail

Line up with C-1 to form complete pattern

ADD SEAM ALLOWANCE

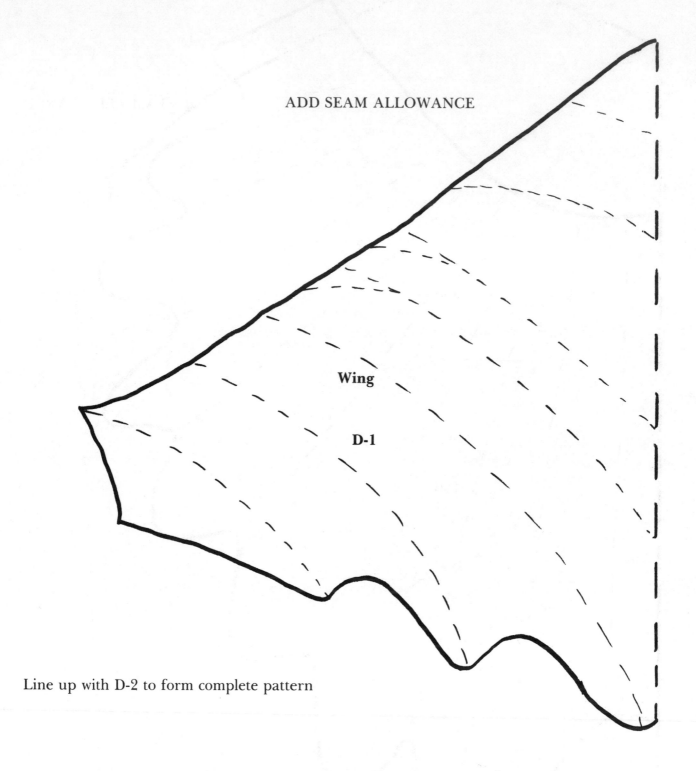

Wing

D-1

Line up with D-2 to form complete pattern

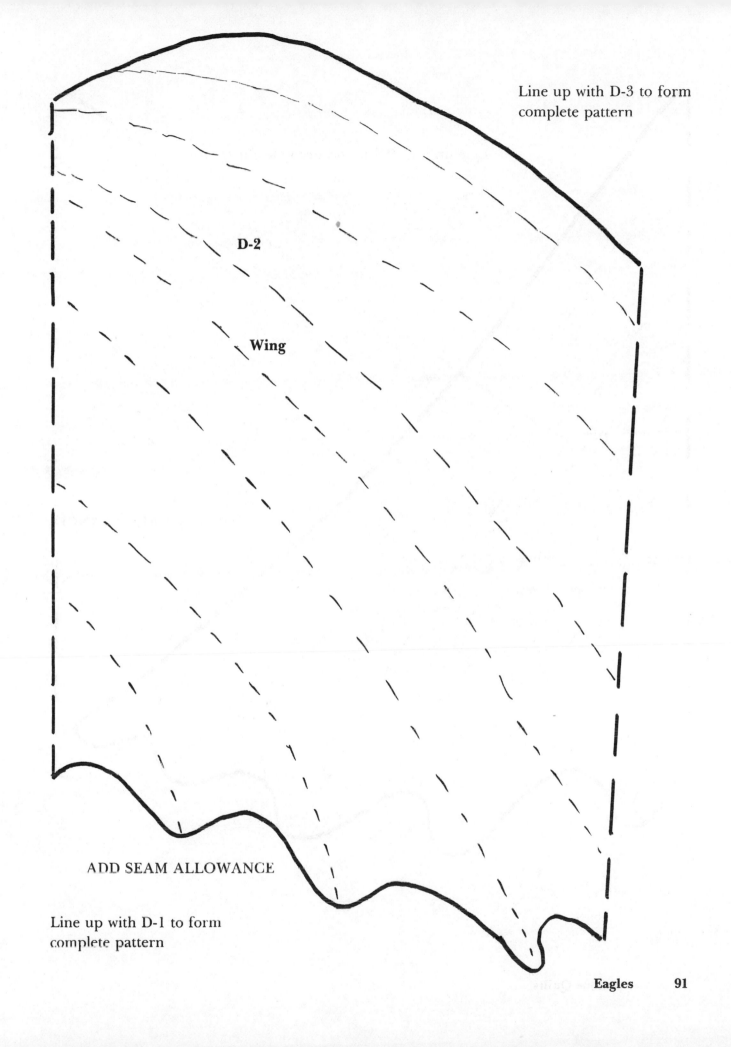

Line up with D-3 to form
complete pattern

D-2

Wing

ADD SEAM ALLOWANCE

Line up with D-1 to form
complete pattern

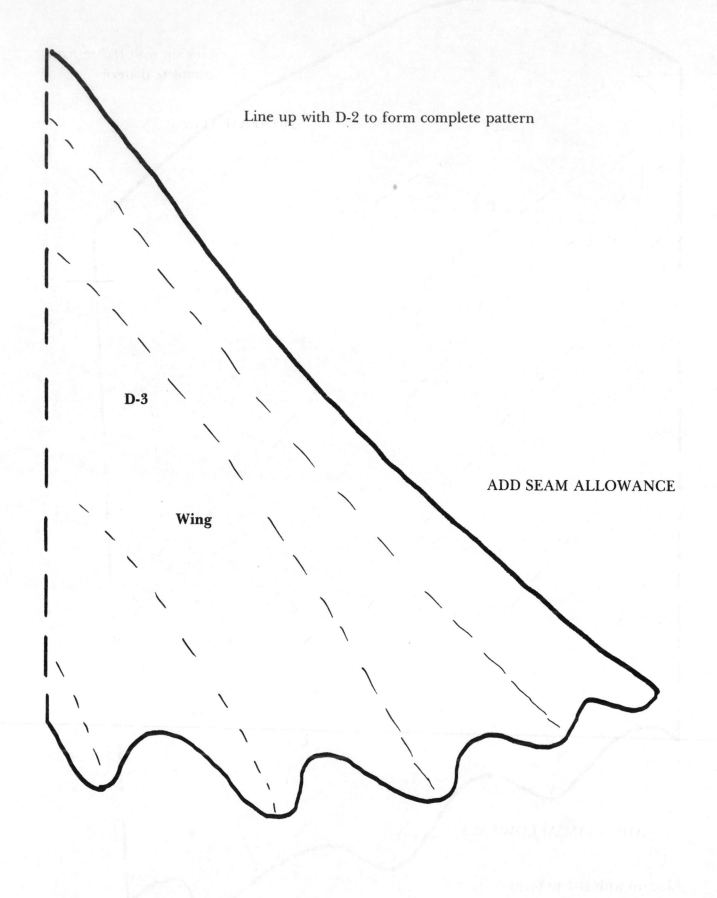

Line up with D-2 to form complete pattern

D-3

Wing

ADD SEAM ALLOWANCE

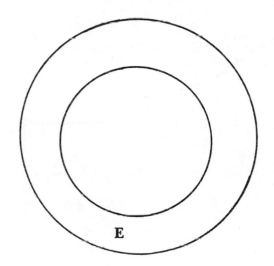

E

ADD SEAM ALLOWANCE

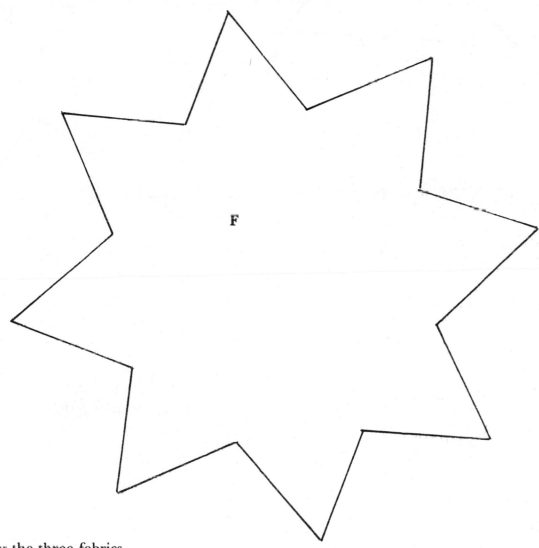

F

16 needed using the three fabrics
1 Gold for center of quilt

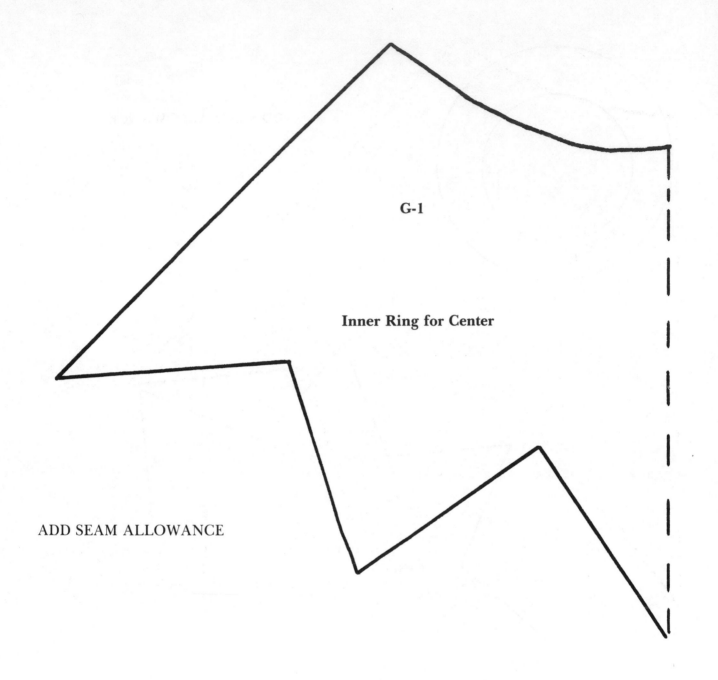

G-1

Inner Ring for Center

ADD SEAM ALLOWANCE

Line up with H-2 for complete pattern (This makes one-quarter of the center circle; cut out four and seam together)

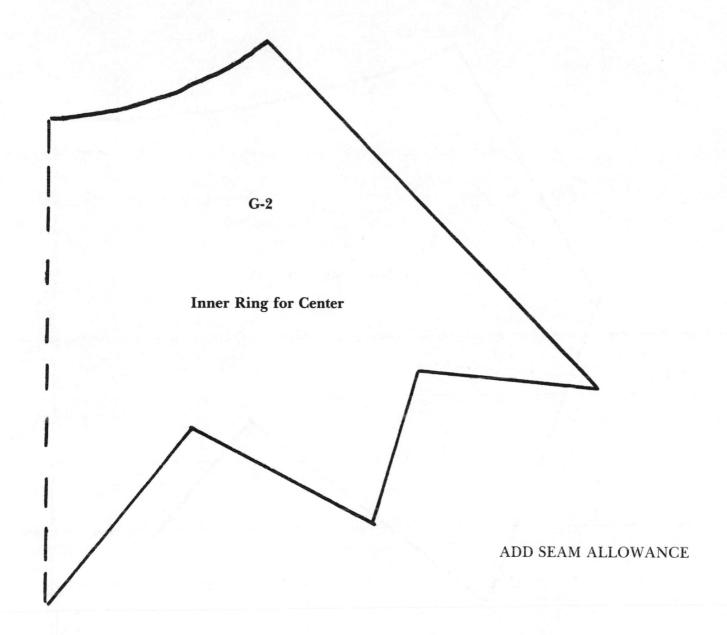

G-2

Inner Ring for Center

ADD SEAM ALLOWANCE

Line up with G-1 for complete pattern (one-quarter of circle)

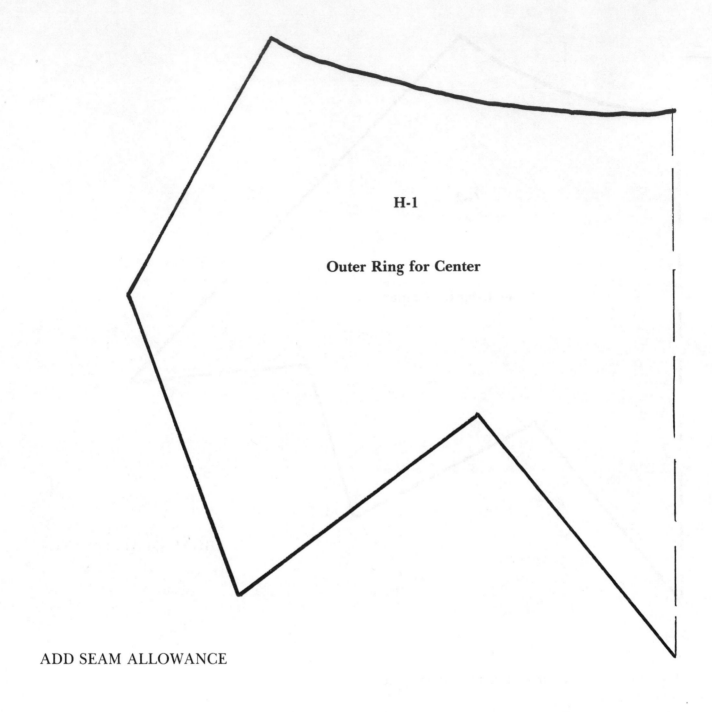

H-1

Outer Ring for Center

ADD SEAM ALLOWANCE

Line up with G-2 for complete pattern (this makes one-quarter of the circle; cut out four and seam together to complete)

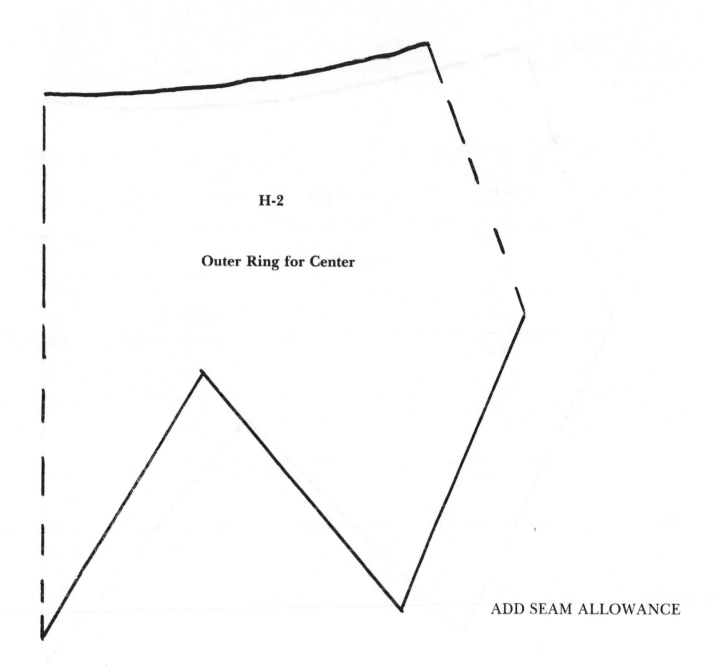

H-2

Outer Ring for Center

ADD SEAM ALLOWANCE

Line up with H-1 to complete pattern for one-quarter of the circle

Line up with H-2
to complete

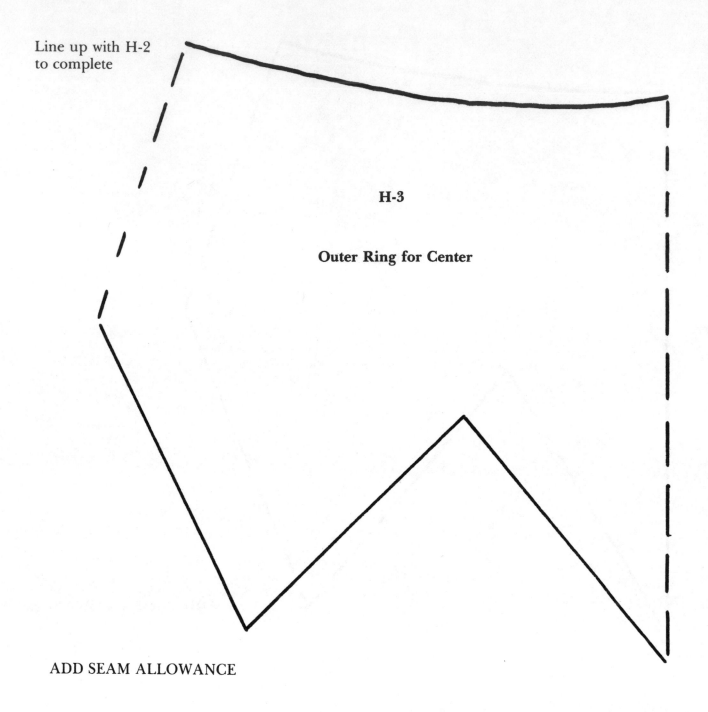

H-3

Outer Ring for Center

ADD SEAM ALLOWANCE

Line up with H-4 for complete pattern

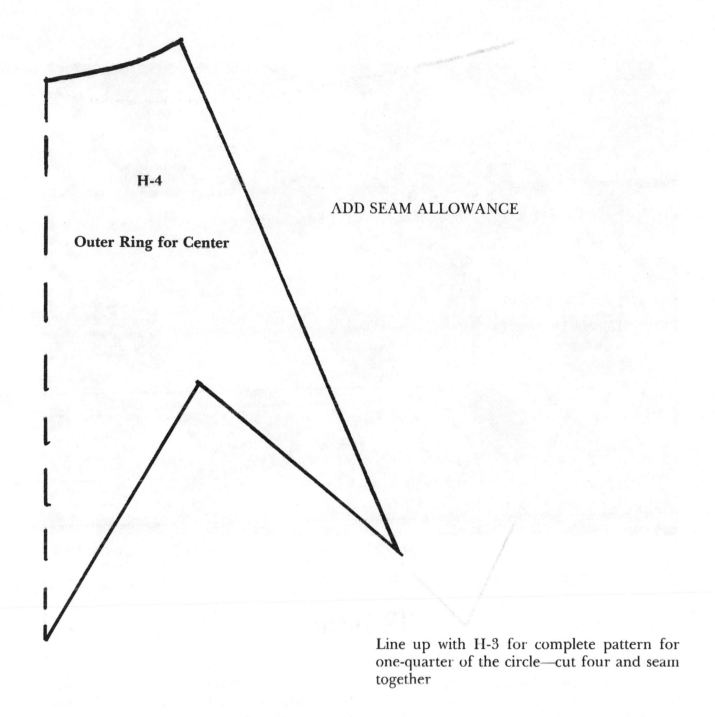

H-4

Outer Ring for Center

ADD SEAM ALLOWANCE

Line up with H-3 for complete pattern for one-quarter of the circle—cut four and seam together

Courtesy of the Geauga County Historical Society, Burton, Ohio

Thistle

This quilt comes from the Geauga County Historical Society in Burton, Ohio, and like the other quilts from their collection, I don't have any documented background other than it was made by Polly Henry. Her name is embroidered in the quilting.

I included this quilt because I like the block design. It appears to be an appliqué translation of some of the early crewel embroidery designs used for bed hangings. However, I don't care for the way the quilt is set. Even though the blocks are all going in the same direction, it appears too busy and haphazard

I'm providing two ways in which to set this quilt, the first being to arrange the blocks so that the leaf of each of four blocks meet at the center. You need thirty-six 16″ blocks, set six across and six down. Adding a 6″ border will give you a finished quilt of 102″ × 102″.

The second setting is to alternate the pieced blocks with plain blocks. For this setting you need thirteen pieced and twelve plain blocks, set five across by five down. With the addition of a 6″ border, your quilt measures 86″ × 86″.

FABRIC REQUIREMENTS

VERSION 1	VERSION 2
11 yards White	8 yards White
5½ yards Green	2 yards Green
¾ yard Red Print	¼ yard Red Print
1¼ yards Red	½ yard Red
½ yard Dark Red	¼ yard Dark Red

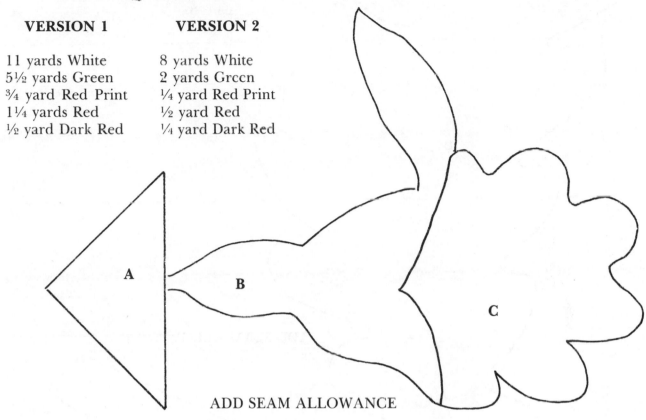

ADD SEAM ALLOWANCE

QUILTING Quilt along all seamlines. Background quilting is closely spaced diagonal lines.

	PIECES PER QUILT	VERSION 1	VERSION 2
A	1 Green	36	13
B	1 Green	36	13
C	1 Red Print	36	13
D	1 Green	36	13
E	1 Green	36	13
F	1 Red	36	13
G	2 Green	72	26
H	2 Green	72	26
I	2 Green	72	26
J	2 Green	72	26
K	2 Red Print	72	26
L	2 Dark Red	72	26
M	8 Green	288	104
N	2 Red	72	26

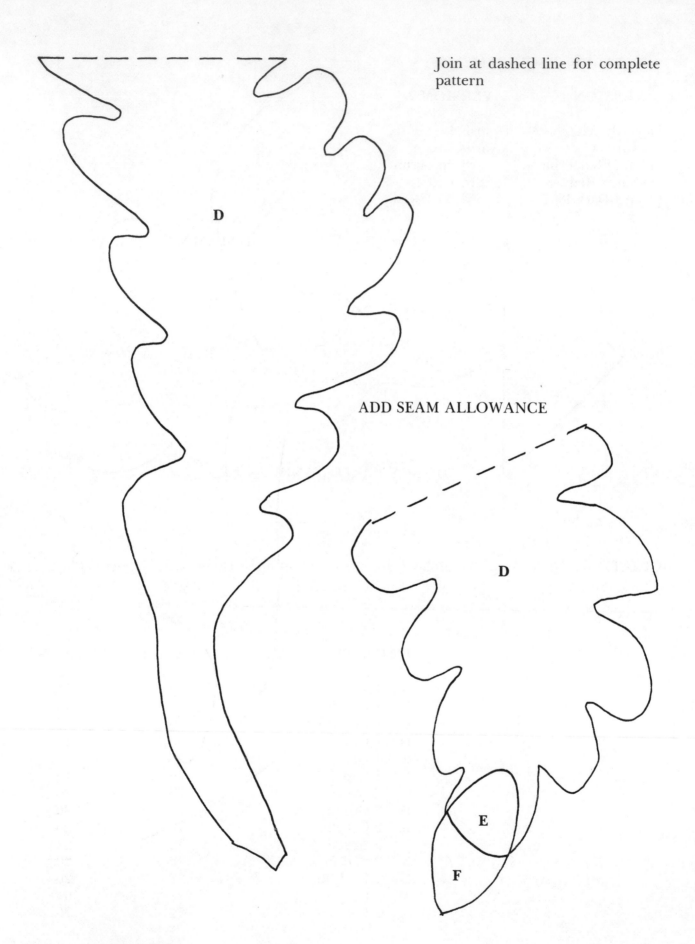

Join at dashed line for complete pattern

ADD SEAM ALLOWANCE

D

D

E

F

ADD SEAM ALLOWANCE

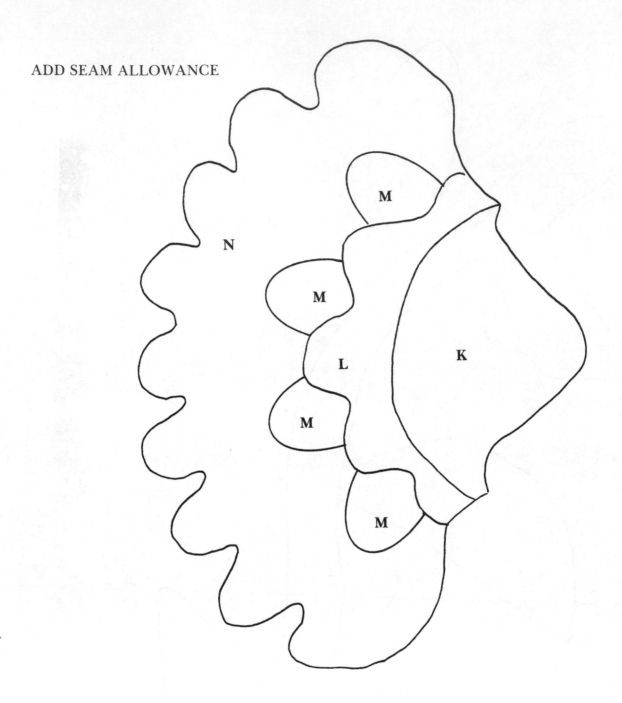

From the Collection of the Mercer Museum, courtesy of the Bucks County Historical Society

Snowflake

Pennsylvania Dutch designs are usually recognizable because of their bold designs and strong colors. At the time many of these quilts were made, the color schemes were considered rather bizarre by those outside the community, but to our eye, being used to modern graphics as we are, they are quite pleasing. Unlike the Amish, who are sometimes lumped with them, the Pennsylvania Dutch did not limit themselves to geometric forms and many of their quilts were lavishly embellished with hearts, flowers, and birds.

In this quilt, the delicate geometric form of the snowflake makes a bold statement in green, red and yellow. It has been enlarged to a 21" block, and the red and yellow zigzag border adds to the dynamics of the design. The border is a 13½" strip of printed fabric. A border print would work nicely on this quilt, if you adjust the size of the border to accommodate the print chosen. The finished quilt measures 90" × 90".

The pattern given is one-eighth of the total design. To make a full-size pattern, trace around the segment given, move the paper over enough to line up the traced portion with the pattern and trace again, repeating until all eight segments have been drawn.

You could also treat this like a cut-paper design. To use this method, you need a very sharp pair of scissors. Fold a 20" square of yellow fabric in half, then in quarters, then fold the resulting square diagonally so you have eight layers of fabric. Lay the pattern segment on the fabric and cut out. To prevent shifting of fabric, baste the layers together loosely.

Zigzag border

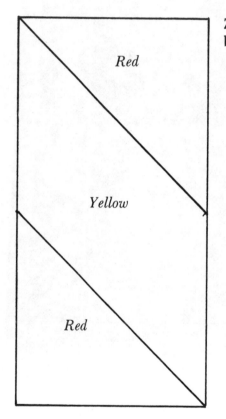

Red

Yellow

Red

ADD SEAM ALLOWANCE

FABRIC REQUIREMENTS

3⅛ yards Green
4¼ yards Yellow
1½ yards Red

For the border you need 156 yellow pieces and 312 red pieces. Sew the pieces together as shown in the pattern, then join to form a zigzag.

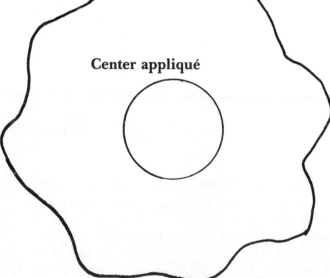

Center appliqué

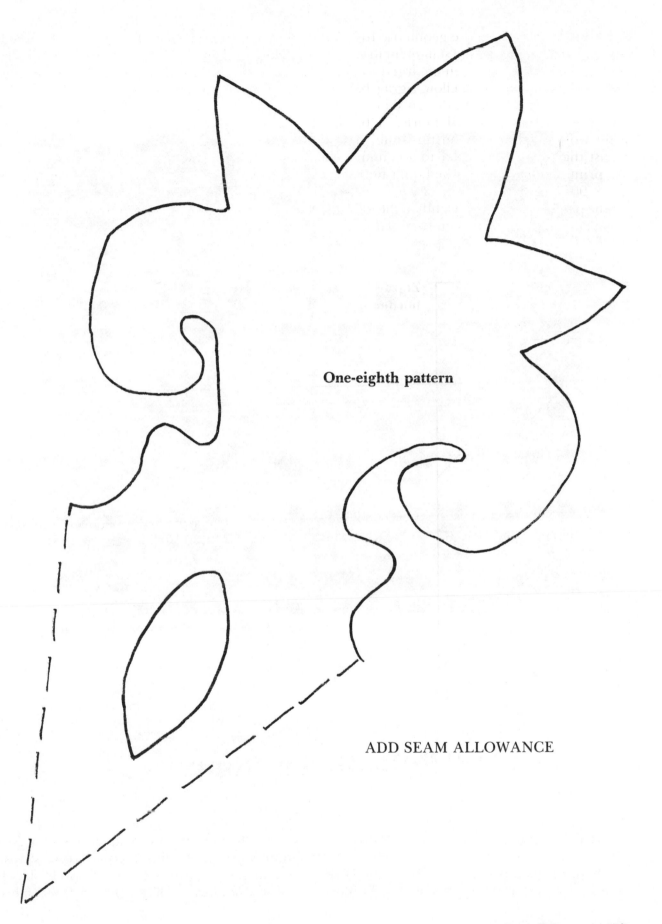

One-eighth pattern

ADD SEAM ALLOWANCE

From the DAR Museum, Washington, D.C.

Full-Blown Poppy

This very feminine quilt was made by Lucy Howland Bassett Thatcher of Lee, Massachusetts, in 1860.

The information I received from the DAR Museum says that the border is a preprinted tape, but I have supplied a pattern for the roses. The border pattern alone would make a stunning quilt set with alternate plain strips.

The quilt measures 83″ × 89″; twelve blocks 19″ square, with a 13″ border on three sides.

ADD SEAM ALLOWANCE

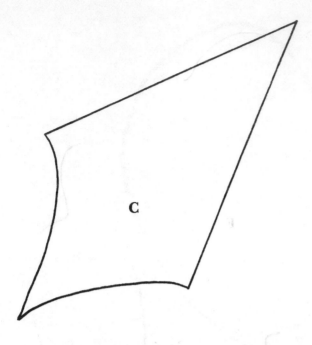

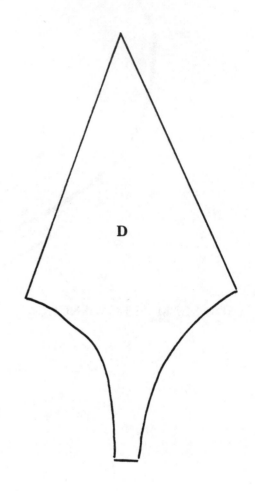

ADD SEAM ALLOWANCE

FABRIC REQUIREMENTS

5¾ yards White
¼ yard Rose
1 yard Pink

2¾ yards Green
16 yards Green bias-fold tape (border)

		PIECES PER BLOCK	PER QUILT
A	1	Rose	12
B	4	Pink	48
C	4	Green	48
D	4	Green	48
E	1	Green	12
F	2	Green	24

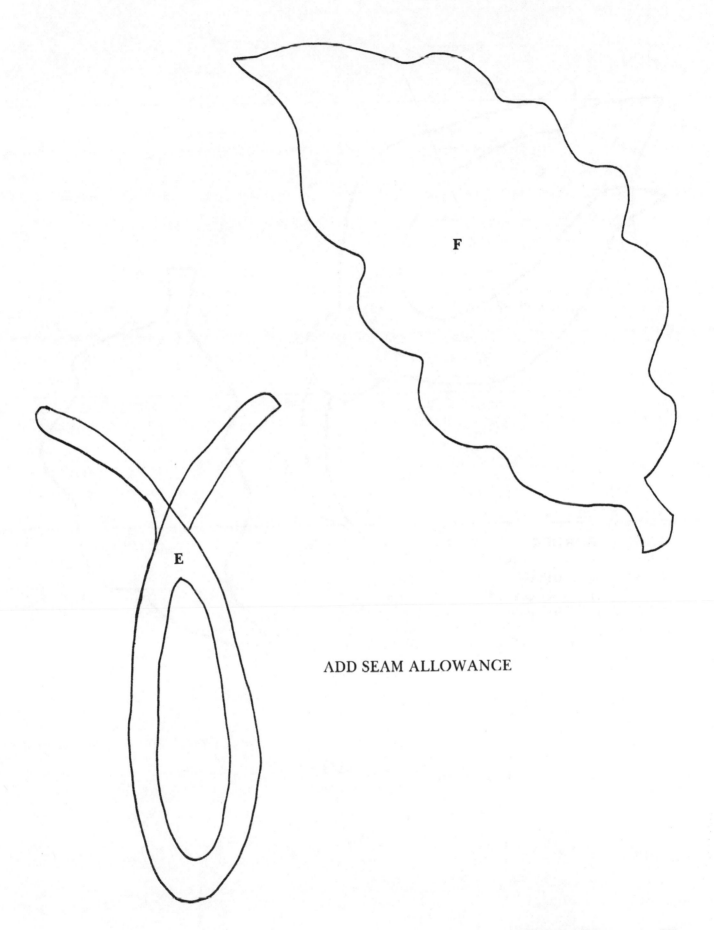

F

E

ADD SEAM ALLOWANCE

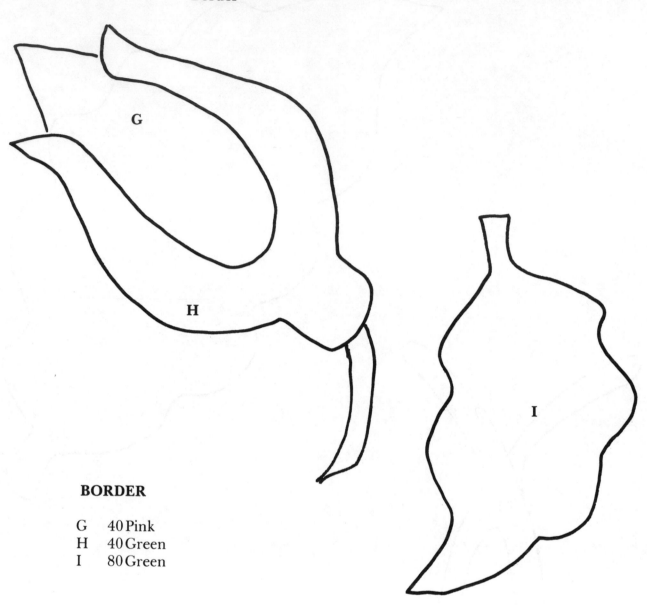

BORDER

G   40 Pink
H   40 Green
I   80 Green

ADD SEAM ALLOWANCE

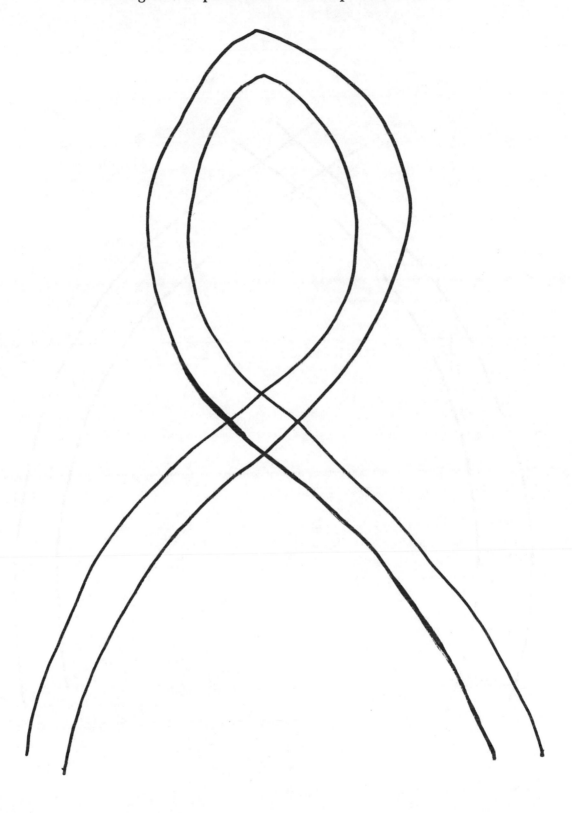

Diagram for placement of bias tape on border (continued)

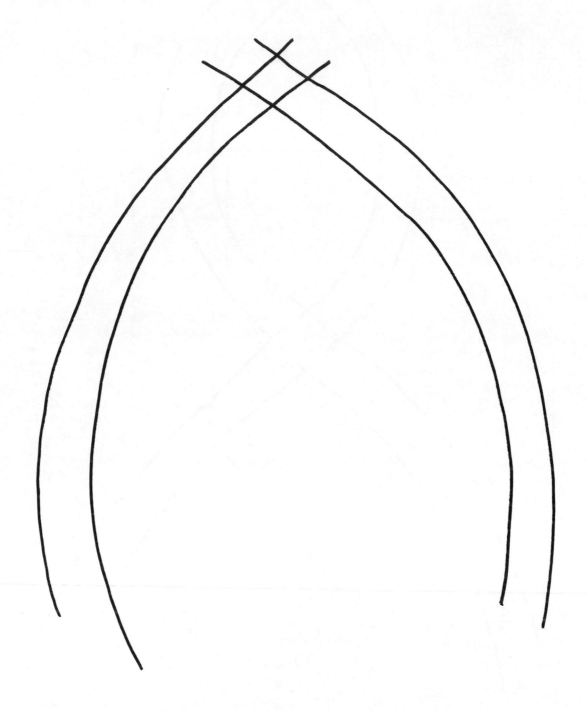

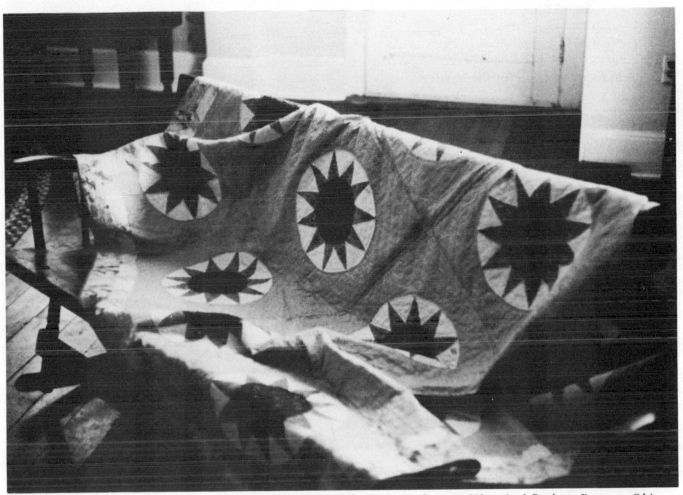

Courtesy of the Geauga County Historical Society, Burton, Ohio

Sunburst II

This quilt is in the possession of the Geauga County Historical Society in Ohio and the only information I have about it is the knowledgeable opinion of one of the trustees that it predates 1860. However old it is, it's a nice pattern that would lend itself well to many color schemes. A light greyish-blue was used for the background of the blocks, with the suns in navy blue and an orange print.

QUILT SIZE   92″ × 92″   16″ block

A	1 Dark Blue print	25
B	11 Orange print	275
C	11 White	275

25 Light Blue 16″ squares (plus seam allowance)

The border is 6″ wide.

FABRIC REQUIREMENTS

⅞ yard Dark Blue
1⅝ yards Orange
1⅝ yards White
6¼ yards Light Blue
1¾ yards are needed for the border

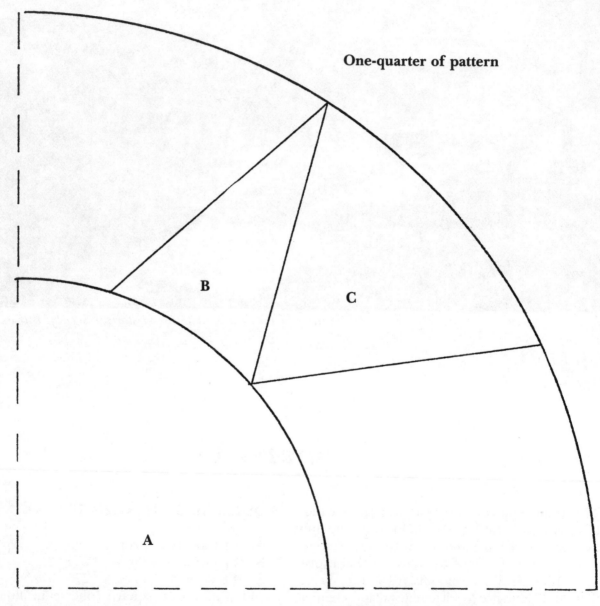

One-quarter of pattern

B

C

A

ADD SEAM ALLOWANCE

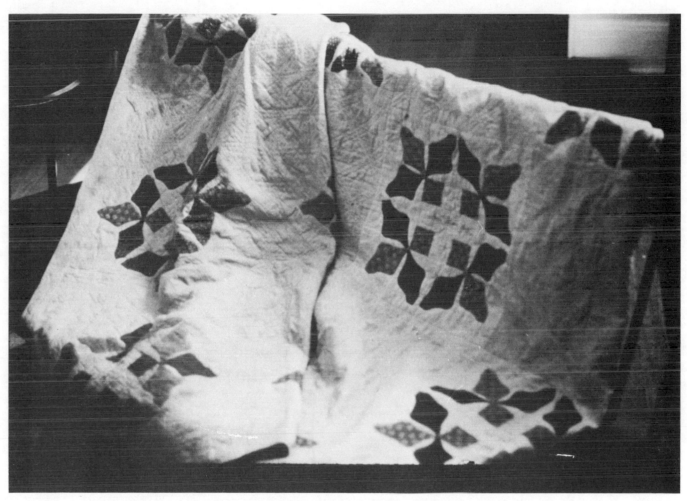

Courtesy of the Geauga County Historical Society, Burton, Ohio

Honeybee

This old favorite is from the Geauga County Historical Society in Ohio and dates to about 1850. This version was set on the diagonal with alternate plain blocks. This would also make an excellent pattern for an album quilt with space for signatures in the center of each block.

QUILT SIZE 85″ × 102″

30 pieced blocks, 20 plain blocks, 18 half-blocks
and 4 quarter-blocks

A 4 Pink   120
   5 White   150
B 4 Pink   120
C 8 Green   240

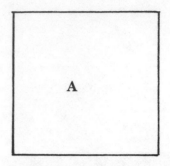

FABRIC REQUIREMENTS

8 yards White
1½ yards Pink
1¼ yards Green

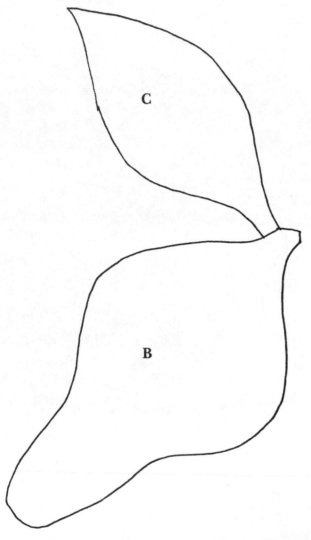

ADD SEAM ALLOWANCE

Piece the center nine-patch, using Part A. Make
Pattern D to measure 3¾″ × 4½″. Cut out two
for each block (total of 60) and sew to top and
bottom of block. Make Pattern E to measure
3¾″ × 12″ (add seam allowances) and seam to
remaining two sides of block. Appliqué B and C
to outer edges of block.

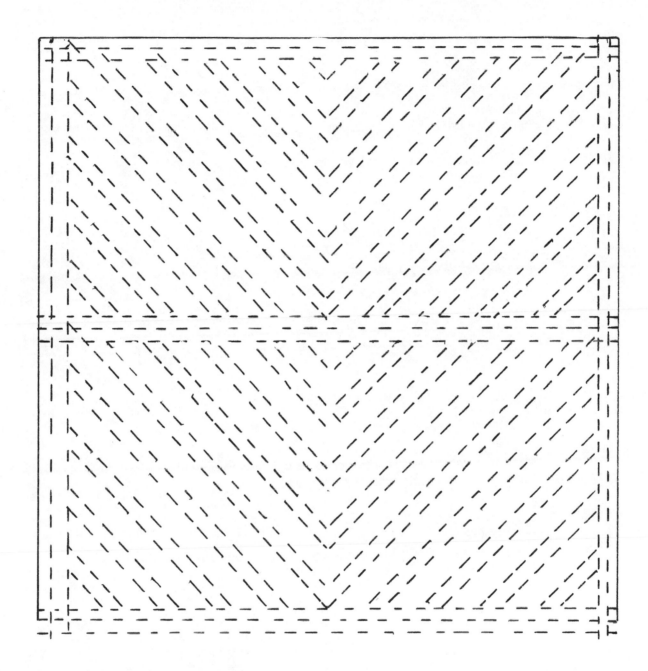

QUILTING For the appliqué blocks, quilt around each piece. Follow this line for each succeeding row, both into the piece, and towards the edge of the block. For the plain blocks, use the pattern given.

Strip Quilts

With the exception of the Amish "Bars" quilt pattern, strip quilts are a rarity. However, as you can see from the following examples, the strip quilt can be as beautiful as any pieced design. In addition, it is very quick to make. If you prefer quilting to piecing, the strip quilt is the one for you.

The quilt on the preceding page was made in 1775. It is made up of chintz fabric, cut in strips of equal width, alternating dark and light printed fabric, and finished with an equal border at top and bottom. This type of quilt can be made to any size desired merely by adding or subtracting strips, or by altering the width of the strips.

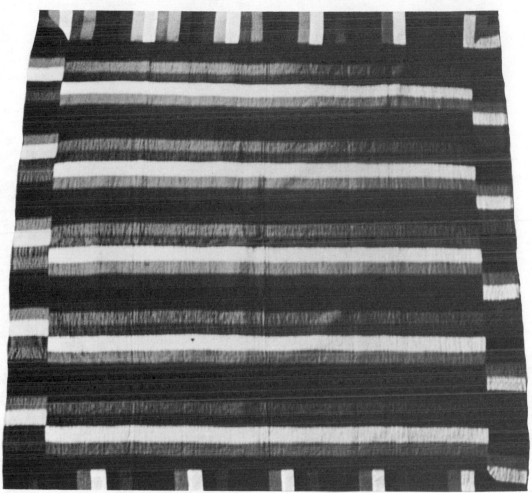

From the Collection of the Mercer Museum, courtesy of the Bucks County Historical Society

Bars

The Bars quilt is typically Amish with its strong colors and geometric design. Strips of gold, red, brown, grey, teal blue, green and cream were cut to equal widths and stitched in a repeating pattern. The border uses the same strips, cut shorter. On the vertical sides, the border strips are slightly offset.

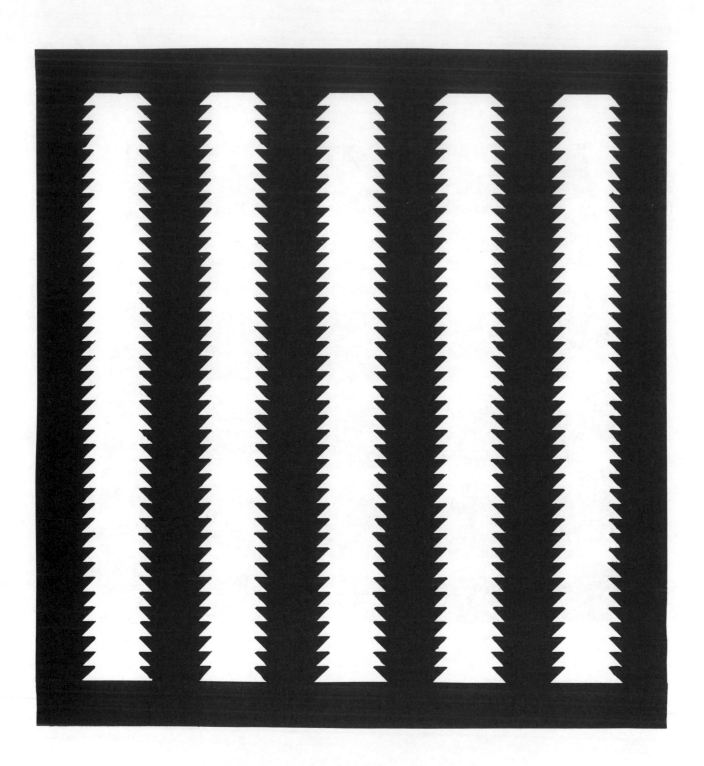

Tree Everlasting

The design, Tree Everlasting, was made around 1850. The bold simplicity of the design makes it popular with many, and it will make up beautifully in any light/dark color combination.

The quilt measures 75″ × 90″ and requires 4½ yards red and 4¼ yards white fabric. The amount of fabric given allows for the strips to be cut without piecing.

PATTERN PIECES A 400 Red   400 White

The following strips include seam allowance:

5 strips of White 5½″ × 80½″
6 strips of Red 5½″ × 80½″
2 strips of Red 5½″ × 90½″

Piece together the red and white A-pieces, and join into strips 40 units long. Set the pieced strips on each side of the white strips, then join to the red strips. Add the 5½″ × 90½″ strips to top and bottom.

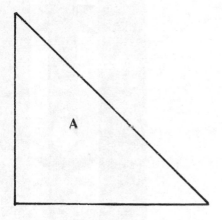

Pattern for Tree Everlasting

Shooting Star

This final example is of Black origin. The example I saw was made by Ginny Rimbert of Demopolis, Alabama, around 1880. Another quilt using a similar pattern made by Harriet Powers, also a Black woman, in 1898, is in the collection of the Boston Museum of Fine Arts. The quilt is a pictorial representation of a meteor shower that occurred on November 13, 1833. The event became a part of Black lore, and was incorporated into such Black spirituals as "The Day the Stars Fell." It was also used by slaves who had seen the event as a time-fixing device.

The quilt measures 75" × 96" and takes 4¼ yards white and 2½ yards of red fabric.

Piecing Diagram

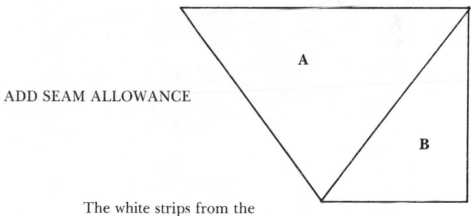

PATTERN PIECES

A   48 White
B   104 Red
C   16 White
D   8 White

8 Strips of White 2½" × 11½" (includes seam allowance)
32 strips of White 2½" × 13½"
 5 strips of Red 5½" × 80½"
20 strips of Red 3½" × 12½"

ADD SEAM ALLOWANCE

The white strips from the top to the first star are 11" long, all others are 13".

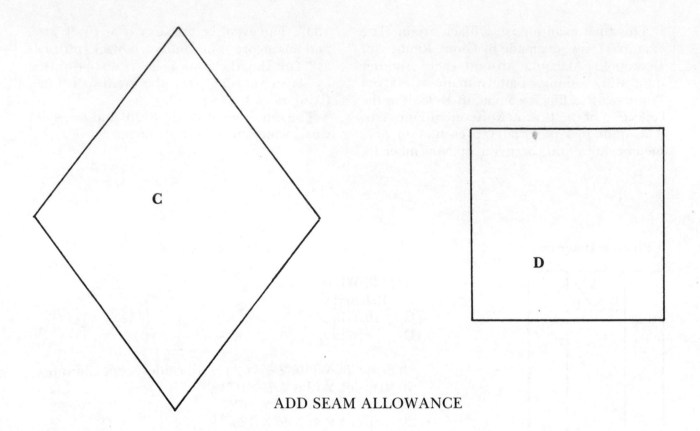

C

D

ADD SEAM ALLOWANCE

Above is the very feminine appliqué quilt, Full-Blown Poppy (pages 108–114). At right is an appliquéd Sunburst II (pages 115–116). This pattern is sometimes called Rising Sun.

Here are two examples of reverse appliqué. At left is Princess Feather I (pages 131–135). Below is Sunburst III (pages 142–150). Note the fine Princess Feather quilting.

H

Reverse Appliqué

The feather pattern has long been a favorite quilting motif, but its use as an appliqué is somewhat rare. It takes a fine seamstress to achieve a smooth finish on the feathers.

The three quilts that follow all date to the mid-nineteenth century and though there are similarities, each uses either an unusual technique or setting.

The first two quilts are from the DAR Museum, and both include reverse appliqué in the top. The second quilt, shown on page 136, in addition to the reverse appliqué, has a very striking arrangement.

Reverse appliqué is achieved by stacking any number of colors, one on top of the other, then cutting through the layers until you reach the color you want to show. The edges on top are turned under and stitched down. For both of these quilts, only one layer is used, that being the feather appliqué. The design in the center is cut out, allowing enough fabric for turning under. It is then stitched in place like the rest of the appliqué.

From the DAR Museum, Washington, D.C.

Princess Feather I

QUILT SIZE   87″ × 87″

FABRIC REQUIREMENTS

    White 6¼ yards
    Red 1½ yards
    Green 2 yards
    Gold ¼ yard

PIECES REQUIRED

A	4 Red	D	46 Green
B	16 Red	E	43 Gold
	16 Green	F	21 Red
C	12 Green	G	42 Green
	12 Red		

4 blocks 33½″ square

Cut out

A

ADD SEAM ALLOWANCE

The quilting follows the shape of the appliqué pieces.

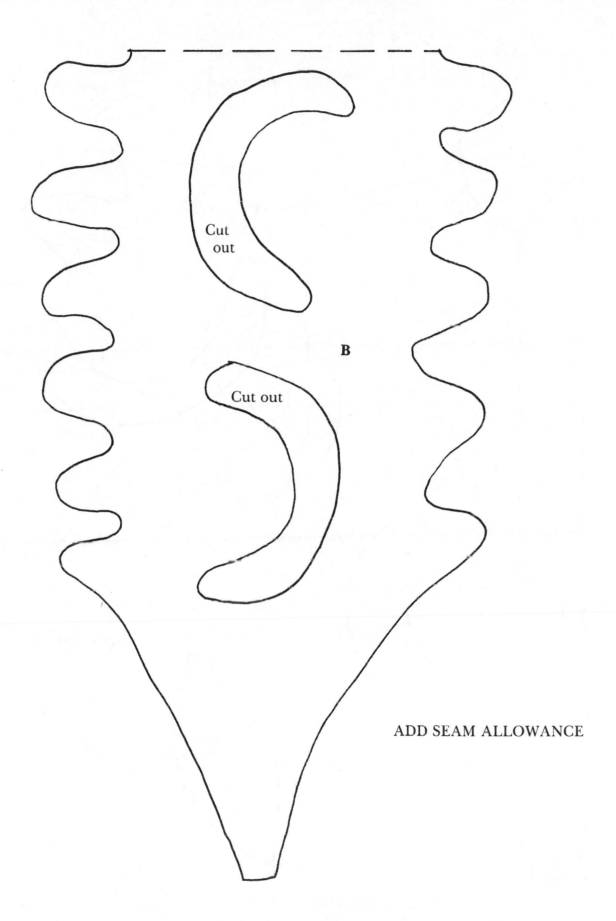

Cut
out

Cut out

B

ADD SEAM ALLOWANCE

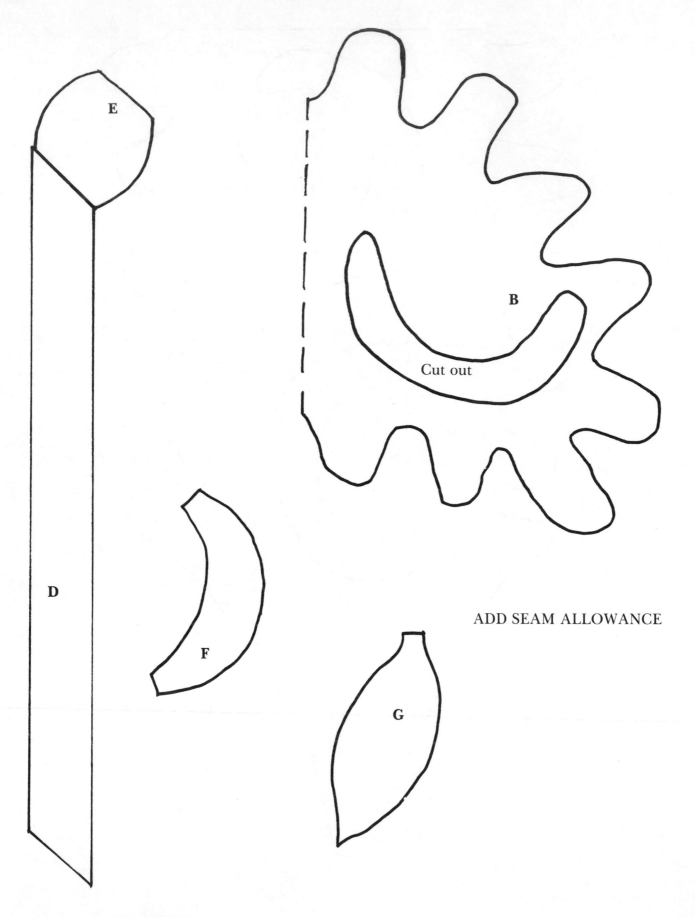

E

B

Cut out

ADD SEAM ALLOWANCE

D

F

G

Border is 10½″ wide

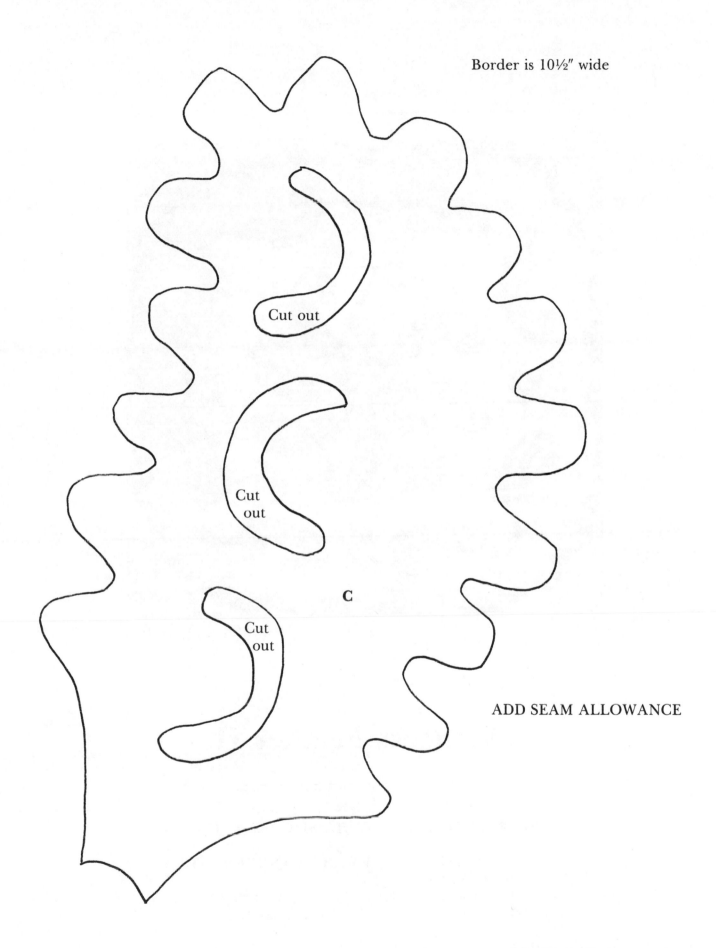

Cut out

Cut
out

C

Cut
out

ADD SEAM ALLOWANCE

From the DAR Museum, Washington, D.C.

Princess Feather II

PIECES REQUIRED   **QUILT SIZE**   90″ × 90″

   A   1 Red   **FABRIC REQUIREMENTS**
   B 16 Red
   C   4 Red   6 yards White
   D 35 Red   4 yards Red

Piece fabric together for the background. Or you could use a sheet and eliminate seaming the fabric. You might also want to lay the fabric out on the bed to arrange the appliqués so the feather circle and border fall in the center of the bed. Then arrange the scalloped border around this.

This quilt also uses reverse appliqué. Cut out the pieces marked on the pattern, allowing enough fabric to turn under. Whipstitch in place as you do the rest of the appliqué.

One-quarter of pattern

A

Cut out for center

ADD SEAM ALLOWANCE

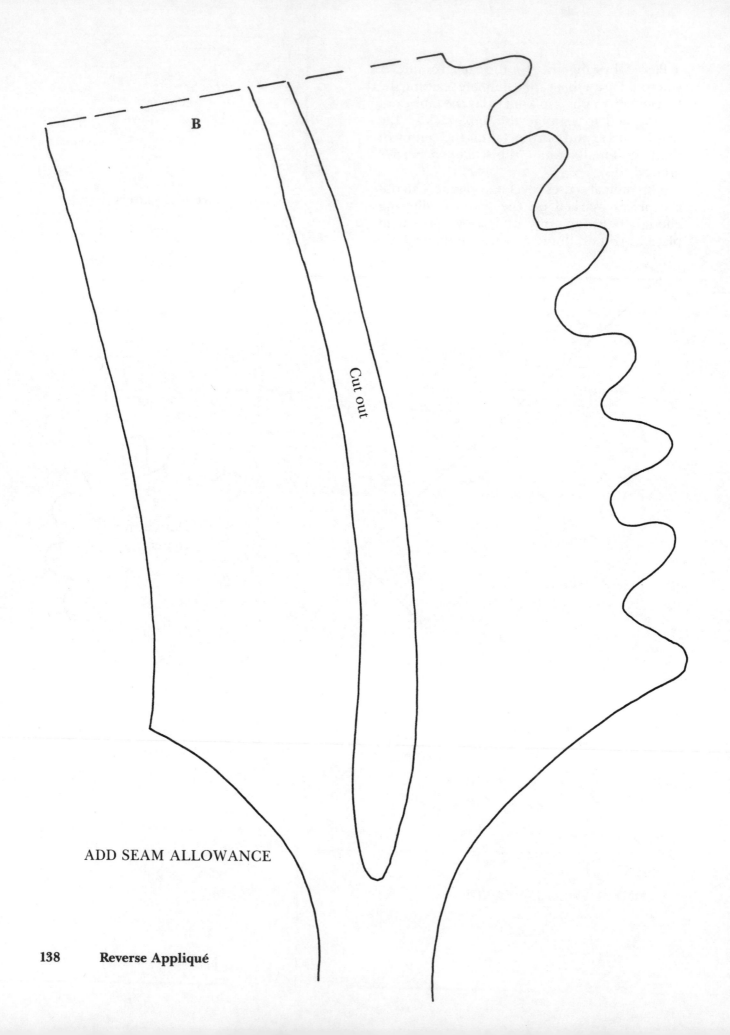

B

Cut out

ADD SEAM ALLOWANCE

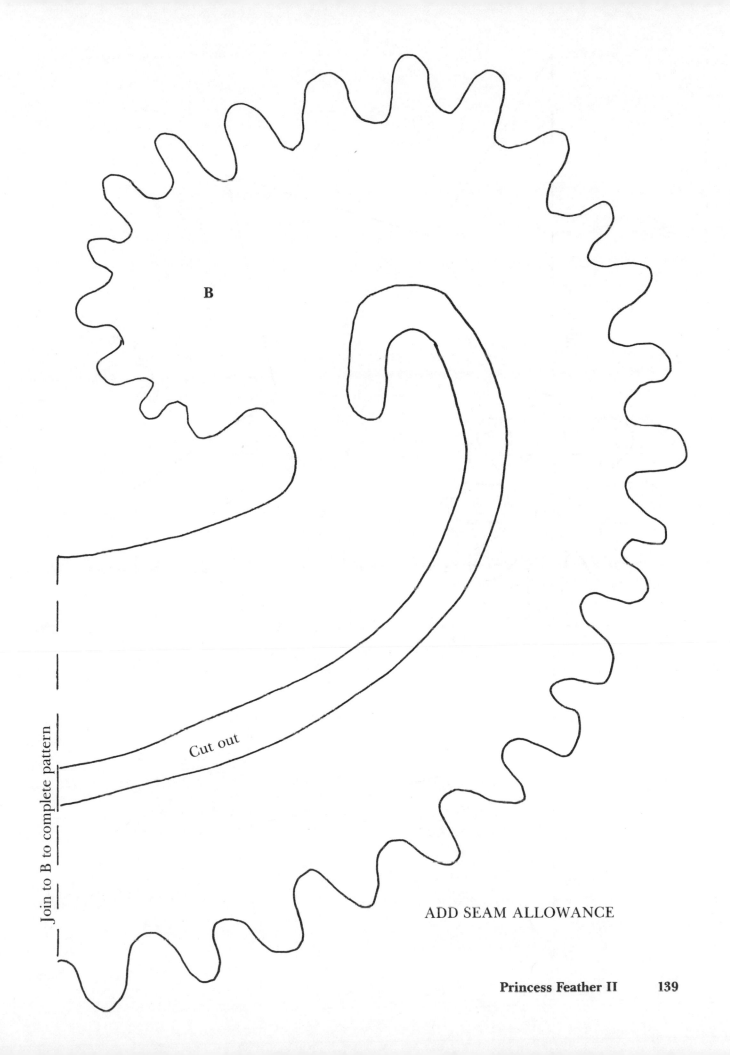

B

Join to B to complete pattern

Cut out

ADD SEAM ALLOWANCE

Princess Feather II 139

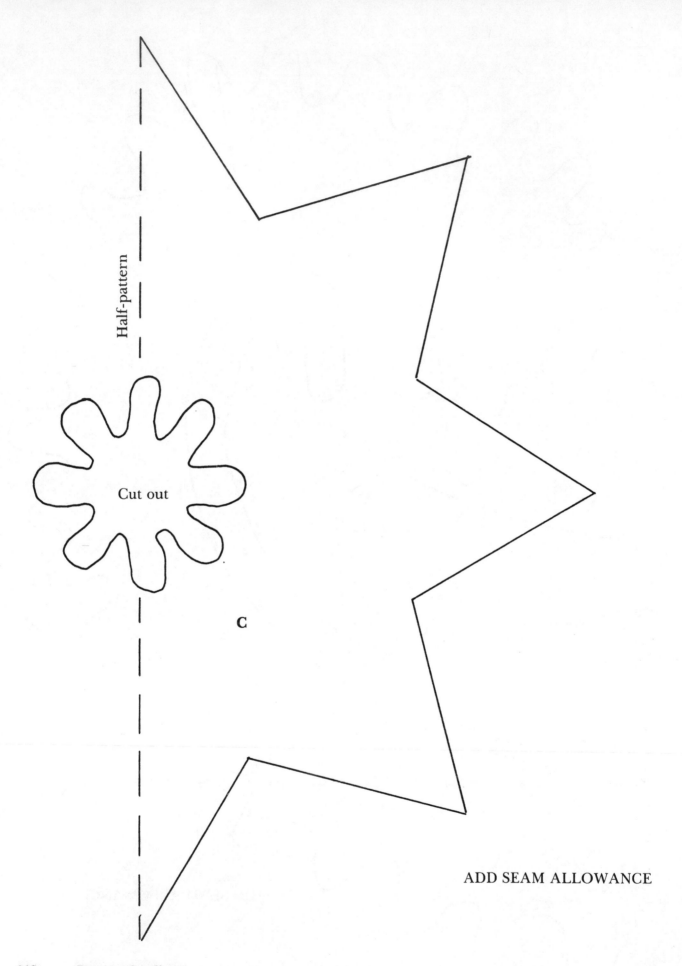

Half-pattern

Cut out

C

ADD SEAM ALLOWANCE

ADD SEAM ALLOWANCE

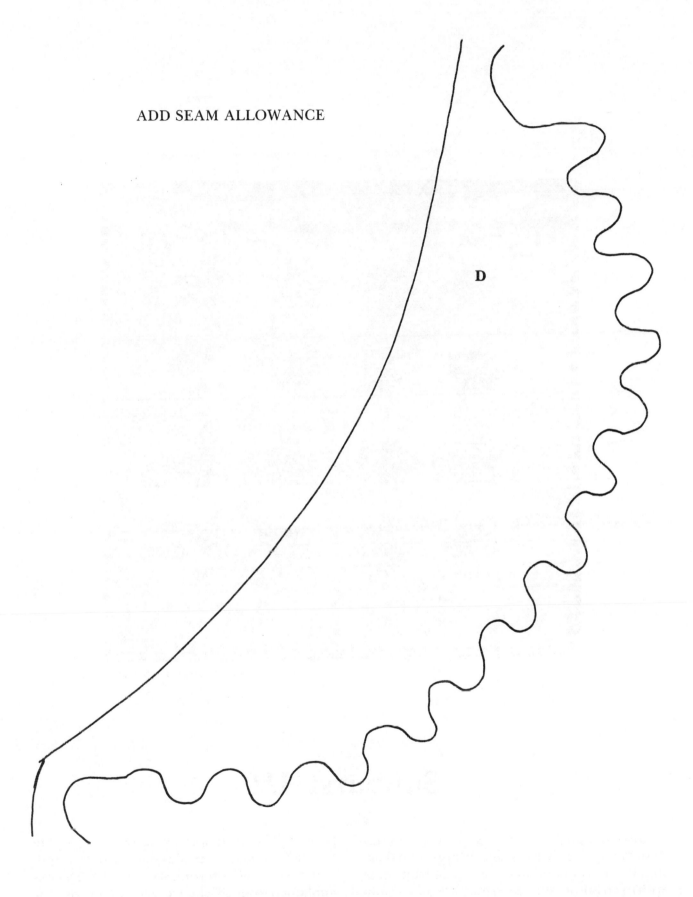

D

From the Smithsonian Institution

Sunburst III

In this example, the Sunburst pattern is of secondary importance to the fine background quilting. It could almost have been an all-white quilt with its elaborate stuffed Princess Feather quilting between the blocks and the serpentine feather border. The quilt was made by Ann Sophie Shriver of Funkstown, Maryland around 1840.

It is 94″ × 94″, utilizing sixteen pieced blocks appliquéd to an 18″ square, with a 7″ border for quilting, and a 2″ Sawtooth border.

FABRIC REQUIREMENTS

3 yards Red Print
8¾ yards White

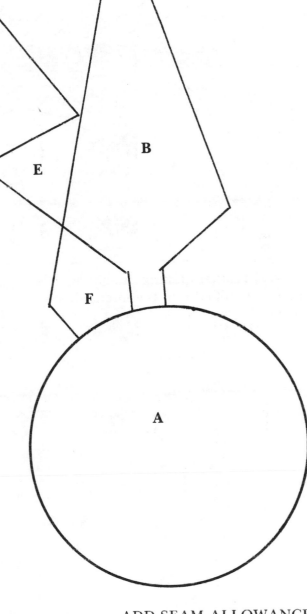

ADD SEAM ALLOWANCE

Piece the Sunburst and appliqué it to an 18″ square, plus seam allowance. Set the blocks together, add the borders, then mark the quilting designs. The Sunburst is quilted in circular rows, two rows beyond the outer points. The Princess Feather and Feather Vine border are both stuffed.

PIECES PER BLOCK		PER QUILT
A	1 Red Print	16
B	10 Red Print	160
C	10 Red Print	160
D	20 White	320
E	10 White	160
F	10 White	160
G	For border Red and White each	180

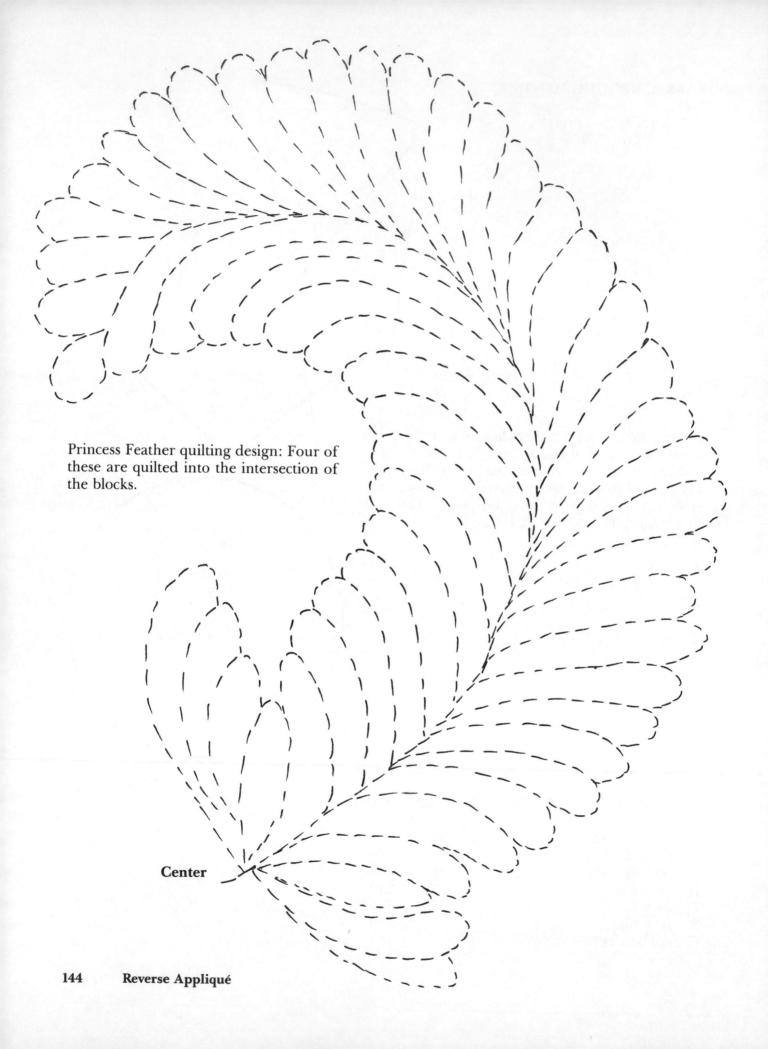

Princess Feather quilting design: Four of these are quilted into the intersection of the blocks.

Center

Using a felt-tip marker, trace this pattern onto white paper. Turn the paper over, and follow the lines for the reverse design. Position the Princess Feather design between these two.

This side faces the edge of the quilt.

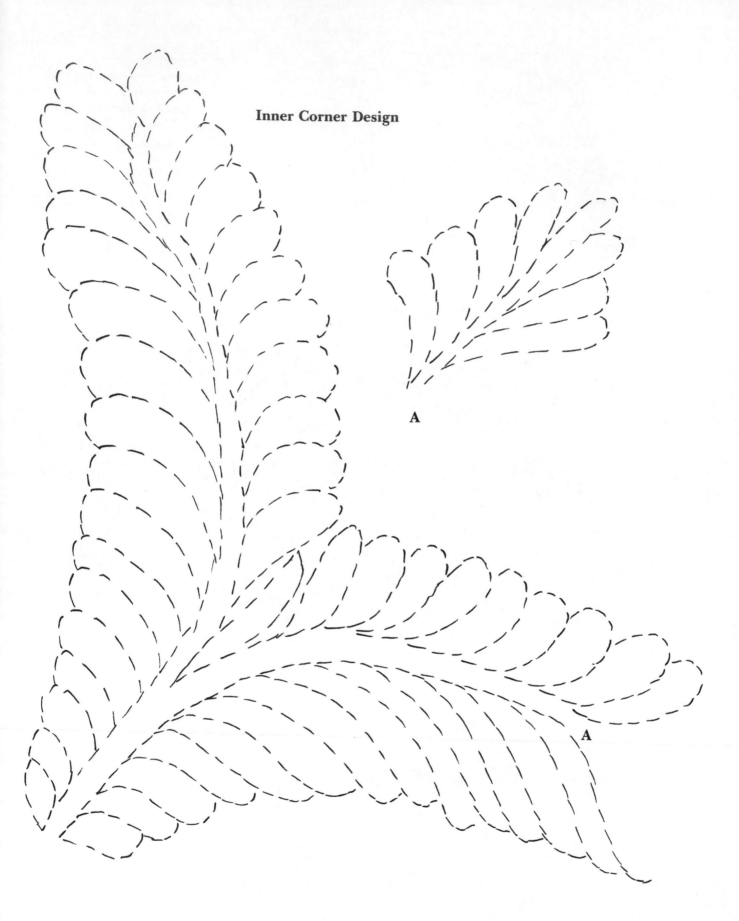

Inner Corner Design

A

A

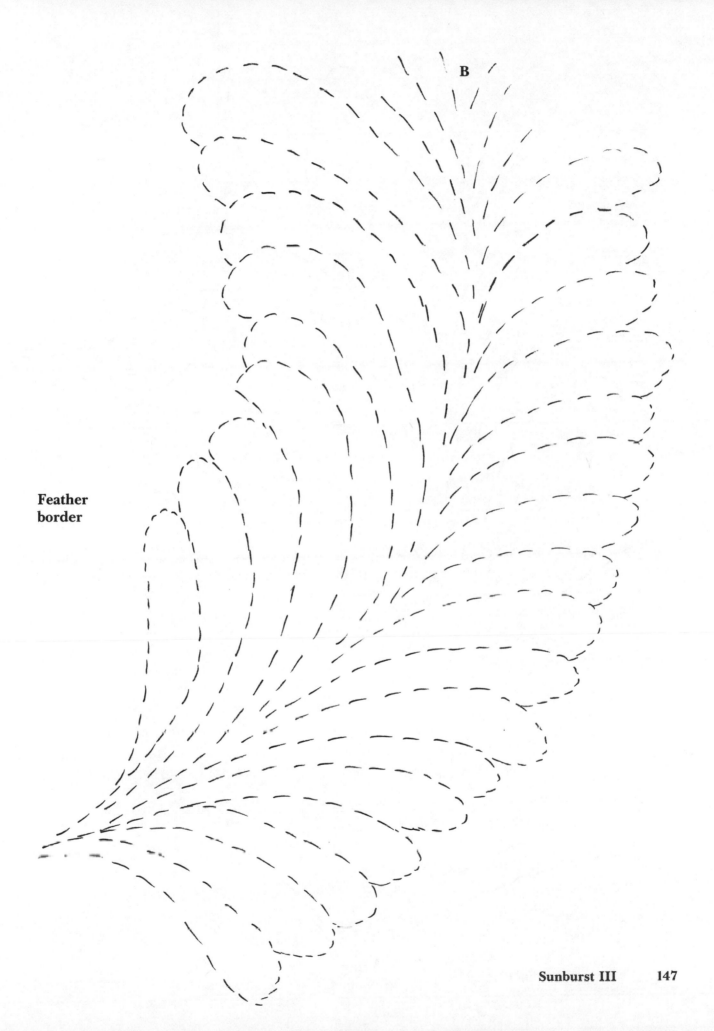

Feather border

B

C

B

D

C

D Corner

Album Quilts

An album quilt is a collection of blocks, each one usually made by a different person, assembled into one quilt. Most album quilts are appliquéd, but many contain pieced blocks as well as appliqué. Several names are used to describe album quilts, each designating the purpose for which the quilt was made.

Autograph quilts are usually made by one person who then asks friends and relatives to sign the blocks. The Smith Autograph Quilt, with signatures collected over a period of 100 years is an excellent example of this type.

The bride's quilt was generally made by friends of the bride. A theme may have been chosen, or each person could make up their own block. Since it was a bridal quilt, it usually contained doves, cupids and hearts. The bride's mother set the blocks together, then invited all those who had contributed a block to a quilting bee to finish the quilt before the wedding. It was considered bad luck for the bride to work on the wedding quilt so she acted as hostess at the quilting bee.

Friendship quilts or presentation quilts were usually made as a gift for a minister or other prominent person, or for a friend who was moving away. Each person made a block, and often signed it or embroidered a verse on the block.

Another type not always recognized is the freedom quilt. This was a quilt presented to a young man when he reached the age of 21. Because of the variety of patterns used, it is difficult to say which quilts were freedom quilts, but if an early quilt has a strong masculine design, it may have been such a quilt.

Memory quilts were usually made in honor of someone who had died, the blocks being made up from the clothing of the deceased person. The colors are usually dark and somber. One such quilt depicts the family burial ground with names embroidered on coffins to show which family members had died.

The sampler is also a type of album quilt. Many women used to make up a sample block of a pattern they had seen and liked so they wouldn't forget it. What better way to put these blocks to use than to assemble them into a quilt, a kind of catalogue of the blocks at their disposal.

The Baltimore album quilt can be any of the foregoing types, but it is distinctive due to the elaborateness of the design and the fine workmanship. The best examples were made in Baltimore between 1840 and 1850, hence the name. Most of the blocks were original creations of their makers, depicting elaborate fruit and floral designs, birds and baskets, patriotic themes and historical scenes. As an example of the workmanship that went into the blocks, in one quilt, a bird design is made up of twenty different fabrics to show the shading and contour of a real bird.

Any block with some plain space can be used for an autograph quilt. On the following pages you will find a variety of album quilts, two of which emulate the Baltimore type, although only one was made in Maryland. Due to space limitations, from these three quilts I chose the blocks that I felt were the most graceful or had the widest appeal. Each of the blocks can be used by itself to make a whole quilt, or you can make up one of each block for your own album quilt.

ALBUM VERSIONS 1, 2 and 3

This group of three quilts spans a time period of 141 years, which certainly attests to the popularity of the pattern, especially when you consider that quiltmakers are still using the pattern today. Although this is a very simple four-patch design, as you can see from the examples it is a very versatile pattern and lends itself to many interpretations.

The first quilt was made in 1745 by Jane Schmuck. It now resides with the Geauga County Historical Society in Burton, Ohio.

It is a simple, utilitarian quilt made of dark blue and cream homespun. The blocks are set straight with alternate plain dark blue blocks. The quilting is minimal and quite plain, just a straight running stitch to hold the layers together.

The second version, also from the Geauga County Historical Society, was made in 1886 as a Friendship Quilt. A small blue and white print and white cotton was used for the pieced blocks. The completed blocks are set on the diagonal with alternate plain white blocks. The drawings and messages on the white blocks are in india ink.

The quilting is plain, straight-line quilting, but the arrangement adds interest to the overall quilt. The pieced blocks are quilted so that the lines run across the block. On the plain white blocks, the quilting runs up and down the block.

The third quilt, ca. 1840, from the DAR Museum in Washington, D.C., is much more elaborate. Brown print scrap fabrics were used for an eight-point star in the center of each block, with a half-star on each edge. The blocks are set on the diagonal with an alternate plain white block. The border is made up of a Sawtooth strip, a plain blue strip, a white strip, another blue strip and finally a second Sawtooth strip to finish.

The quilting is very elaborate and quite fine. A feather pattern runs between the small dark squares, forming a square that meets in the center of the white block. The rest of the white block is filled in with a closely quilted circular design. The pieced block is quilted in straight lines diagonally across the block.

Courtesy of the Geauga County Historical Society, Burton, Ohio

Album Version 1

QUILT SIZE 94″ × 102″

NO. OF BLOCKS 66 Pieced, 66 Plain, 3″ border

FABRIC REQUIREMENTS

7½ yards Dark Blue
2 yards White

PIECES PER BLOCK		PER QUILT
A	1 Dark Blue	66
B	4 White	264
C	4 Dark Blue	264

66 Plain Dark Blue 8″ squares (plus seam allowance)

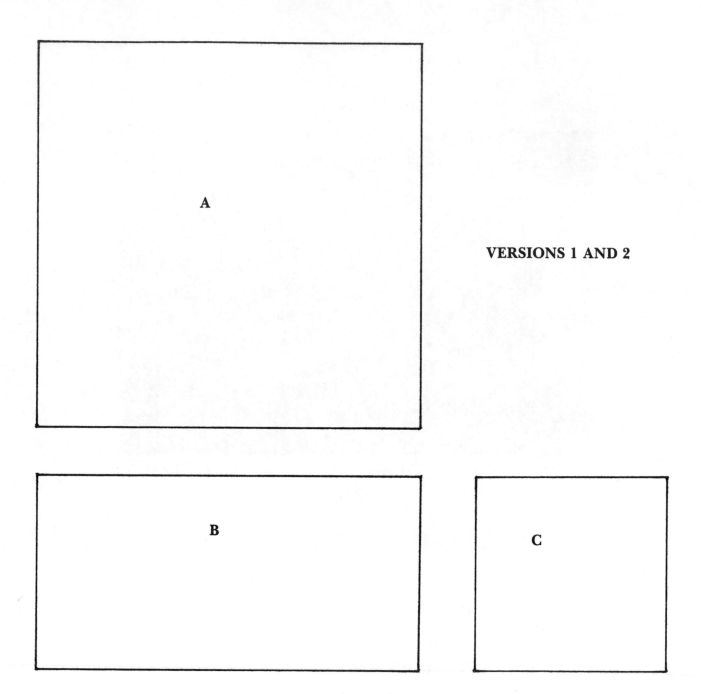

A

VERSIONS 1 AND 2

B

C

ADD SEAM ALLOWANCE

Courtesy of the Geauga County Historical Society, Burton, Ohio

Album Version 2

NO. OF BLOCKS 48 Pieced, 35 Plain

QUILT SIZE 69″ × 92″

PIECES PER BLOCK		**PER QUILT**
A	1 Dark Blue	48
B	4 White	192
C	4 Dark Blue	192

35 White 8″ squares (plus seam allowance)
24 White half-squares
4 White quarter-squares

FABRIC REQUIREMENTS

5¼ yards White
1½ yards Blue

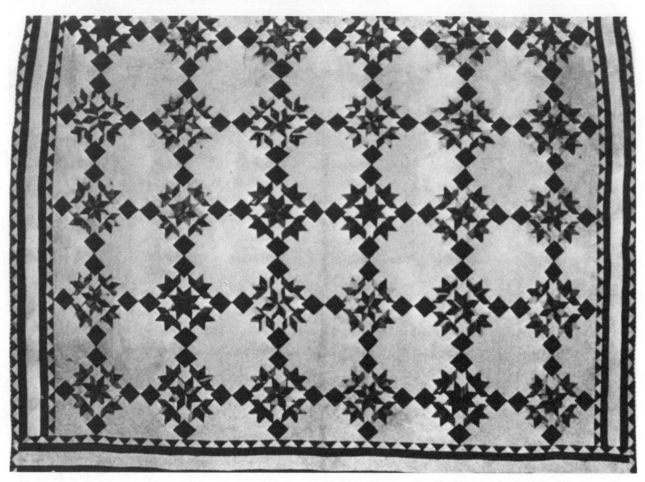

From the DAR Museum, Washington, D.C.

Album Version 3

PIECES PER BLOCK	PER QUILT	QUILT SIZE	84½″ × 99″

A   24 Scrap   720

B   8 White   240

NO. OF BLOCKS   30 Pieced, 20 Plain

C   12 White   360

D   8 White   240

E   4 Dark   120

   20 White 10¼″ squares (plus seam allowance)

   18 White half-squares

    4 White quarter-squares

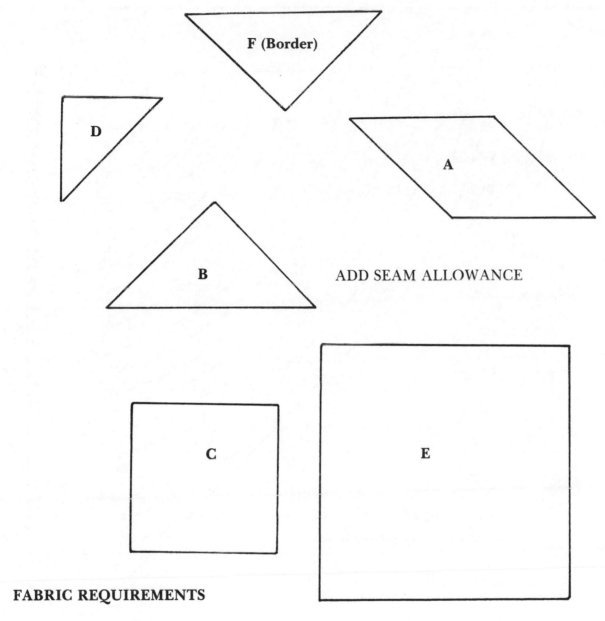

ADD SEAM ALLOWANCE

FABRIC REQUIREMENTS

7 yards White
2 yards Dark
1¼ yards Red

BORDER

Part F in red and white, 1″ white for Sawtooth border
Dark inner border, 1″ wide, plus seam allowance
White middle border, 2″ wide, plus seam allowance
Dark outer border, 1″ wide, plus seam allowance
Sawtooth border, 1″ wide

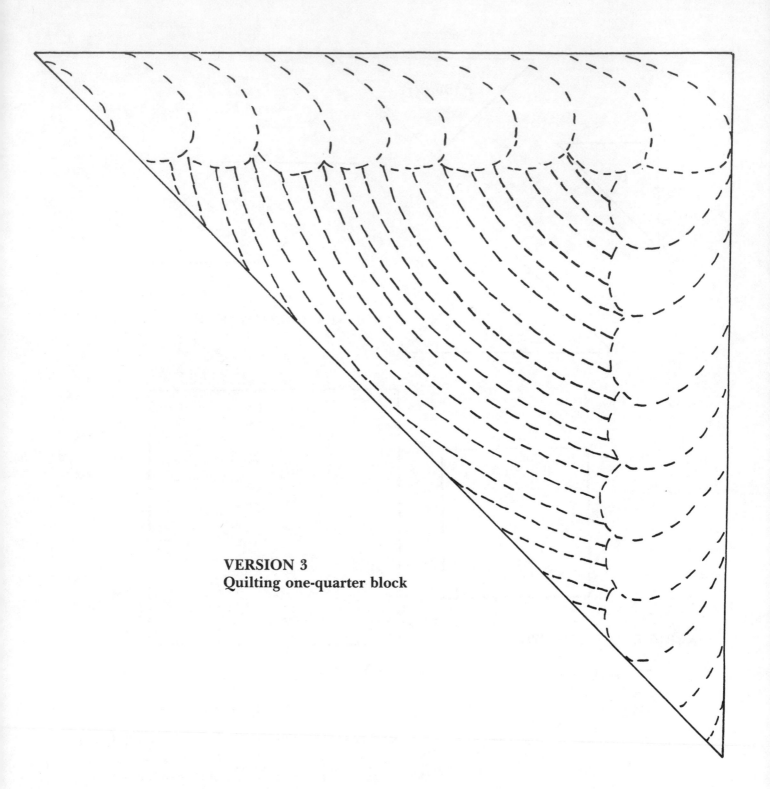

VERSION 3
Quilting one-quarter block

Smith Autograph Quilt

This quilt was started in 1840 by Mary Caroline Wooley Smith of Cincinnati, Ohio. The white patch was appliquéd to a 9″ scrap block. Over a period of 100 years, the white patches were autographed by friends and relatives. It wasn't until 1950 that the quilt was finally set together and quilted by Mrs. Smith's granddaughter, Mrs. Russell Wilson.

I had seen a picture of this quilt previously, but it wasn't until Carolyn Shine, Curator at the Cincinnati Art Museum, pointed it out to me that I noticed the secondary pattern of sunbursts that form where the blocks join together. Since each block was different, you had wildly varying colors and patterns joining to form the sunburst, so that in many cases it was totally lost. By converting the pattern to an all-pieced design, you can control color placement so that each sunburst will have the same fabric throughout, making a much more dynamic design. It can be worked as a scrap design although a two-color design makes a very pretty quilt.

The quilt measures 84″ × 93″, set nine blocks down and eight across. A 6″ border is added. Seventy-two blocks are needed to complete the quilt. For a scrap quilt, you will need 4 yards of white and 1¾ yards for the border. For a two-color quilt, you will need 4½ yards of color fabric.

If you wish to make the original appliqué, draw a 3″ square in the center of a large piece of paper. Lay the pattern Part A on each side of the square, and using carbon paper, draw it attached to the square. Cut out the finished drawing in one piece. The appliqué is sewn to a 9″ block.

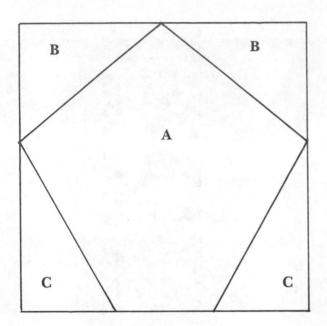

ADD SEAM ALLOWANCE

The squares are 3″

Piecing diagram for scrap quilt

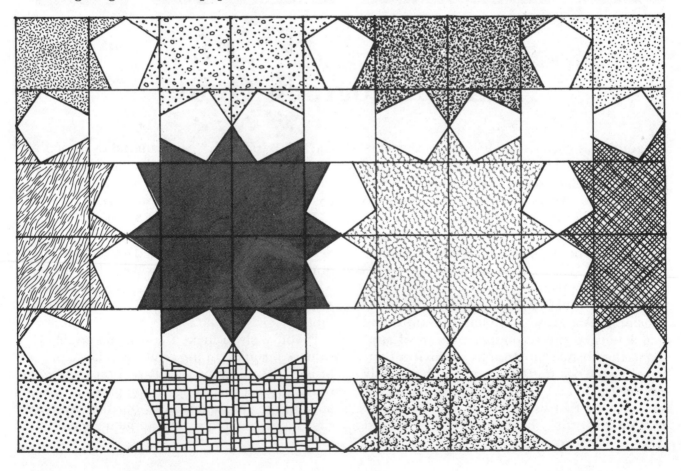

From the Smithsonian Institution

Bride's Quilt

This lovely quilt was made by Elizabeth Jane Baile of Carroll County, Maryland. Miss Baile, who married Levi Manahan on October 30, 1851, wrote in ink on the quilt, "Commenced June, 1850, Finished October 30, 1851."

I found the blocks in this quilt to be the most gracefully designed of the many album quilts I researched. There is a light airiness to them, which is lacking in most quilts of this type, that I found very appealing. Most of the blocks would make beautiful quilts if used alone.

Starting with the Rose Wreath in the upper left-hand corner as number 1, I have included patterns for the following blocks: #7 Strawberry Wreath, #17 Grape Wreath, #18 Rose Wreath, #21 Grape Wreath, #22 Bellflower Wreath, #25 Grape Wreath, and the border.

The blocks are 16″ square, with a 6″ border, for a quilt measuring 92″ × 92″.

The quilting is on the diagonal of each block, with the blocks set so that the quilting runs the opposite way from block to block, forming large diagonal squares where four blocks meet.

Block #7 Strawberry Wreath

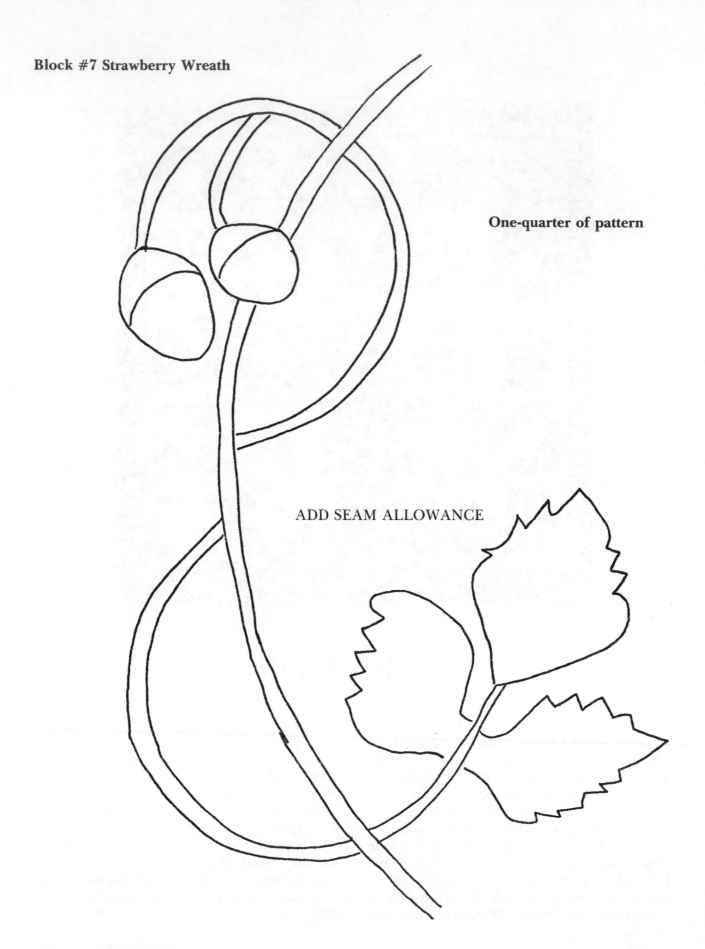

One-quarter of pattern

ADD SEAM ALLOWANCE

ADD SEAM ALLOWANCE

One-quarter of pattern

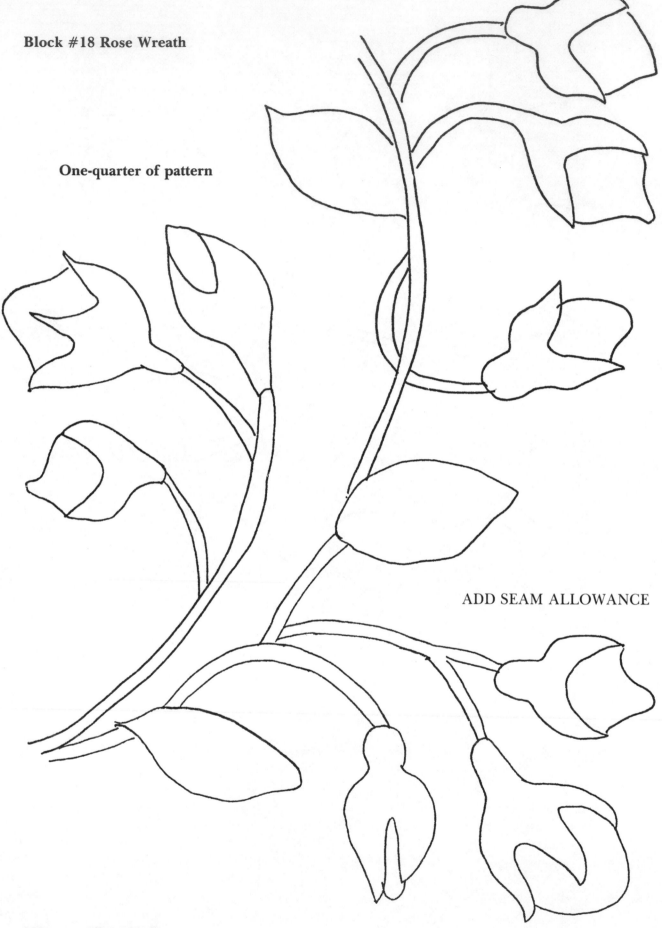

ADD SEAM ALLOWANCE

Block #21 Grape Wreath

One-quarter of pattern

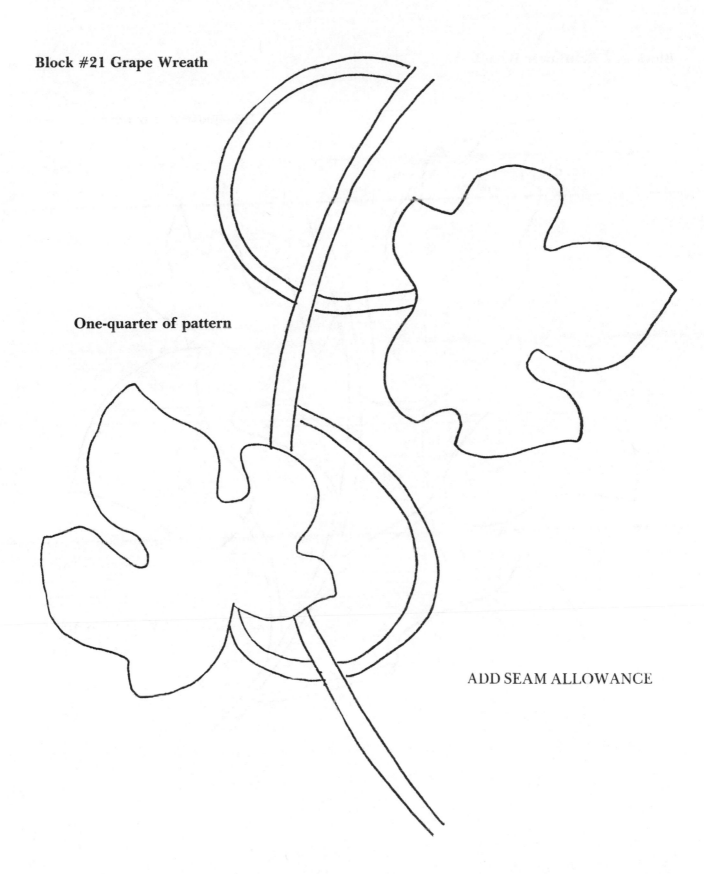

ADD SEAM ALLOWANCE

One-quarter of pattern

ADD SEAM ALLOWANCE

Block #25 Grape Wreath

ADD SEAM ALLOWANCE

B

Border

ADD SEAM ALLOWANCE

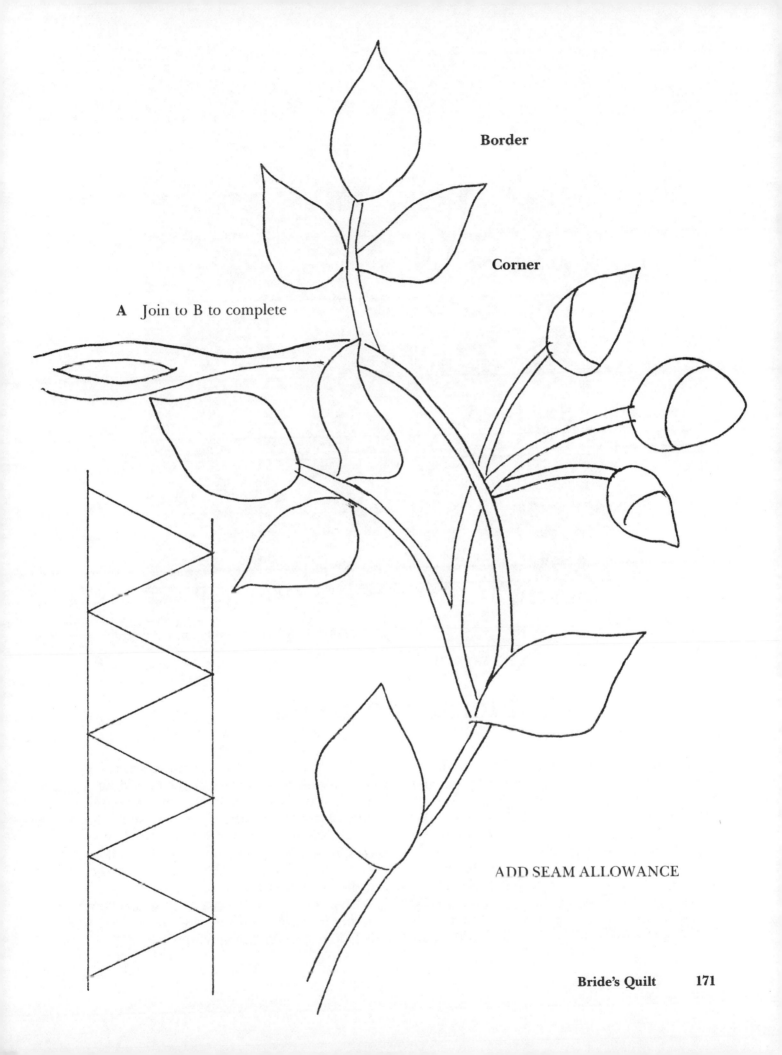

Border

Corner

A Join to B to complete

ADD SEAM ALLOWANCE

From the DAR Museum, Washington, D.C.

Floral and Eagle

This album quilt was made by Cornelia Everhart Wissler of Greensburg, Pennsylvania. She began the appliqué work in 1857 at the age of 22. The quilting was done in 1907 when she was 72. The quilt is now in the collection of the DAR Museum in Washington, D.C.

The florals in this quilt are quite elaborate, containing at least two different fabrics for each flower. In fact, most of the flowers might be easier if done in reverse appliqué.

Using the roses as an example, red frames a yellow center. Cut red and yellow fabric to the outside dimensions of the pattern, adding a seam allowance to the red fabric. Stack the red on top of the yellow, after marking the design for the cutouts on the red fabric. Lay the two pieces in position, turn under the seam allowance on the red and stitch in position. Now cut out the areas that are to be yellow, cutting a little short of the line so you have a seam allowance to turn under. Clip curves where needed. Stitch edges, with a small whipstitch.

A join to A

Block #1

One-quarter of pattern

ADD SEAM ALLOWANCE

ADD SEAM ALLOWANCE

The background blocks are 18″ square. Patterns are given for #1 Floral Wreath, #7 Eagle block, #11 Fruit Bowl block, #15 Wreath with the Blue Bow, and #16 Rose Wreath. The Fruit Bowl block would make up into a lovely wallhanging.

One-quarter pattern

B

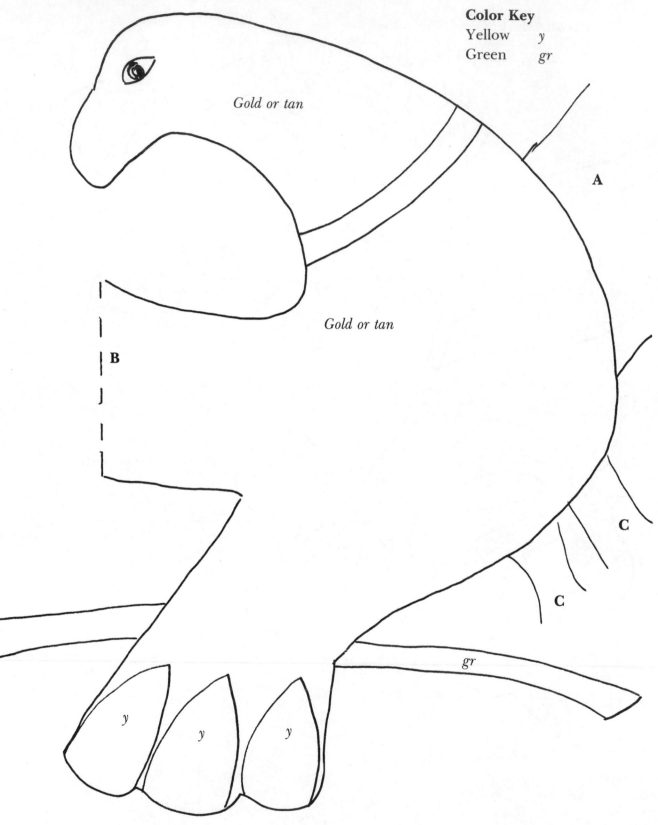

Color Key
Yellow   *y*
Green   *gr*

Gold or tan

A

Gold or tan

B

C

C

gr

y   *y*   *y*

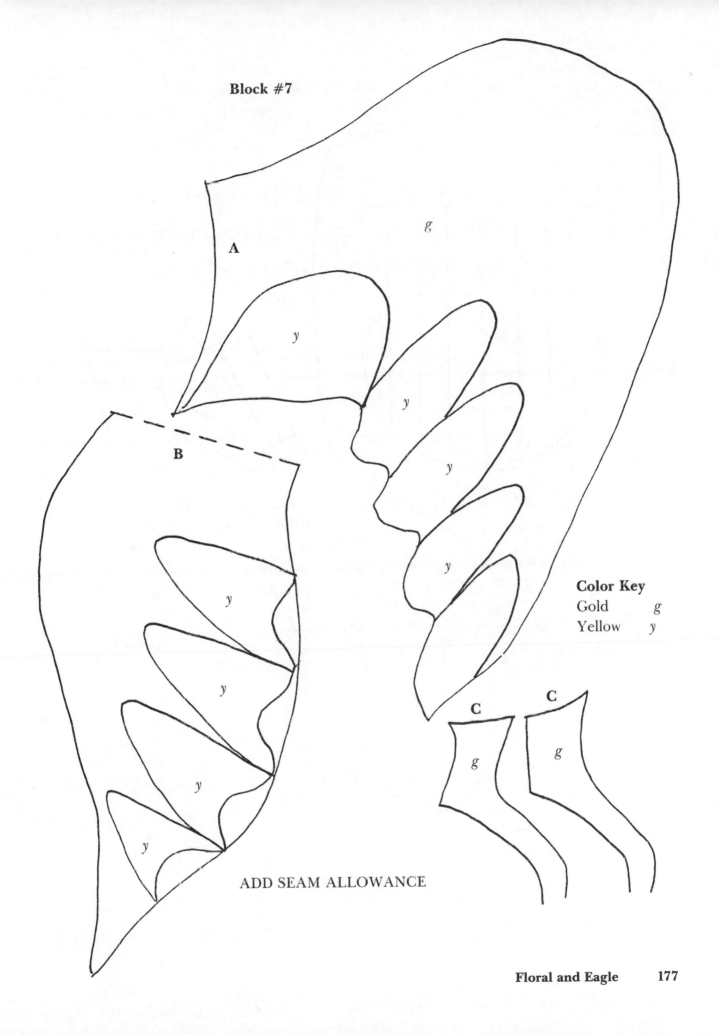

Color Key
Gold   *g*
Yellow   *y*

ADD SEAM ALLOWANCE

Block #7

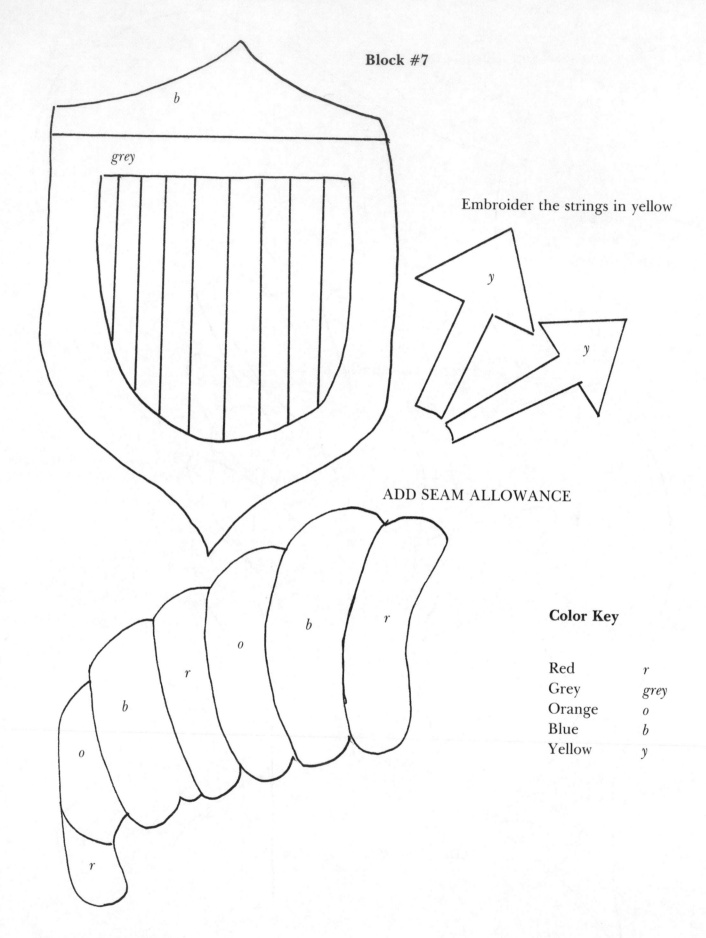

b

grey

Embroider the strings in yellow

y

y

ADD SEAM ALLOWANCE

r

b

o

r

b

o

r

Color Key

Red   *r*
Grey   *grey*
Orange   *o*
Blue   *b*
Yellow   *y*

Block #7

ADD SEAM ALLOWANCE

Color Key
Red r
Green gr

Block #7

ADD SEAM ALLOWANCE

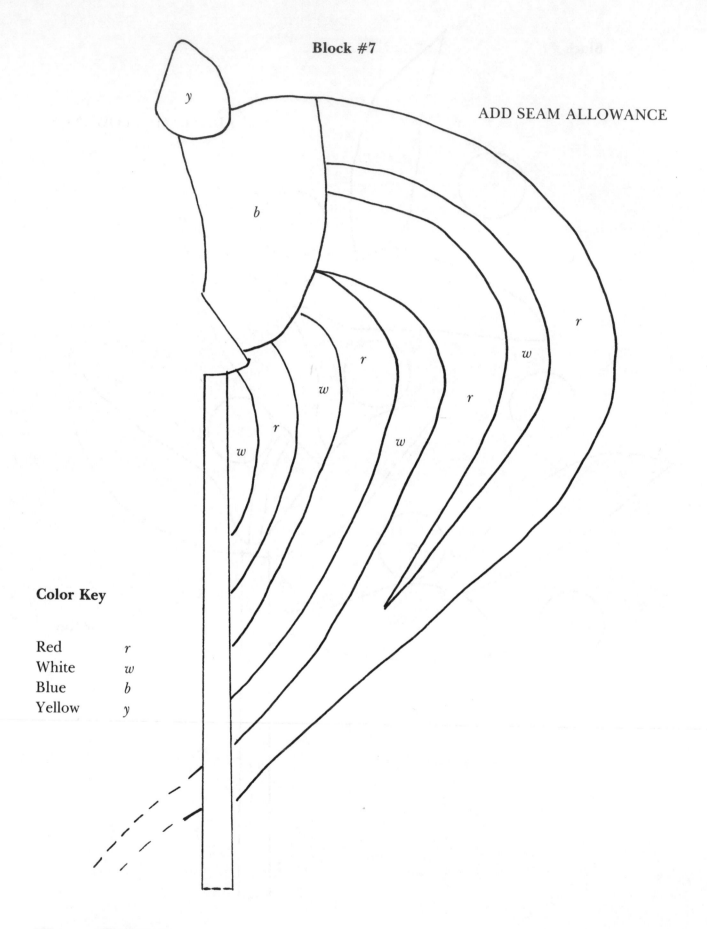

Color Key

Red	*r*
White	*w*
Blue	*b*
Yellow	*y*

Block #7

ADD SEAM ALLOWANCE

Color Key

Red	*r*
Green	*gr*
Orange	*o*
Brown	*br*

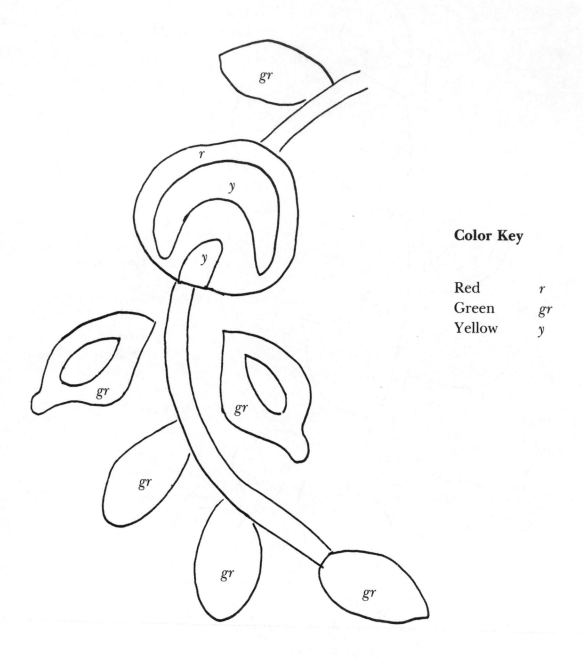

Color Key

Red   *r*
Green   *gr*
Yellow *y*

ADD SEAM ALLOWANCE

ADD SEAM ALLOWANCE

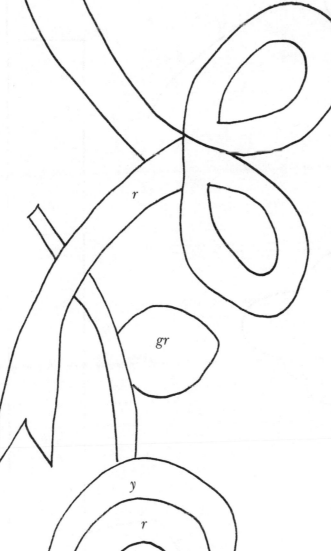

Color Key

Green   *gr*
Red   *r*
Yellow   *y*

Block #11

ADD SEAM ALLOWANCE

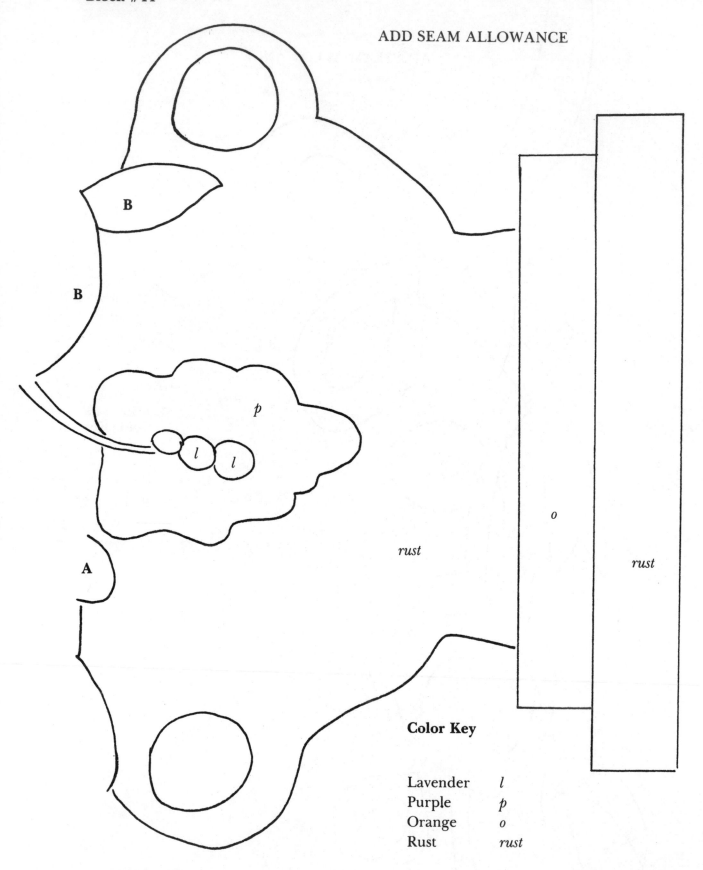

Color Key

Lavender   *l*
Purple   *p*
Orange   *o*
Rust   *rust*

ADD SEAM ALLOWANCE

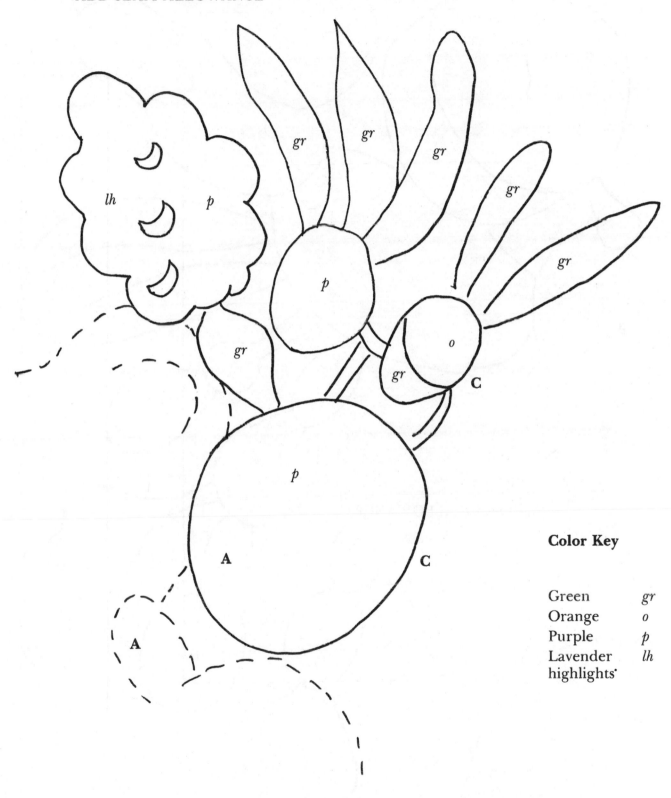

Color Key

Green	*gr*
Orange	*o*
Purple	*p*
Lavender	*lh*
highlights˙	

Block #11

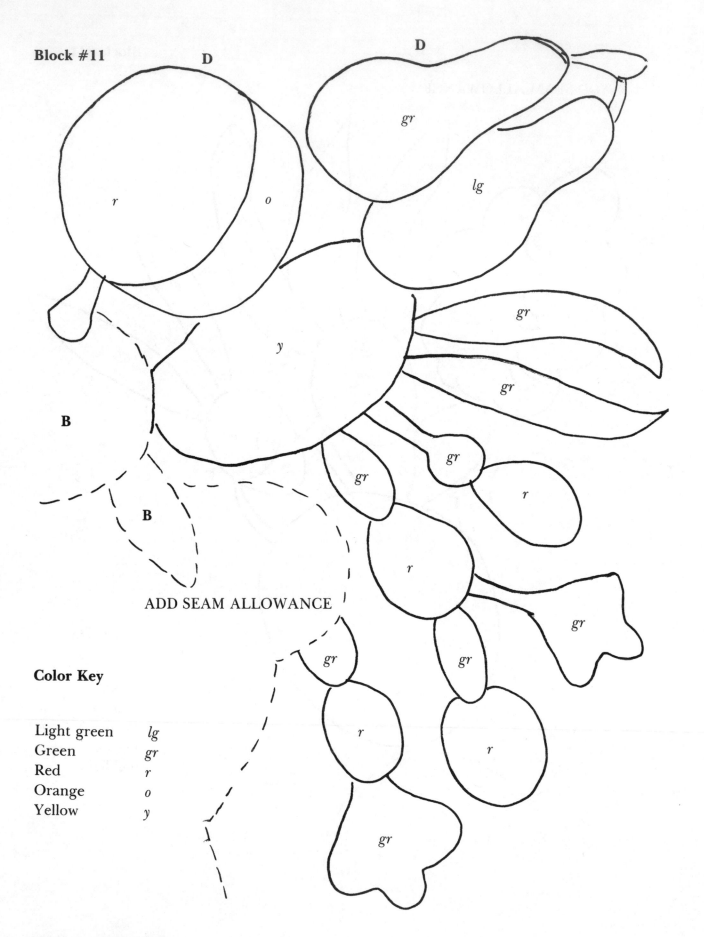

D

D

gr

lg

r

o

gr

gr

y

gr

gr

r

B

gr

r

ADD SEAM ALLOWANCE

gr

B

gr

gr

gr

Color Key

r

r

Light green   *lg*
Green   *gr*
Red   *r*
Orange   *o*
Yellow   *y*

gr

Block #11

Color Key

Green	*gr*
Red	*r*
Orange	*o*
Yellow	*y*
Gold	*g*
Purple	*p*

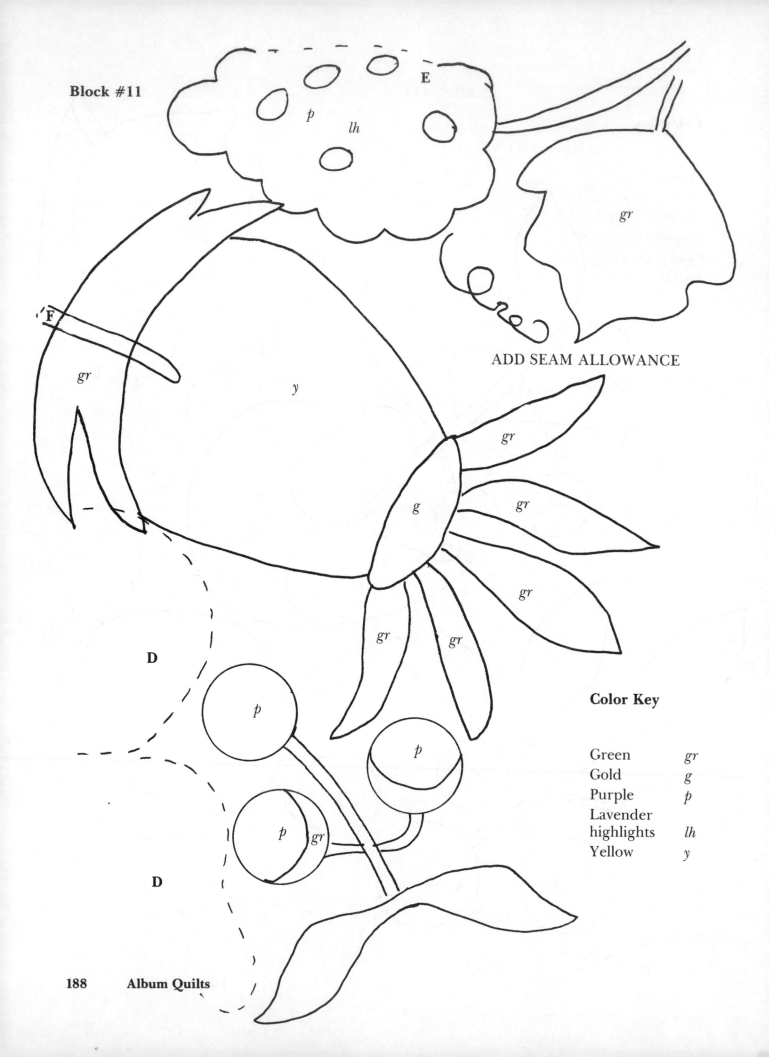

Block #11

E

p

lh

gr

ADD SEAM ALLOWANCE

F

gr

y

gr

g

gr

gr

gr

gr

D

p

p

Color Key

p

gr

D

Green   gr
Gold   g
Purple   p
Lavender
highlights   lh
Yellow   y

Color Key

Green	*gr*
Red	*r*
Orange	*o*
Purple	*p*

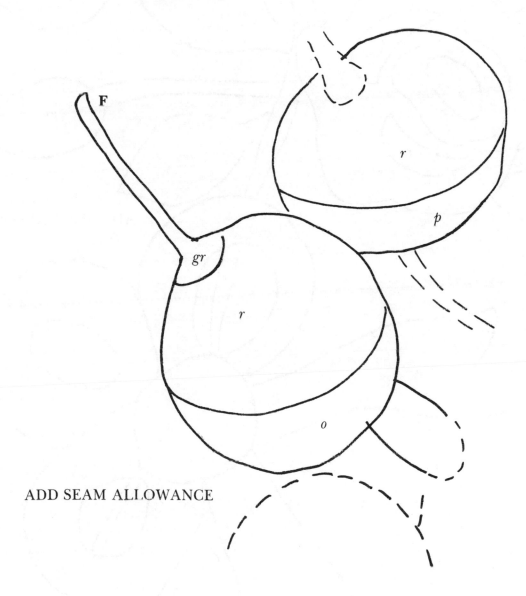

ADD SEAM ALLOWANCE

Block #15

ADD SEAM ALLOWANCE

Color Key

Red   *r*
Yellow   *y*
Green   *gr*
Blue   *b*

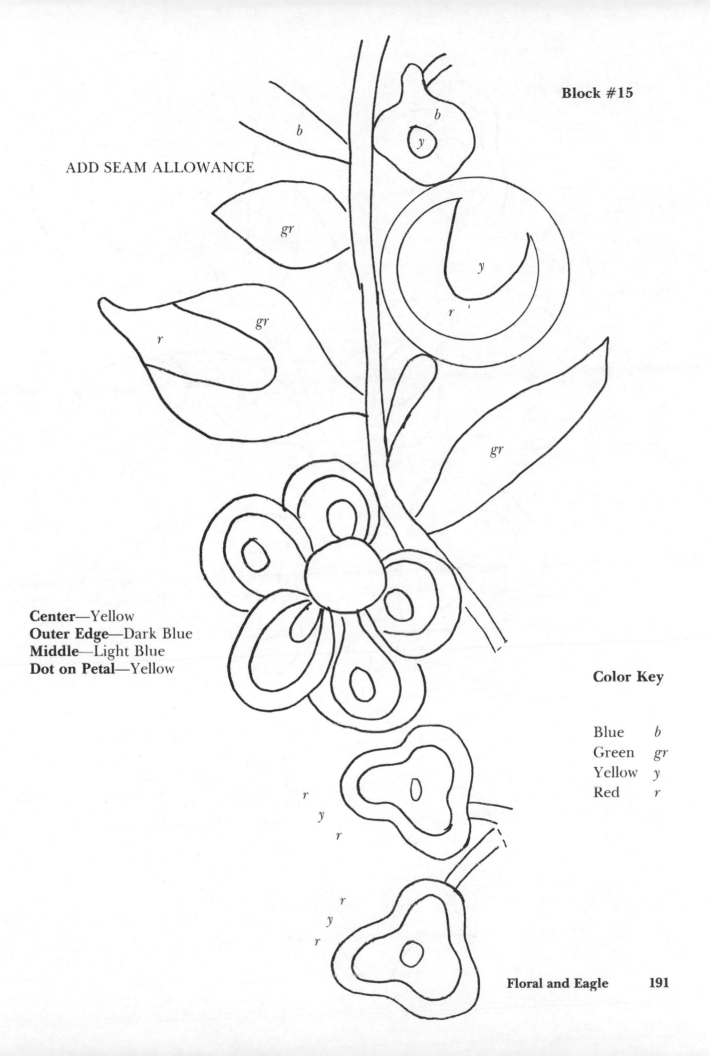

ADD SEAM ALLOWANCE

Center—Yellow
Outer Edge—Dark Blue
Middle—Light Blue
Dot on Petal—Yellow

Color Key

Blue   *b*
Green   *gr*
Yellow   *y*
Red   *r*

Color Key

Red   *r*
Green   *gr*
Yellow *y*
Blue   *b*

ADD SEAM ALLOWANCE

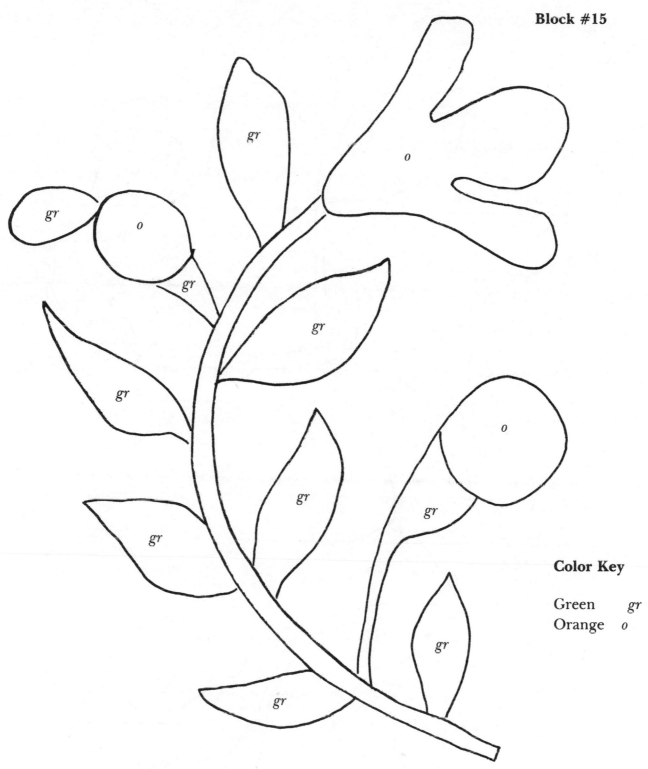

Color Key

Green   *gr*
Orange   *o*

ADD SEAM ALLOWANCE

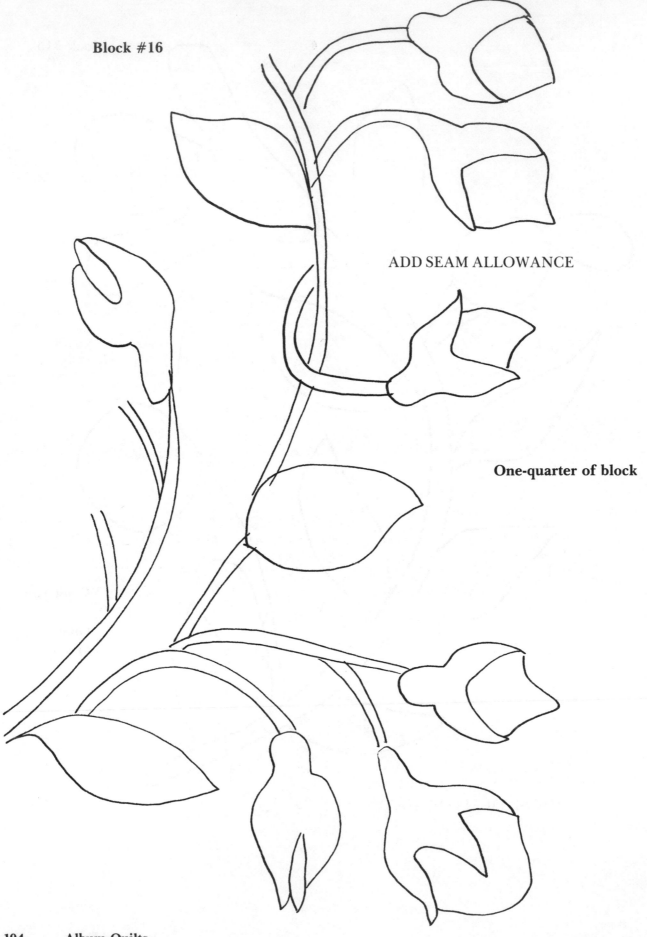

Block #16

ADD SEAM ALLOWANCE

One-quarter of block

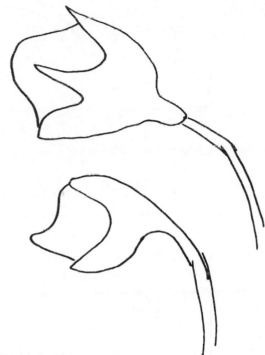

ADD SEAM ALLOWANCE

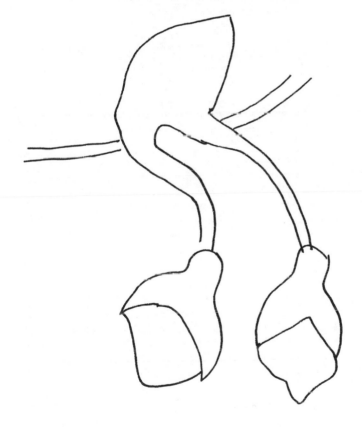

Candlewicking

Candlewicking is a form of needlework that was popular from about 1800 to 1840. Woven candlewick spreads seem to predate the embroidered variety that were being made in the American Colonies during the late 1700's. The woven type was slow to execute and was restricted to geometric forms that could be done on a loom.

Innovative ladies adapted the woven type to hand embroidery, using French knots and a tufted running stitch to create graceful curving designs of flowers, fruits, baskets, feathers and bows, in addition to geometric forms. It was also quick and easy to do, which probably helps explain its long popularity. Candlewicked spreads are not quilted, so when you take the last stitch on the design, you are finished except for washing and drying it to fluff the design.

Candlewicking is quite versatile in both its application and design possibilities. It has been used for curtains, clothing decoration, pillows, bed hangings and spreads. Any design can be adapted to candlewicking; favorite quilt patterns, quilting designs, painting patterns, embroidery patterns, and your own original designs.

Candlewicking is usually done white on white, but with its renewed popularity in recent years, many innovations have come about. Colored background fabric with either matching or contrasting threads to work the design are often used today, with the greatest departure being the use of a variety of colored threads to execute the design.

The term "candlewicking" is derived from the use of leftover candlewicks for sewing the designs. As mentioned, candlewicking has been popular for the past few years and thread has been readily available, but this was not always the case and may not be in the future. Any type of thread can be used for candlewicking, including embroidery floss, crochet thread and yarns of all types, so you are not limited to the availability of actual candlewick threads.

Two main stitches are used in candlewicking, the French knot and the tufted running stitch, depending on the surface texture desired. The French knot will give sharp, concise lines, while the tufted running stitch gives a soft, fluffy appearance, much like chenille, which is a derivative of candlewicking. Other stitches employed are the running stitch, the stem stitch and the satin stitch.

The French knot is made by pulling the needle through the fabric from the back at one of the dots on the pattern. Wrap the thread twice around the tip of the needle, then insert the needle slightly to one side of its entry point and pull to the back.

Tufted candlewicking can be worked in two ways. The first is to use a loose running stitch, leaving a small amount of thread between each stitch. A gauge, such as a crochet hook, can be used to accurately gauge the amount of thread between the stitches. Pull the thread through the fabric, lay the gauge on the line, and take the next stitch, moving the gauge along the line between the stitches as you go. The length of the stitch depends on how dense you want the finished line to be. For a solid line, the stitches should be fairly close together. For individual tufts, use a long stitch so that fabric will show through between the stitches. When the line of stitching is complete, go back and cut the threads between the stitches. The thread will fluff up after washing and drying.

The second method is to use a couching stitch. Lay a bundle of threads along the line to be sewn, then, using a finer thread, tack the bundle at appropriate intervals. Go back and cut between the tacking threads.

When using the tufted stitch, it is imperative that the fabric shrink when washed. Washing in hot water is the final step when doing tufted candlewicking. The hot water shrinks the fabric around the stitches to hold them in place. If this step is omitted, or the fabric does not shrink, the threads will fall out. If only French knots are used in a design, any type of fabric can be used, since shrinking is not needed to hold the threads in place.

You will be using anywhere from four to fifteen strands of thread, so a darning needle with a very large eye is necessary to hold the strands of thread. For ease in working, a loosely woven cloth is the better choice, so the threads won't stick at the eye of the needle when pulled through the cloth. Most cotton or linen fabrics are suitable, always remembering that if you are doing tufted work the fabric must not be preshrunk.

The designs given here are spread over a number of pages and should be transferred to a large pattern sheet before sewing commences. Beginning with the major design element, trace it onto a sheet of paper. Line up the letters shown for continued areas, such as B to B, matching the overlap, and trace this section. Continue with C to C, D to D and so forth, until the pattern is complete. If the design is symmetrical, it is necessary to make up only one-quarter of the overall pattern. Seam the fabric together to obtain the desired size, then transfer the pattern using dressmaker's carbon and a pencil. Most candlewicking patterns are printed in dots, each dot representing a stitch. However, you can use a solid line and gauge the space between the stitches, depending upon the effect you want. In the accompanying patterns, I have used a dashed line to indicate the tufted stitch and dots to indicate French knots.

For the actual sewing, either stretch the spread in a full-size quilt frame, or let it lie loosely in your lap, sewing without a frame. When taking stitches, be sure not to pucker the fabric by drawing the threads too lightly. A small hoop is difficult to use once large portions of the design are completed, because it may not go over the stitches, and if it does, it will crush them.

From the Smithsonian Institution

Tufted Candlewick Spread

This luxurious tufted spread was made by Jemima Ann Beall-Hammond of Frederick, Maryland, around 1800. The finished size is 103″ × 109″, but since it is a repeat pattern, it can be made to any size desired, simply by adding or subtracting elements of the design.

You will need nine yards of a shrinkable fab-

ric pieced together to the above dimensions. The areas to be tufted are indicated by dashed lines on the pattern pages. Use twelve strands of thread, if using candlewicking thread, and space the stitches so that you have a continuous solid line, after the stitches have been cut. If using another type of thread, experiment with various numbers of strands to achieve the desired effect. For the French knots, use four strands of thread.

The outline of the bows, the stems and tendrils are solid lines, so the French knots should touch. There is space between the stitches on the veins of the leaves and flowers and the inner row of the bow.

To make a full-size pattern, lay a large sheet of paper over the basket in the center design and trace. Match B to B, overlapping where shown, and trace. Continue matching the letters, C to C, D to D, and so forth until the pattern is complete. Transfer it to the cloth with dressmaker's carbon and a pencil.

A

B

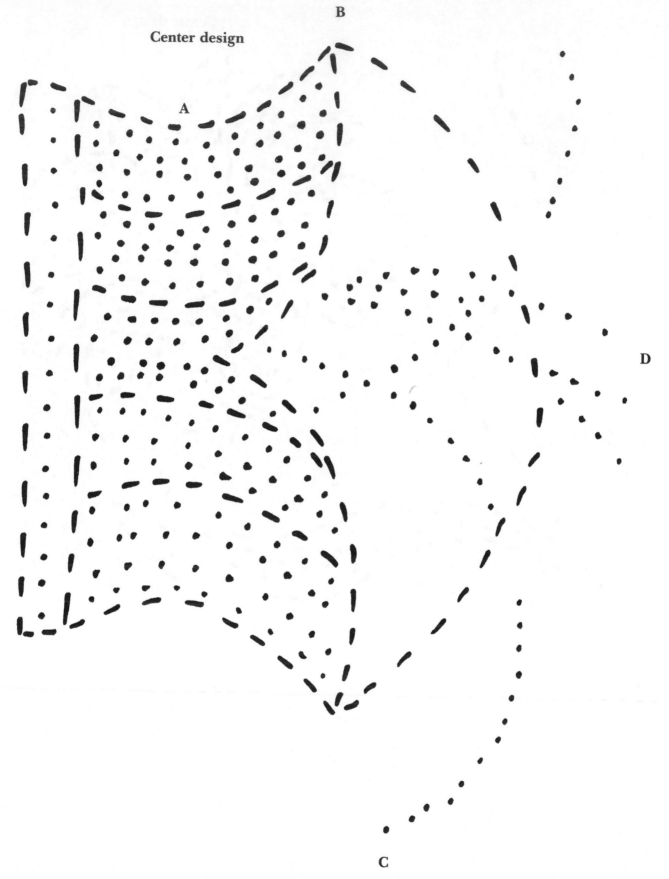

Center design

B

A

D

C

Center design

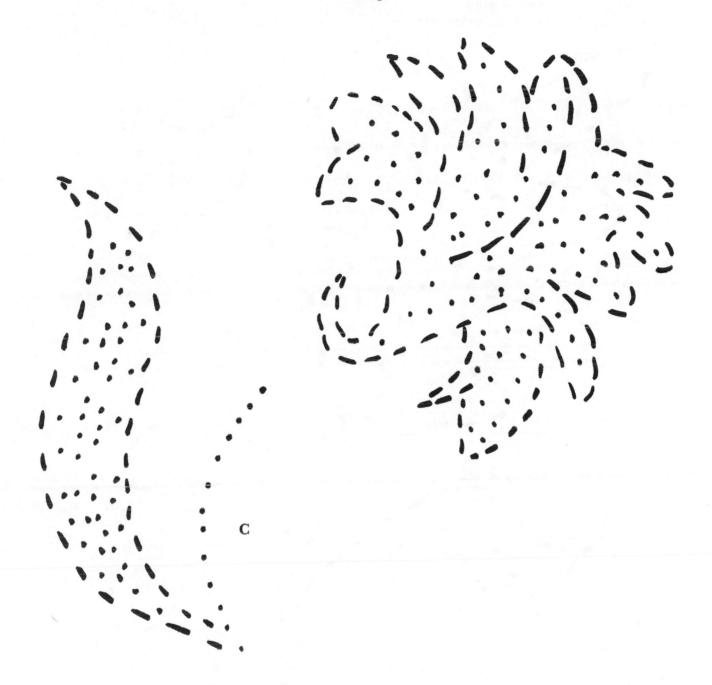

C

Center design

E

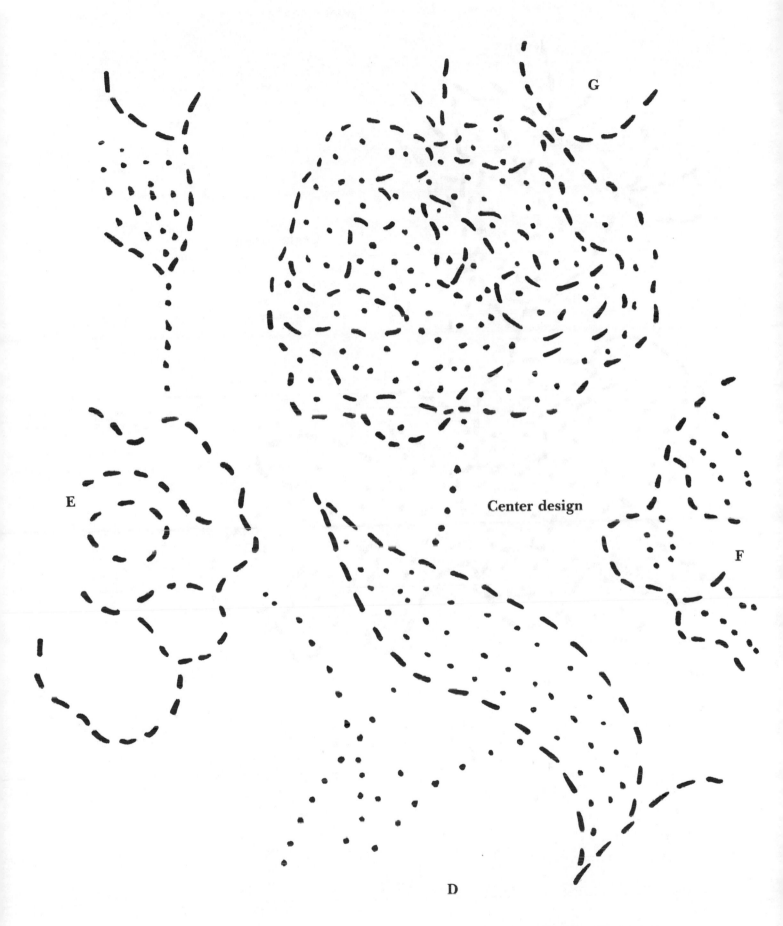

G

E

Center design

F

D

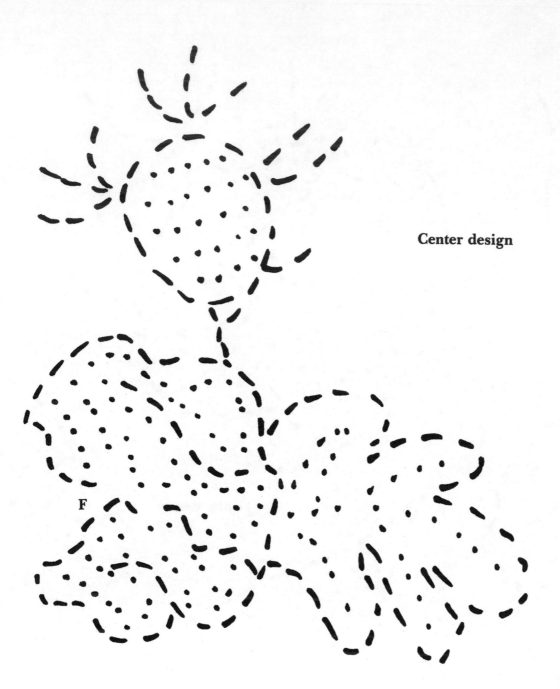

Center design

F

Center design

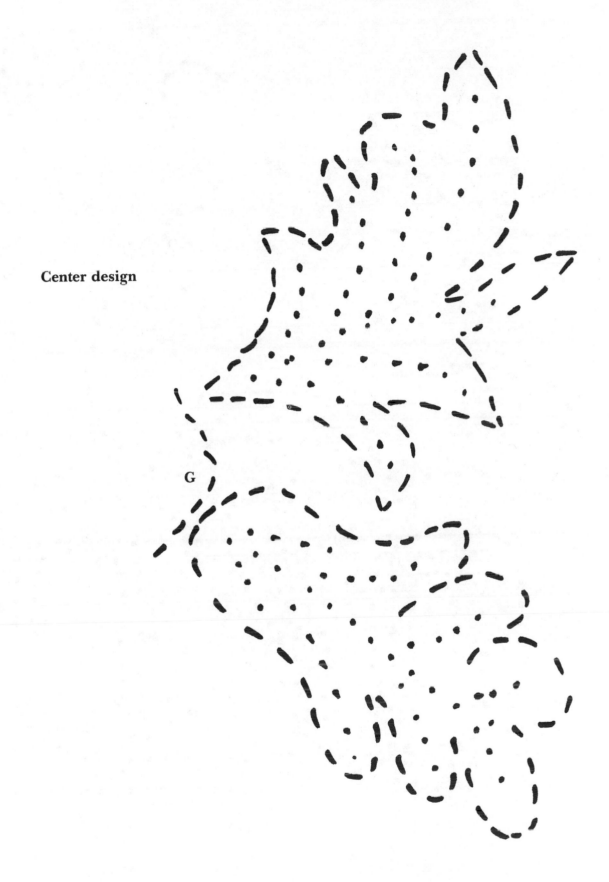

G

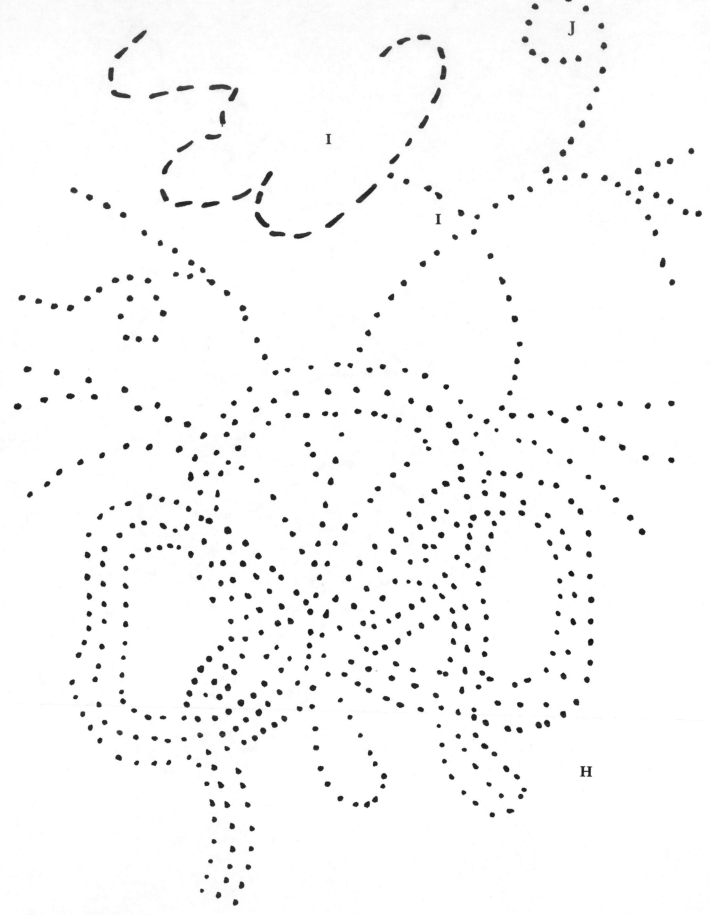

J

I

I

H

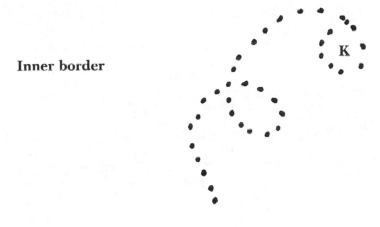

Inner border

Three separate elements

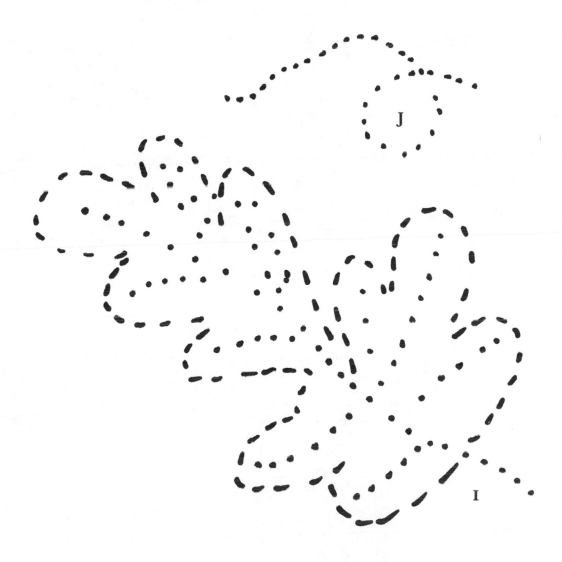

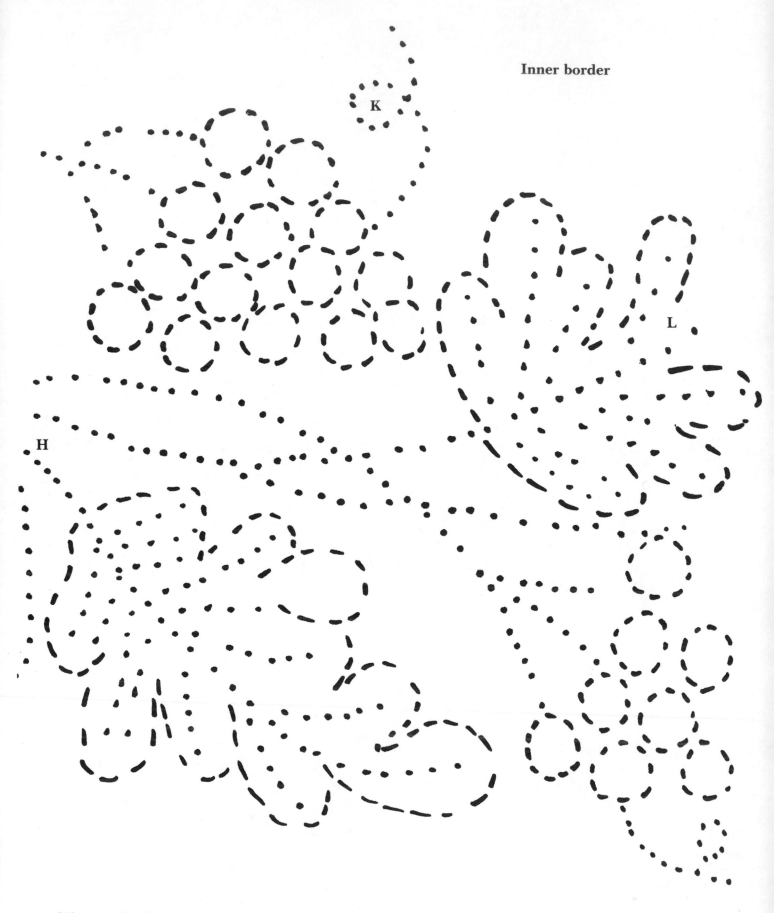

K

L

H

L

M

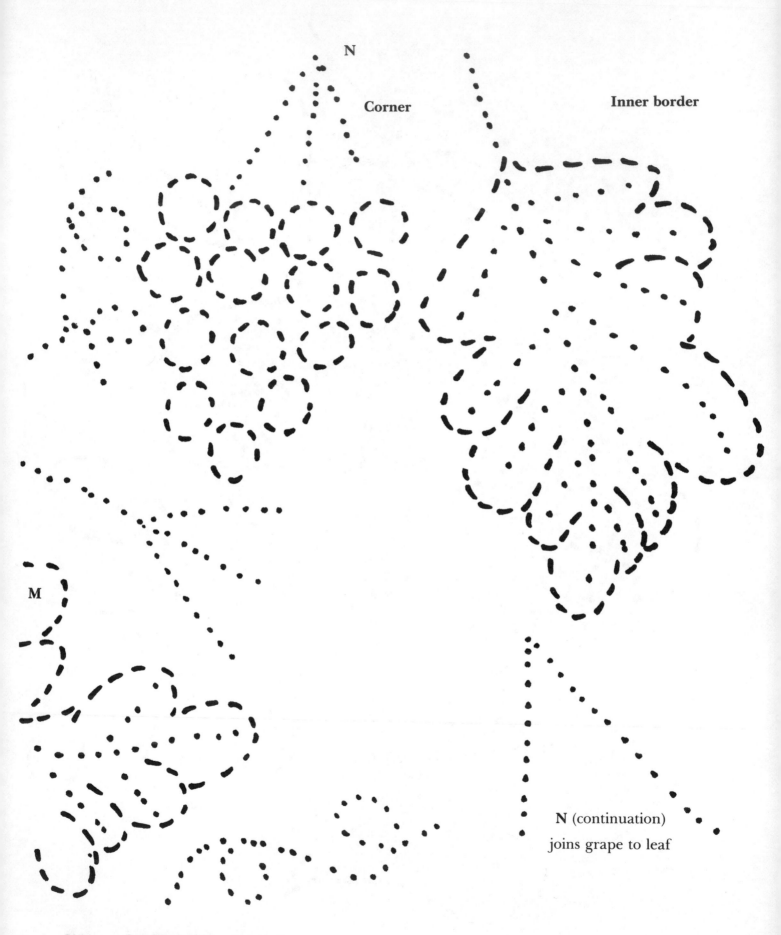

N

Corner

Inner border

M

N (continuation)
joins grape to leaf

Corner

O

Continue adding to pattern to reach desired length

P

O

Corner

P

P

P

Q

R

Q

R

R

From the Smithsonian Institution

French Knot Candlewick Spread

This spread was made by Mary Cushing, of Hingham, Massachusetts around 1813. It is made entirely of French knots, except for the grapes, which are stuffed. The spread measures 65″ by 80″, making it ideal for a twin bed.

You will need 6¼ yards of fabric for the foundation. Since this is done in French knots, it can be any type of fabric. The French knots form a solid line, so that each stitch should touch the one next to it.

To work the stuffed areas, pin a piece of matching background fabric on the back of the foundation, covering the area of the design to be stuffed. Work the French knots three-quarters of the way around a grape, and insert stuffing, being careful not to distort the fabric by using too much stuffing. Complete the circle of French knots. This method makes it easy to insert the stuffing, and also tacks the patching fabric on the back at the same time the stitches are made. When the stuffed area is complete, turn the foundation over to the back, turn under a small seam allowance on the patches, and whipstitch it down to prevent ravelling.

If you wish to eliminate the patches on the back, cut fabric large enough to cover the central portion of the quilt where the stuffed designs are located. By starting in the center and working outward, you can use the above method, or you can revert to the original method of stuffing designs. When using this technique, all stitching is completed first. Then turn the work over to the back, and using a small bodkin, make a small hole in the areas to be stuffed. Push stuffing through the hole with the bodkin to stuff. Smooth the threads back in place when finished.

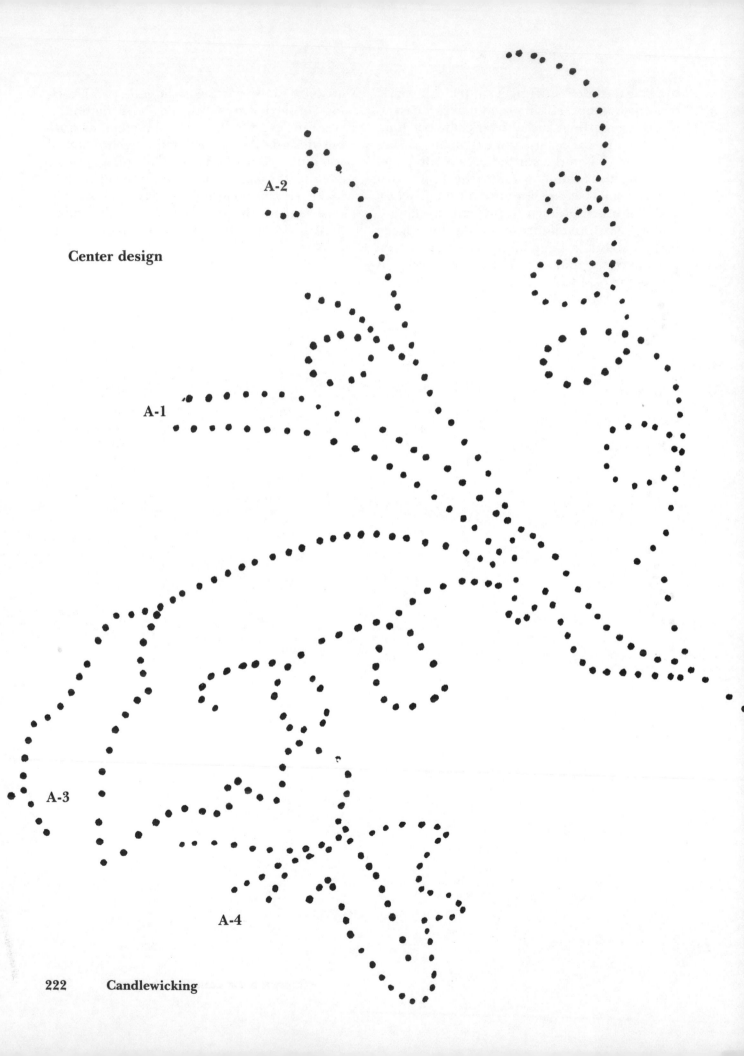

Center design

A-2

A-1

A-3

A-4

Center design

A-6

A-7

A-1

A-2

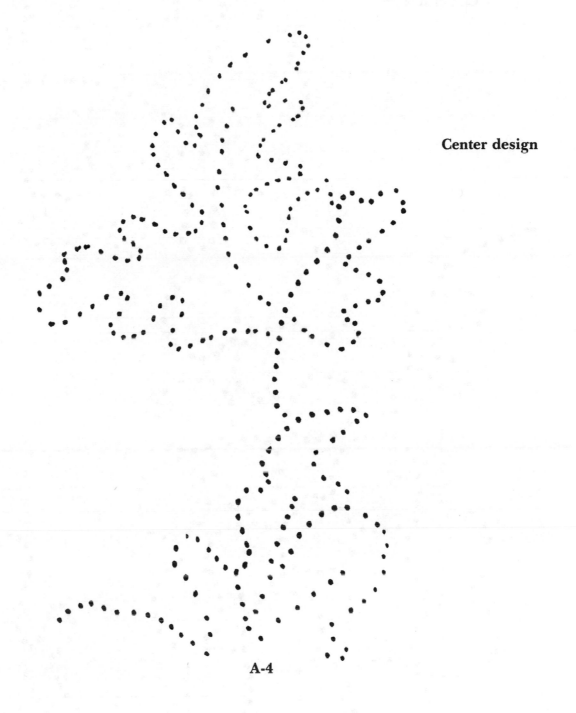

Center design

A-4

Center design

A-5

A-5

A-3

Center design

A-7

A-6

French Knot Candlewick Spread   227

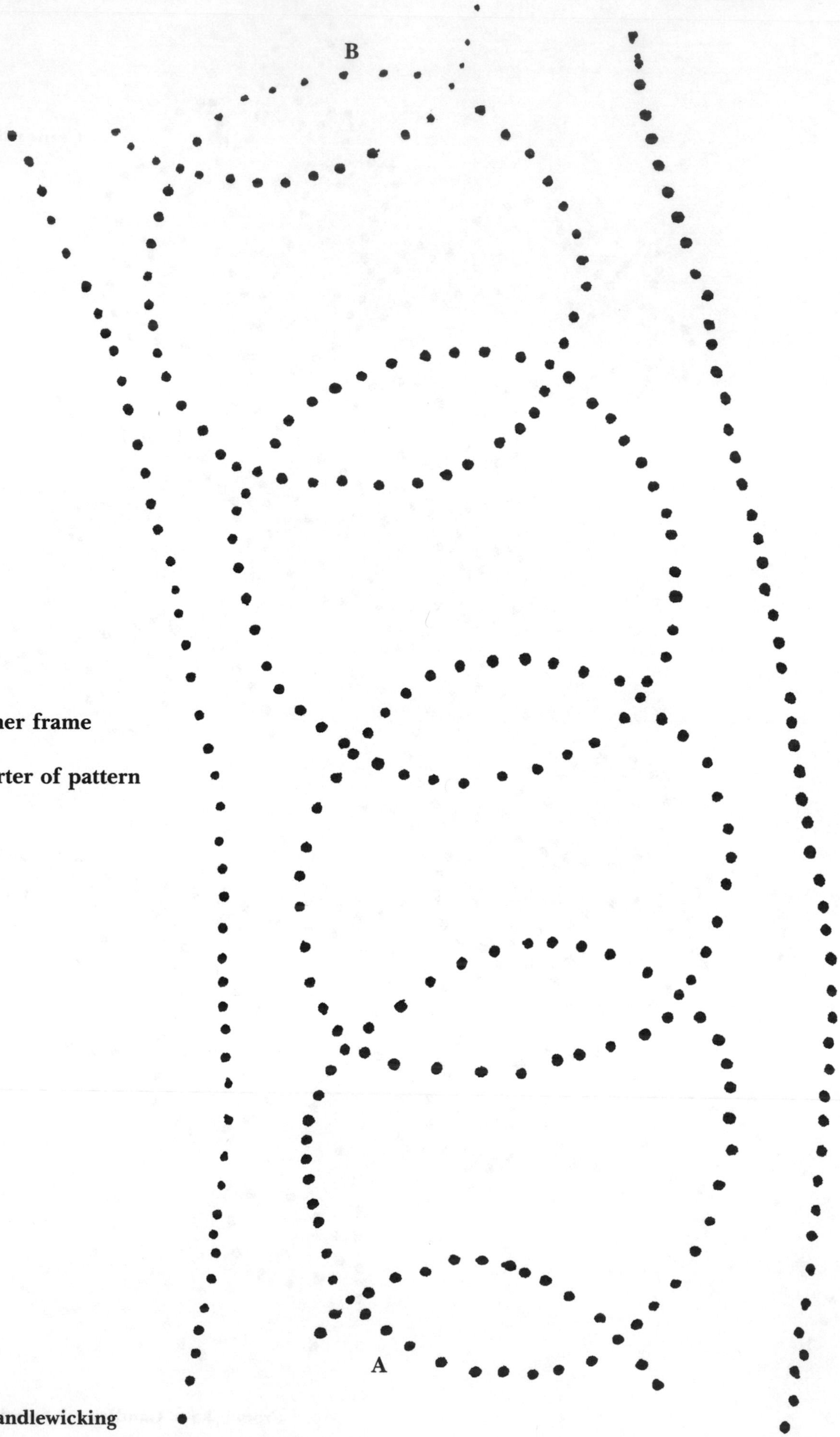

B

Inner frame

One-quarter of pattern

A

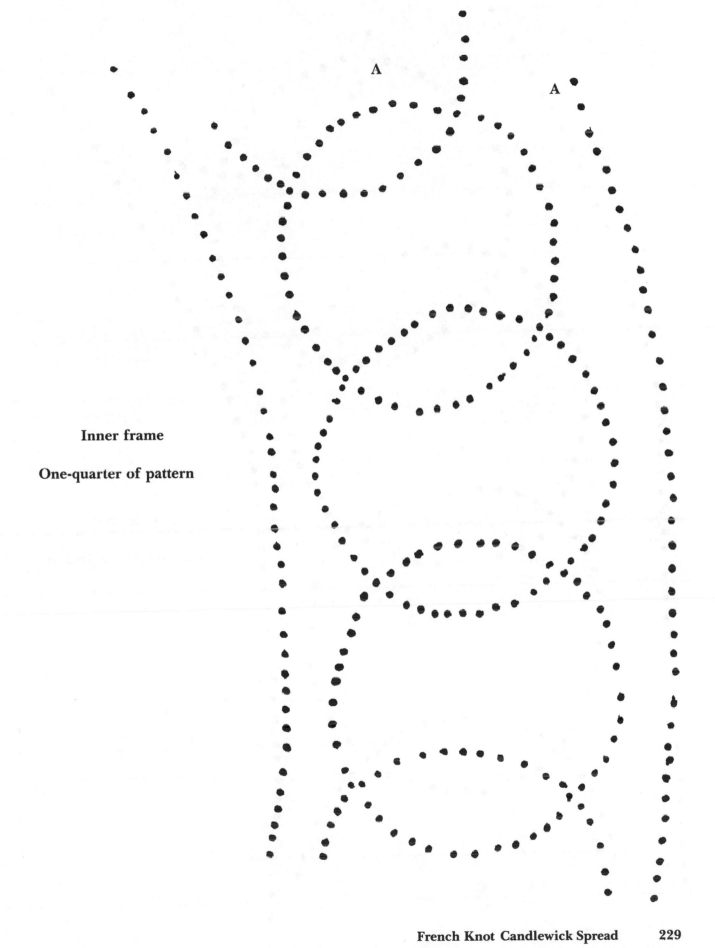

A

A

Inner frame

One-quarter of pattern

French Knot Candlewick Spread   229

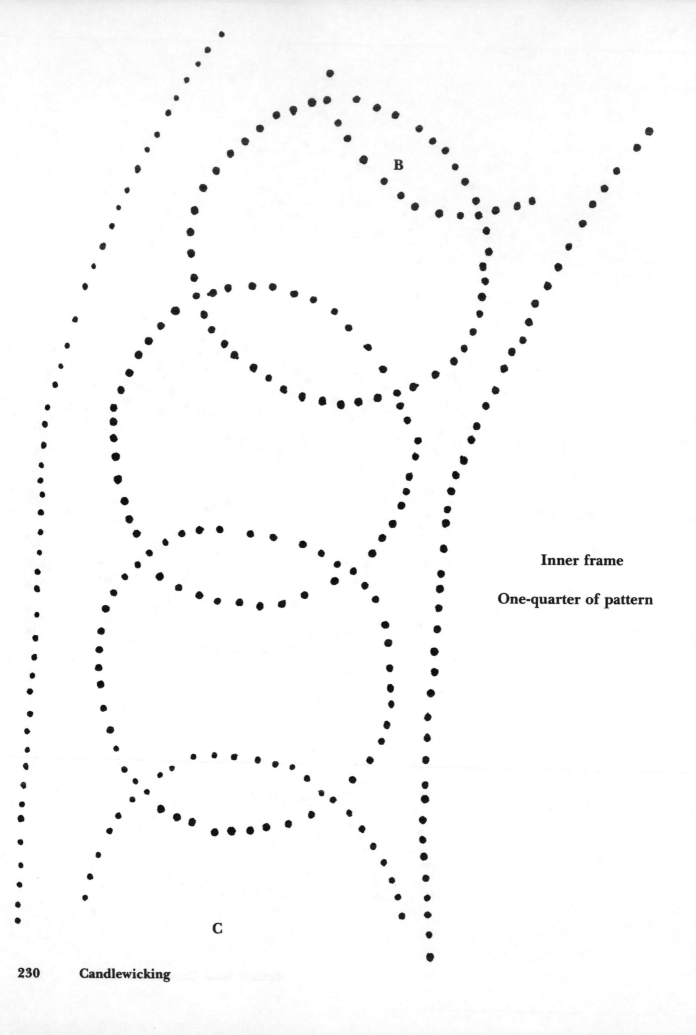

B

Inner frame

One-quarter of pattern

C

Inner frame

C

Inner and outer border

Border corner

Top and bottom borders

Side borders

French Knot Candlewick Spread   235

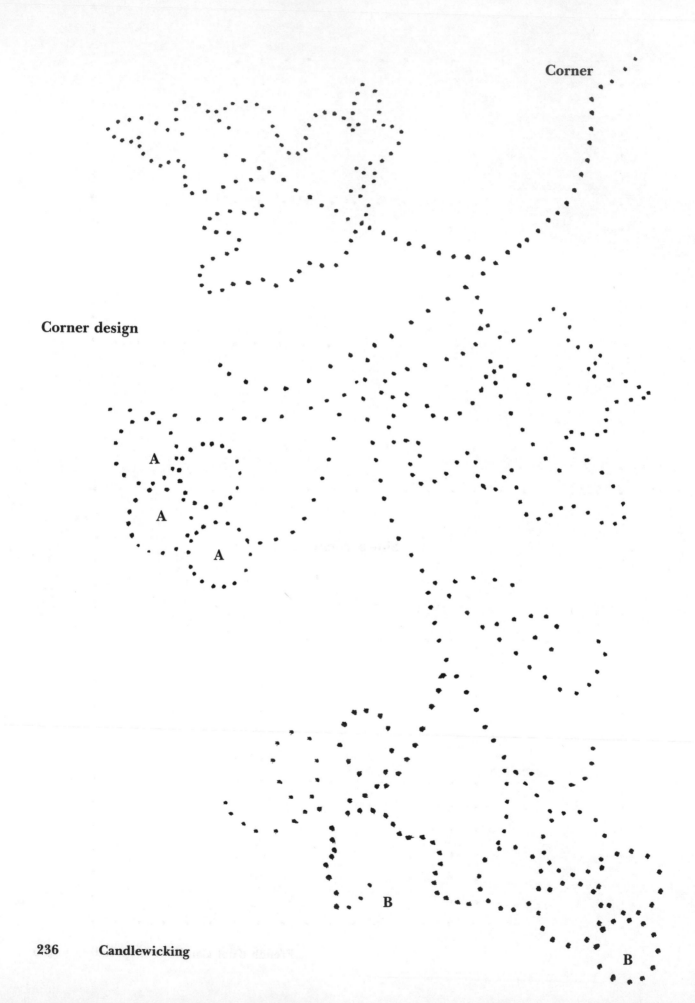

Corner

Corner design

A

A

A

B

B

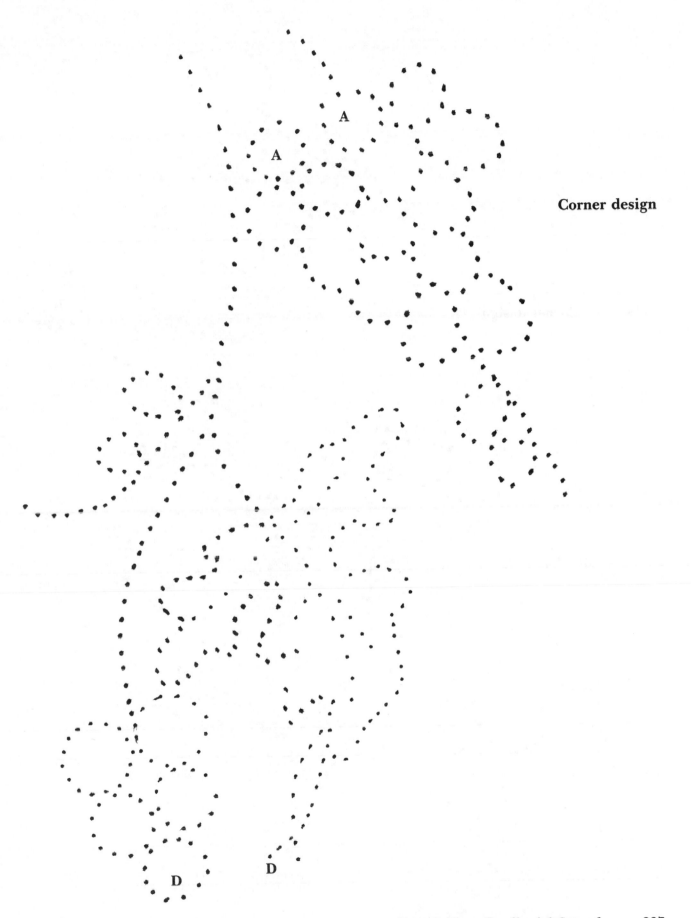

Corner design

A

A

D

D

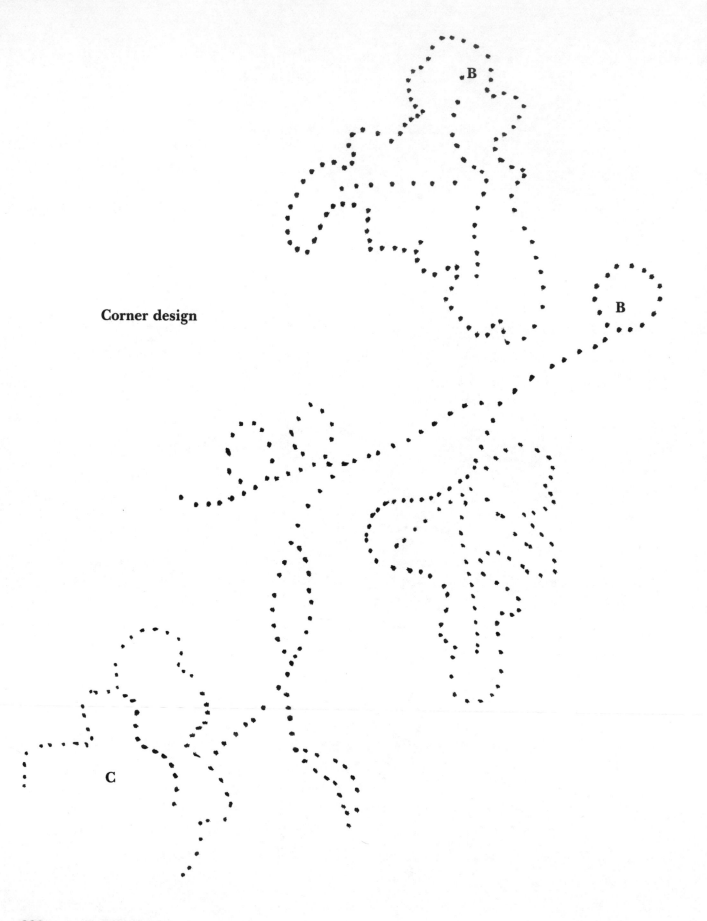

Corner design

C

D

Corner design

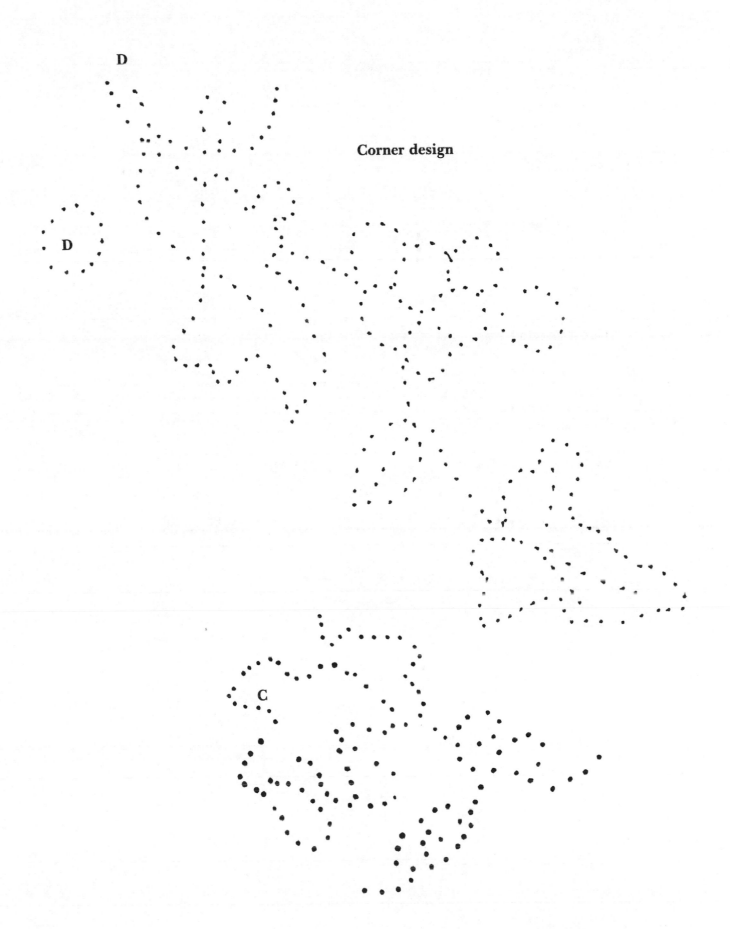

D

C

Quilting and Trapunto

The origins of quilting are not known for sure, but it was probably a very early development. As protection from the cold, two layers of fabric, quilted together, provided greater warmth than a single layer. The earliest known example of a quilted piece is a scrap of rug found in a tomb dating to about 100 B.C. Other evidence indicates that quilted cloth was used in the East and Egypt as long as 3,000 years ago. The earliest surviving examples of European origin were made in Sicily in the early 1400's.

By the early 1700's, American Colonial women of the upper classes had access to imported fabrics from Europe, and like their European relatives, took great pride in their skill with the needle. The all-quilted spread was the perfect way to show off their skills and their artistic abilities. Most all-quilted spreads were the original creations of their makers.

A shiny-surfaced fabric is desirable for an all-quilted spread, since it reflects light and shadow best, which is necessary to show off the finished design to best advantage. In the 1700's, blue glazed wool was commonly used because of its light-reflecting qualities and its ease of sewing. Linsey-woolsey and polished cotton chintz were also used.

We have many examples of the all-quilted spread in museums dating from the early 1700's through the mid-1800's, but after that they were rarely made, falling by the wayside in favor of the patchwork quilt. The elaborate quilting on Amish quilts is the closest we have come in modern times to the all-quilted spread.

A further development of the all-quilted spread came from Italy in the form of trapunto. Certain areas of the design were stuffed so that they stood in bas-relief against the background quilting.

This technique can be used to enhance any quilting pattern, and you will find examples of it throughout the book in conjunction with pieced quilts. Feather wreaths and feather borders were favorite motifs for early quilters, and they were frequently stuffed to add interest to the plain areas of a patchwork quilt. As an example, see the Sunburst with Princess Feather quilting.

The technique can also be used in appliqué work by stuffing certain areas of the appliqué to make it stand out. One example I saw was the President's Wreath pattern. The appliqué blocks were set alternately with plain blocks on which the appliqué pattern was repeated as the quilting motif. The flowers of both the appliqué and the quilted blocks were stuffed for added interest.

The original method of stuffing is to lay two layers of fabric together, no batting is used in the middle, with the design drawn on the top layer. All quilting is done through both layers. The quilt is then turned over to the back and a small hole is made in the backing fabric through which batting is stuffed to pad out the design.

When I first began experimenting with stuffed work, I didn't know that batting was not used. It was a quilt, so it had three layers; or so I thought. It seemed like awfully hard work to punch little wads of stuffing through little holes. And I didn't much like the idea of punching holes in the back of my quilt. So I experimented and developed my own methods.

The first method is for large areas of a design. Before assembling the three layers, determine which areas are to be stuffed. Cut one or two layers of batting to the shape of the design and baste to the back of the top. Then assemble the three layers together and quilt as you normally would. The extra layers will stand above the other areas of quilting. Be careful not to use so many layers that the cloth will distort.

For small areas, I stuff as I stitch. This method can't be used if you use a quilting frame, because the edges of the quilt are fastened down and you can't get under the top layer.

In fact, when doing small areas of stuffed work, I recommend not using a frame at all. Begin your quilting in the center and work towards the edges so that the edges are always free. When you come to a small area to be stuffed, stitch three-quarters of the way around the design. Then lift the top and push stuffing into the stitched area, smoothing it out to fill the whole design. Again, don't overdo the stuffing and distort the fabric. Now finish stitching around the design area.

For straight lines that are to be stuffed, quilt along two parallel lines to form a channel. Thread cord of the appropriate size through the channel.

From the Smithsonian Institution

Quilted Counterpane

This all-quilted spread was made by Esther Wheat of Conway, Massachusetts, in the late 1700's. The quilt measures 91″ × 93″ and is made of indigo blue glazed wool, with a wool filling and wool lining.

The quilting is very elaborate and uses a variety of different feather designs. In this case,

it would be best for you to make a pattern sheet for the whole quilt, rather than just for sections of the quilt. Use the photograph as a reference for placement of the various elements. Trace the patterns, matching the reference numbers for adjoining parts and the overlap for proper placement.

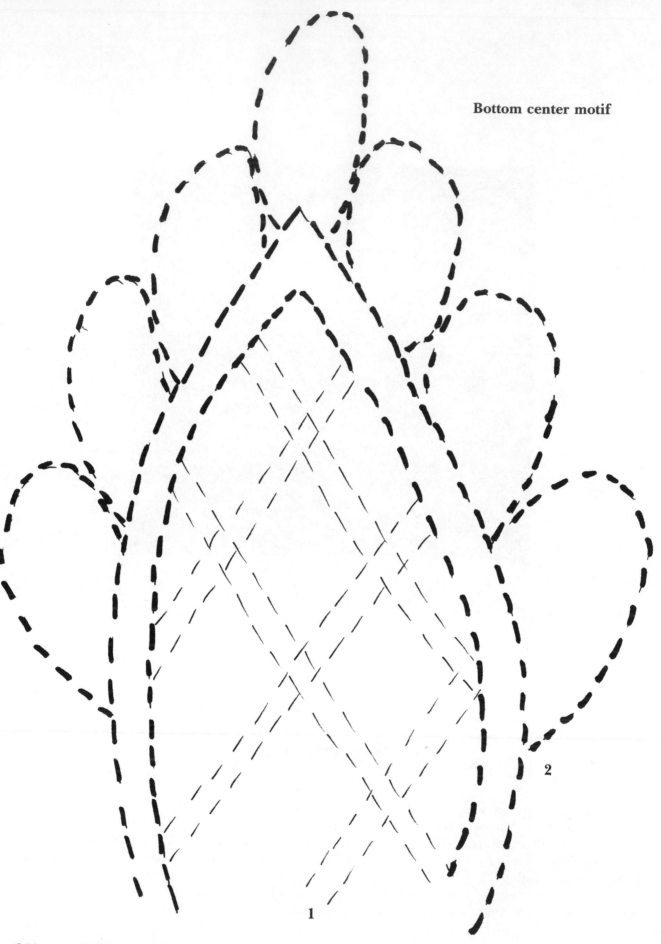

Bottom center motif

1

2

Bottom center motif

Bottom center motif

Bottom center motif

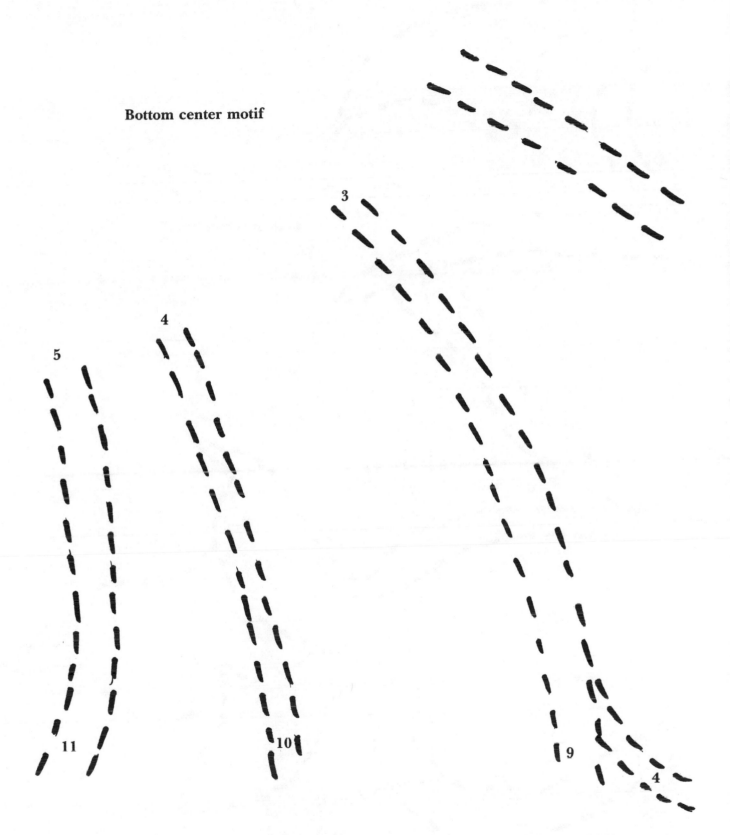

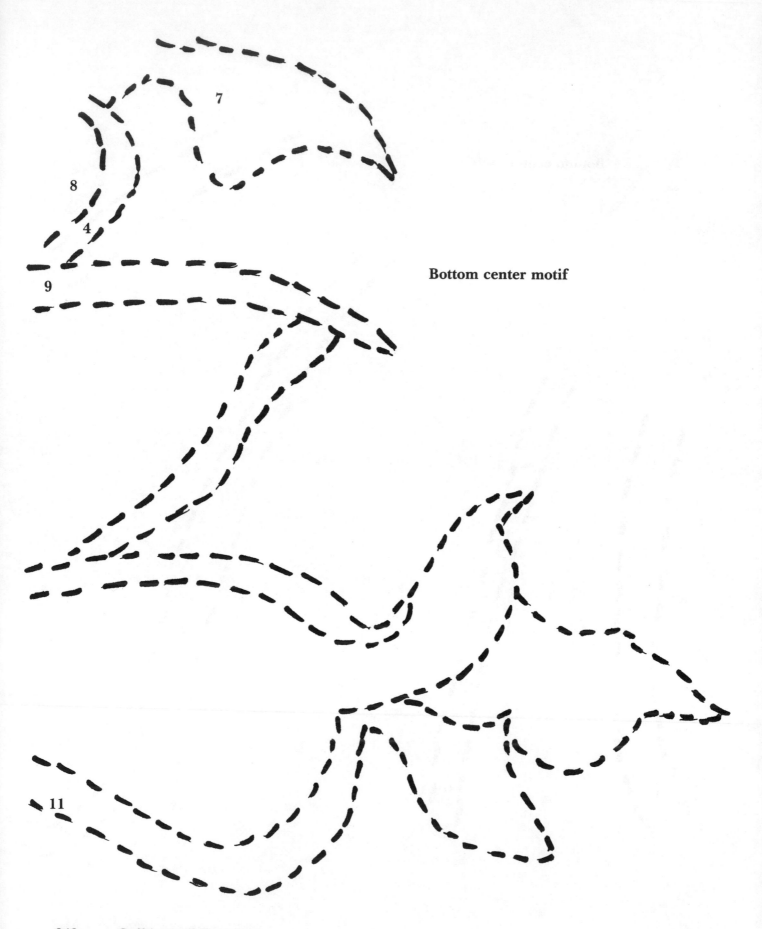

7

8

4

9

Bottom center motif

11

Bottom center motif

Turn completed pattern over
and trace again for
opposite side

2

2

6

8

12

**Flower motif for bottom,
encircled by feather spray**

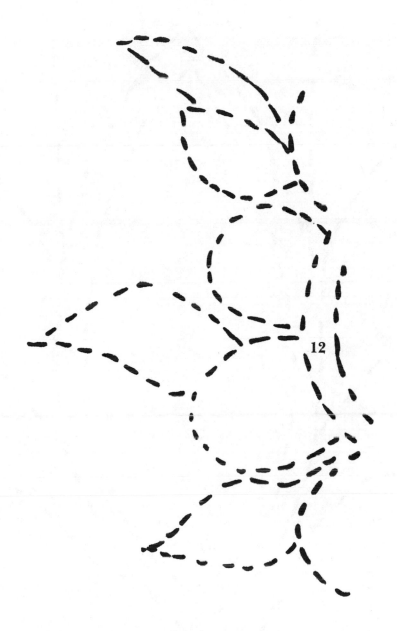

12

Feather spray, center bottom

13

13

Quilting and Trapunto

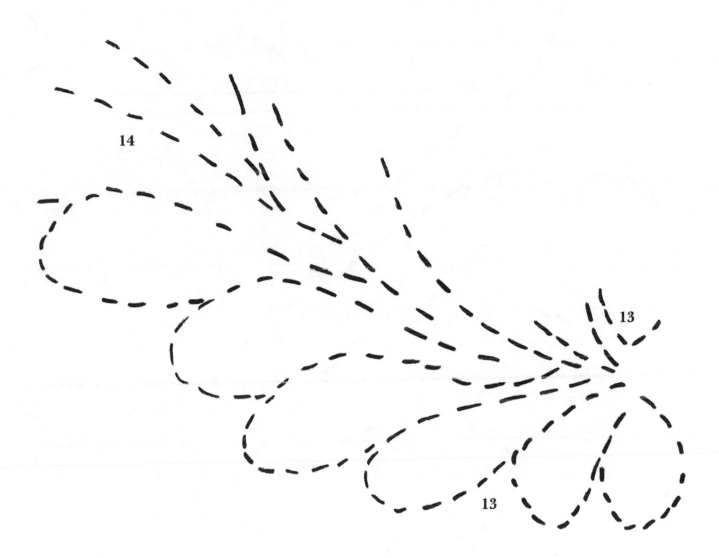

14

13

13

Feather spray, center bottom

Feather spray, center bottom

15

14

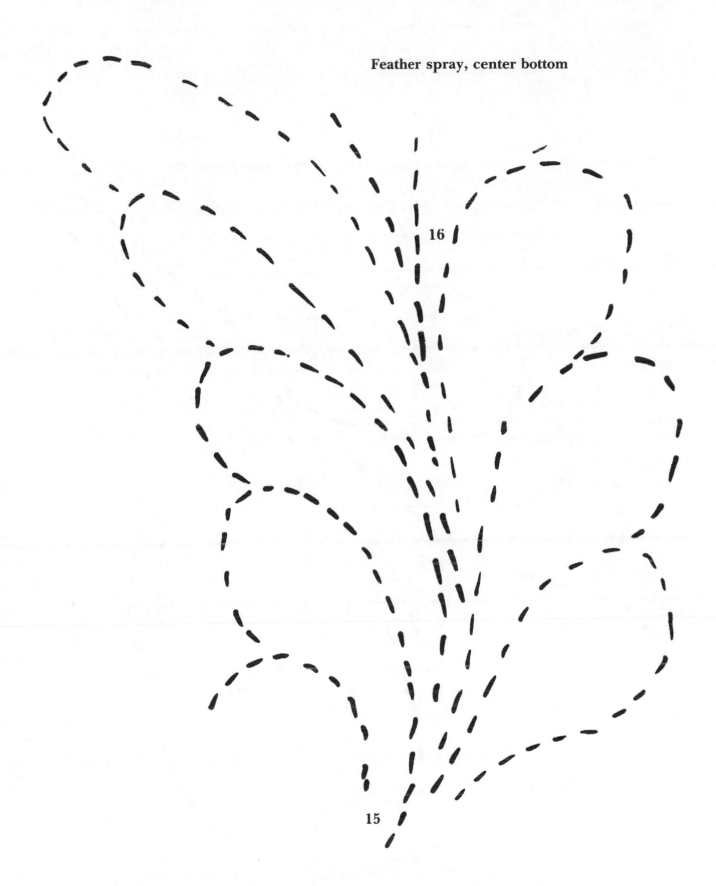

Feather spray, center bottom

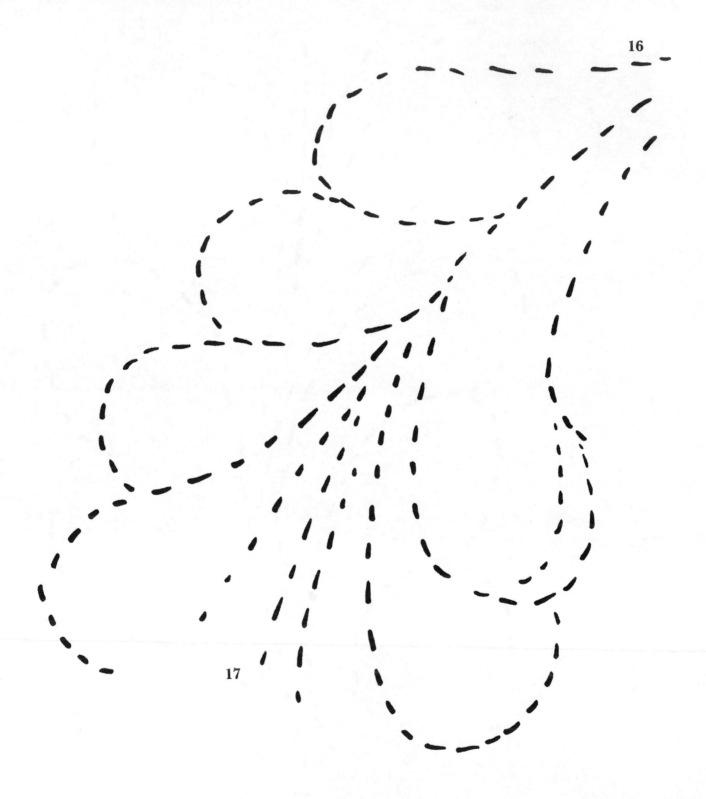

16

17

Feather spray, center bottom

18

18

**Feather spray,
center bottom**

17

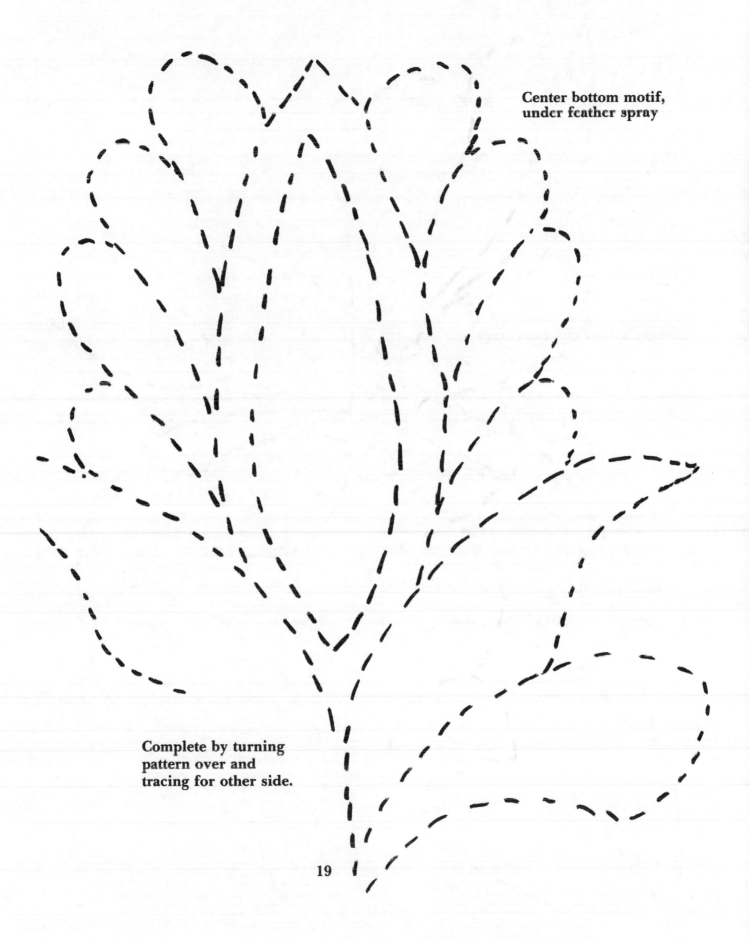

Center bottom motif,
under feather spray

Complete by turning
pattern over and
tracing for other side.

19

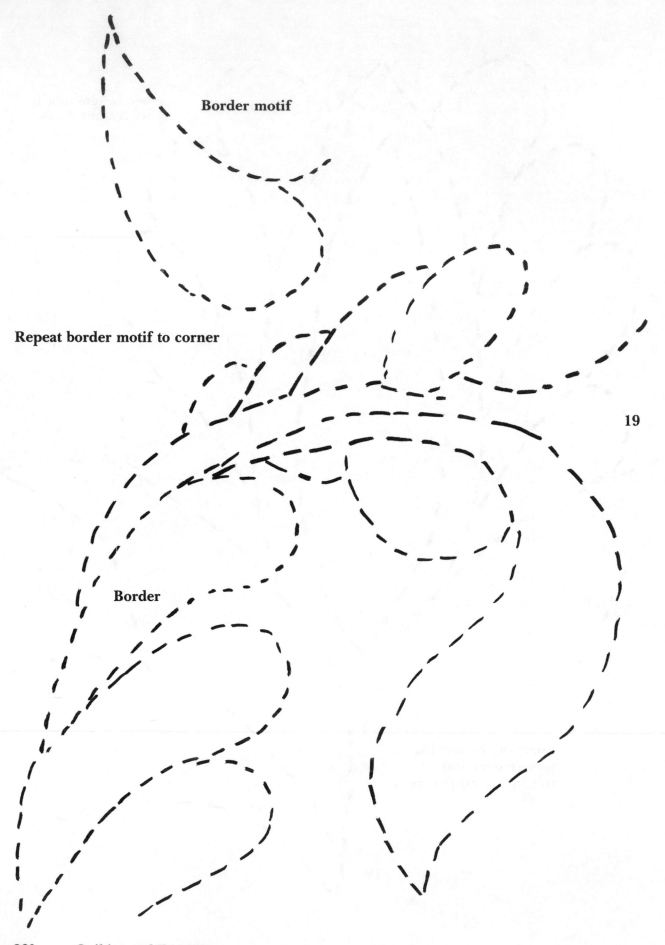

Border motif

Repeat border motif to corner

19

Border

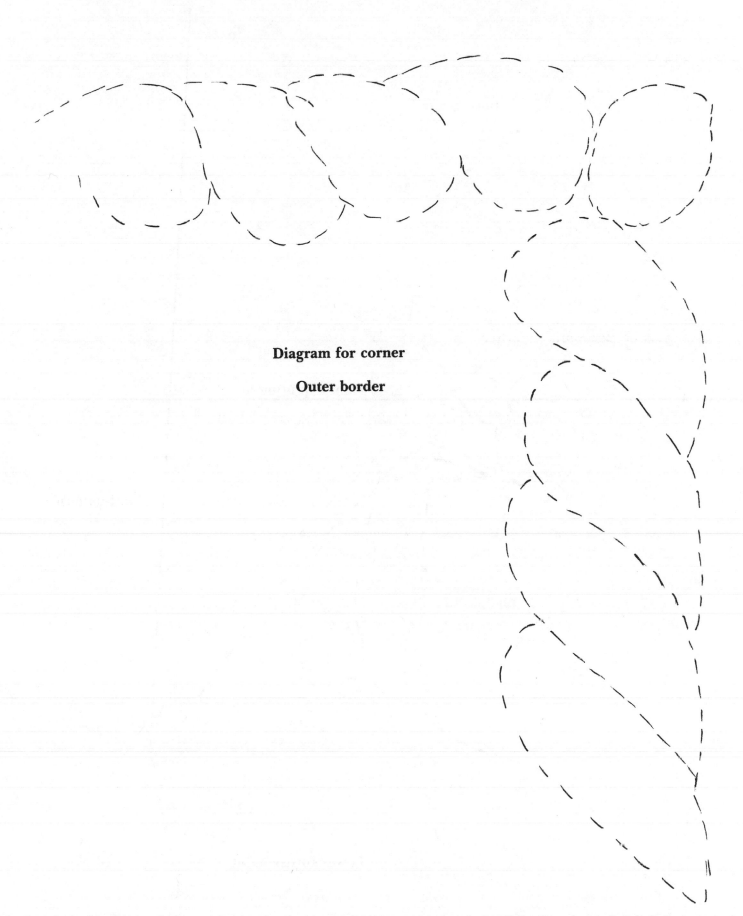

Diagram for corner

Outer border

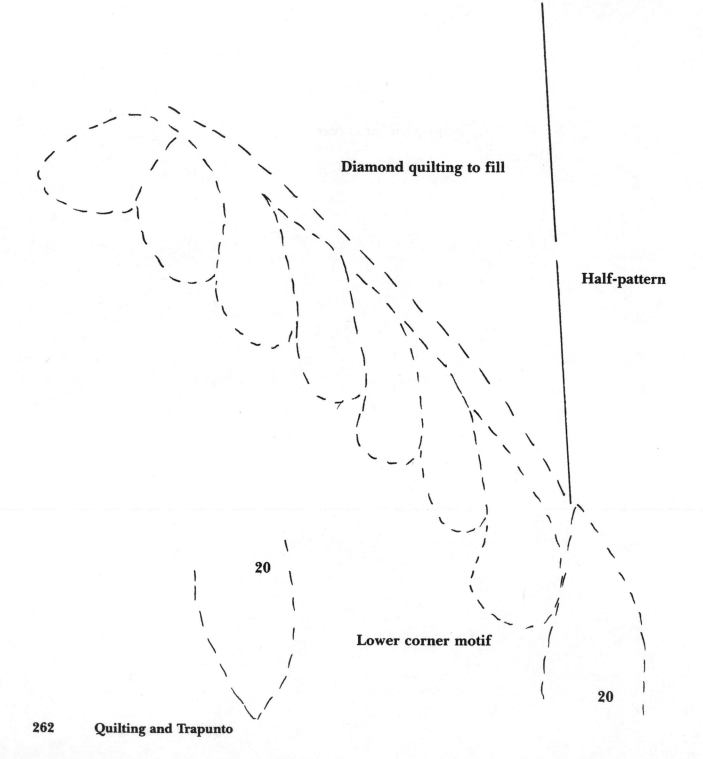

21

Diamond quilting to fill

Half-pattern

20

Lower corner motif

20

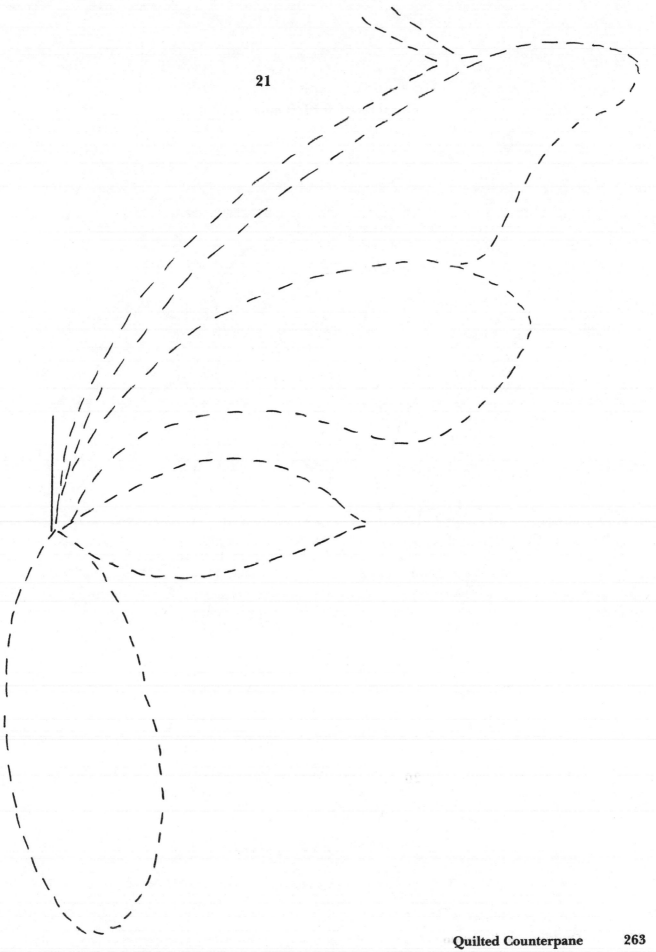

21

22

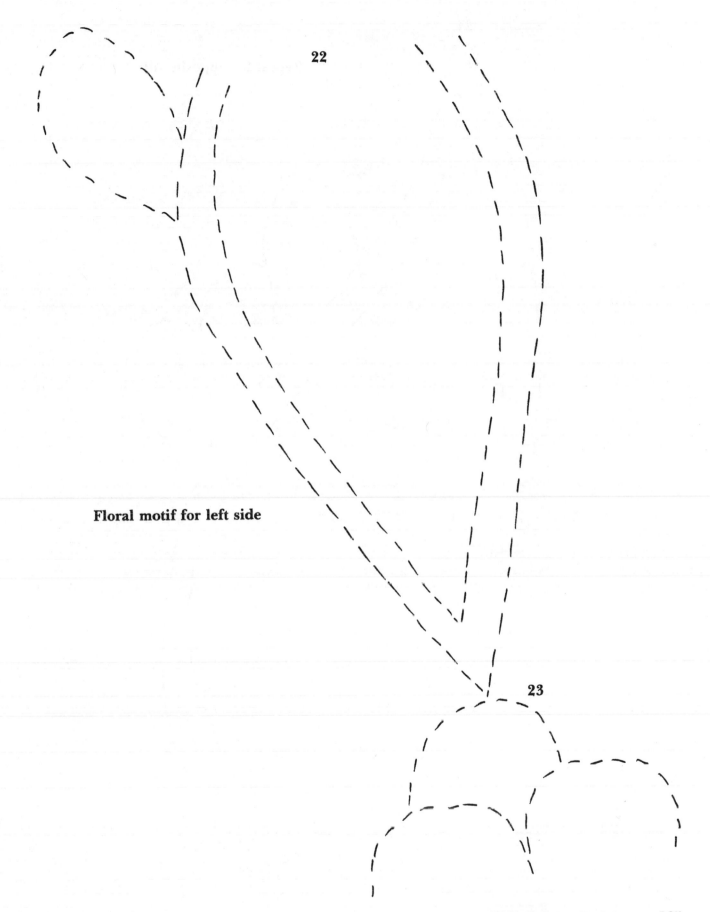

22

Floral motif for left side

23

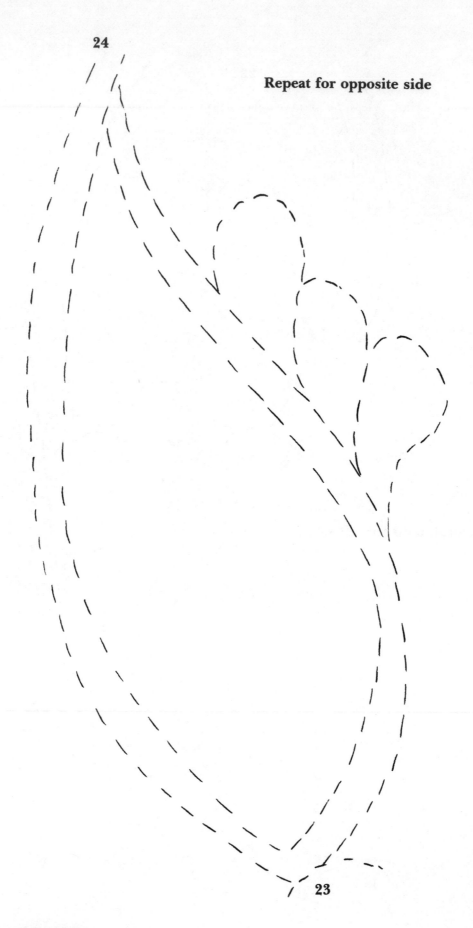

24

Repeat for opposite side

23

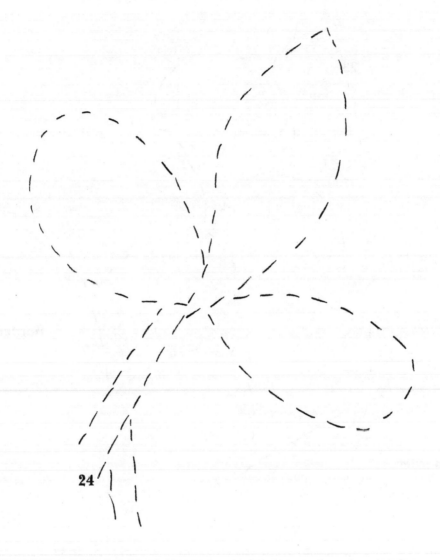

24

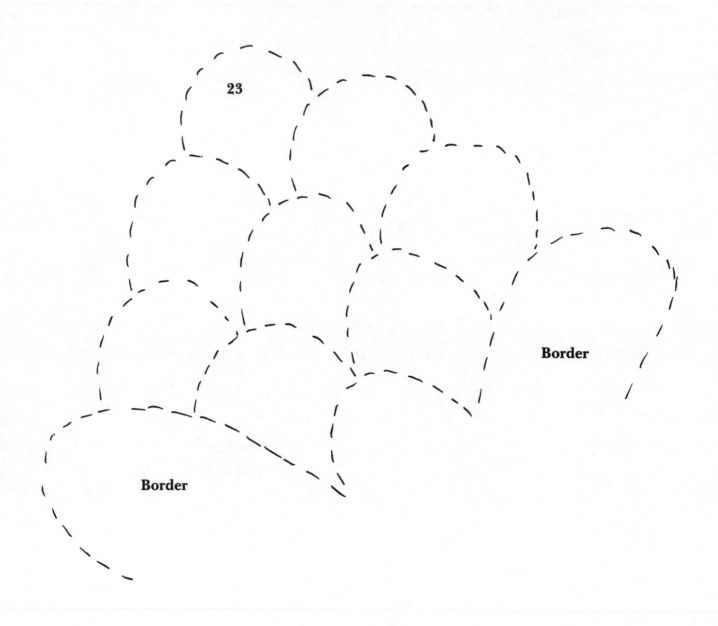

23

Border

Border

25

25

Floral motif, left side
End of feather vine

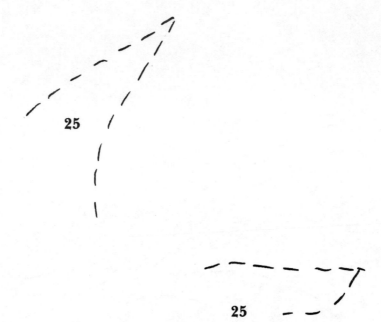

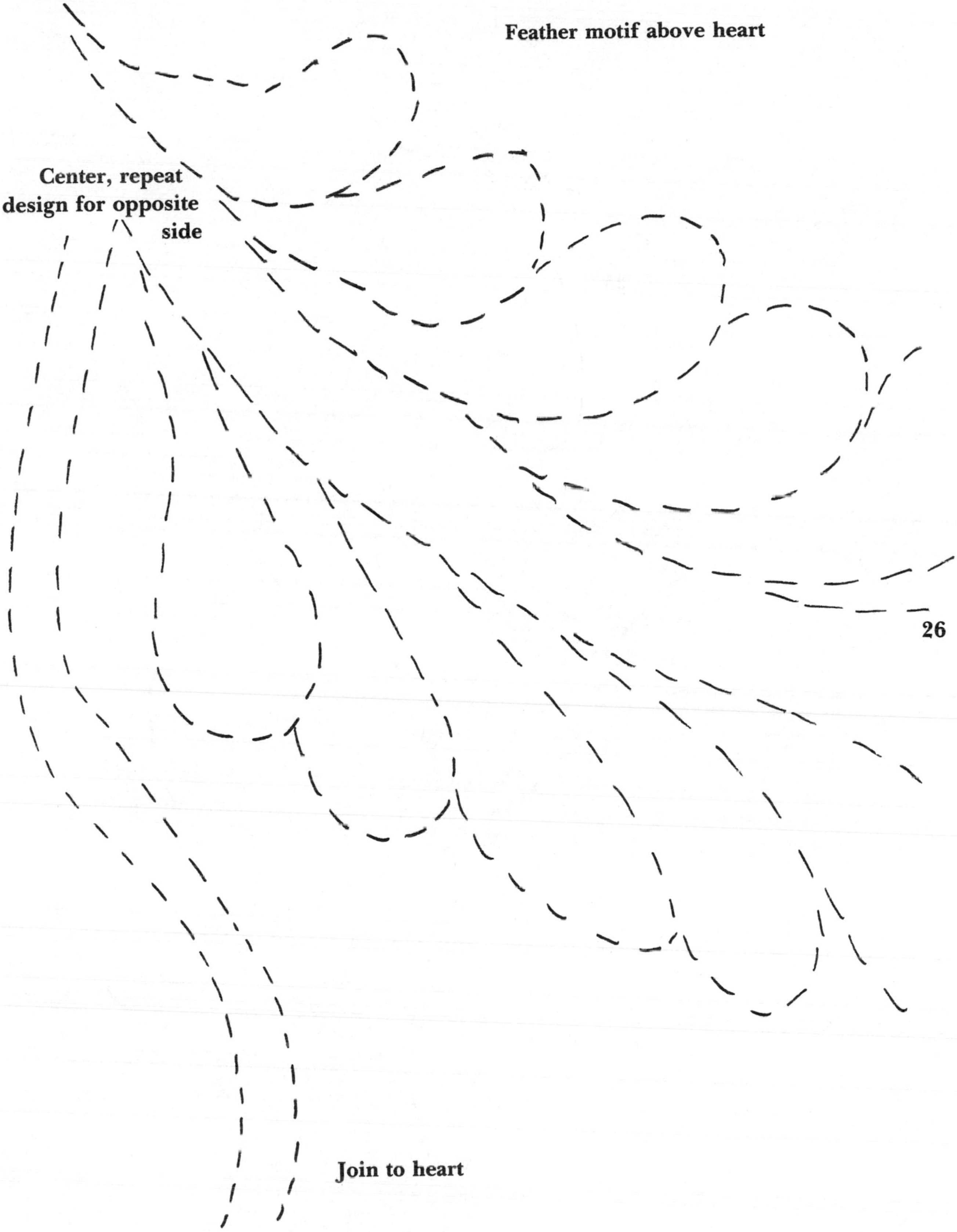

Feather motif above heart

Center, repeat
design for opposite
side

26

Join to heart

26

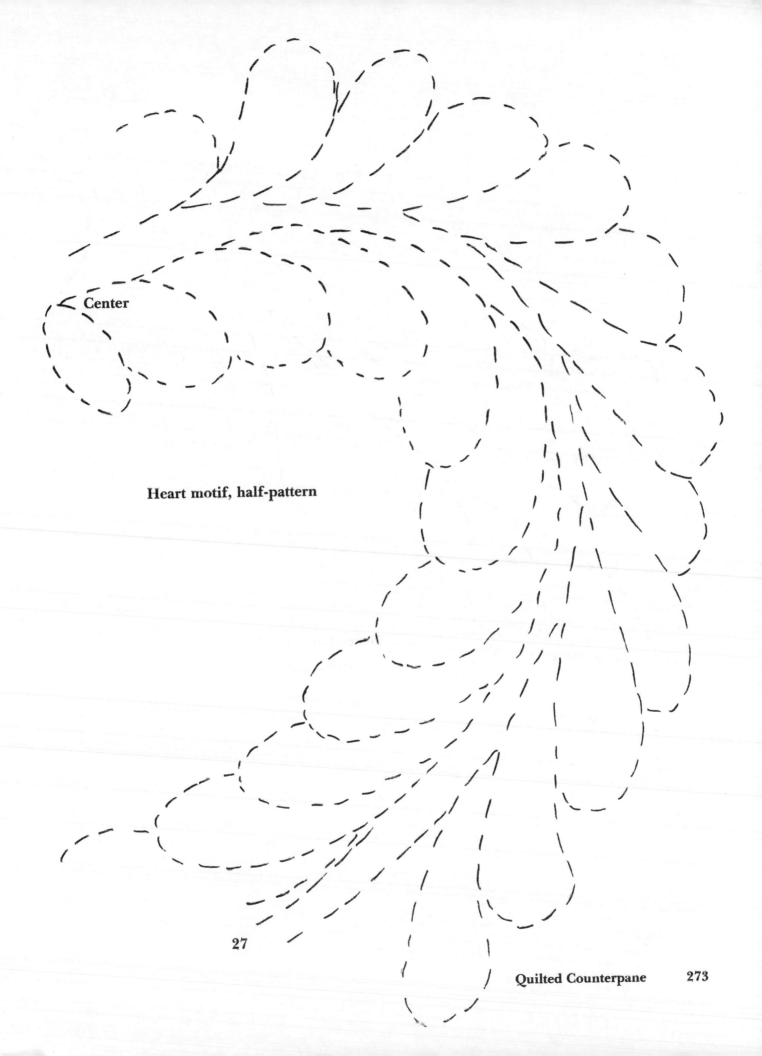

Center

Heart motif, half-pattern

27

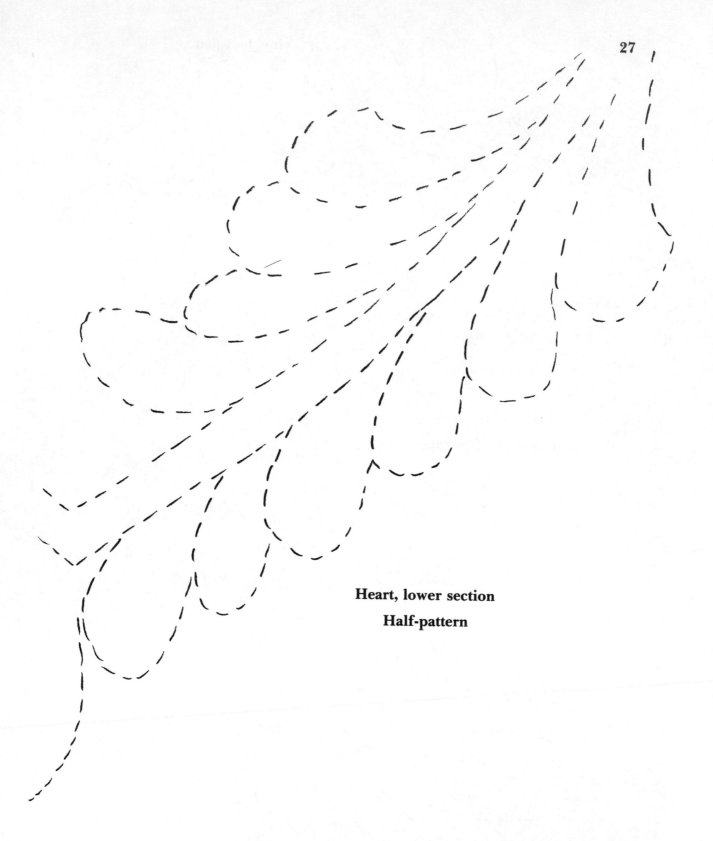

Heart, lower section

Half-pattern

Feather vine, half-pattern

Floral motif

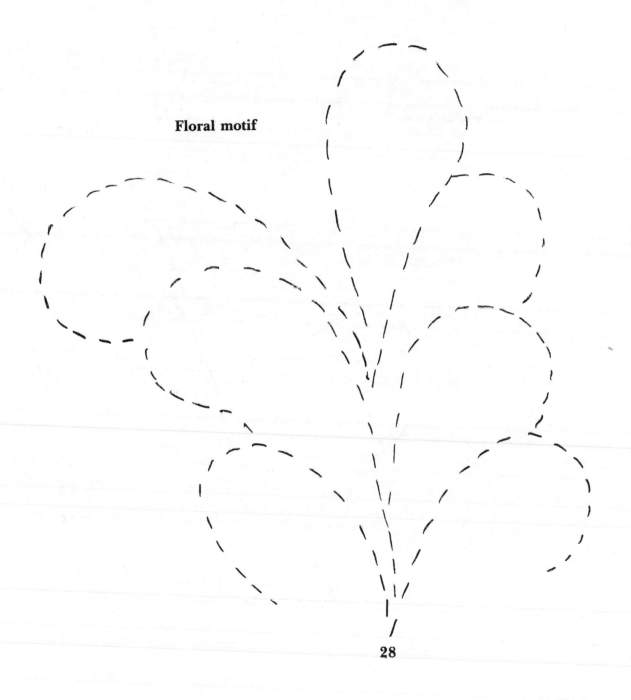

28

Feather vine

28

29

29

Feather vine

30

30

Feather vine

31

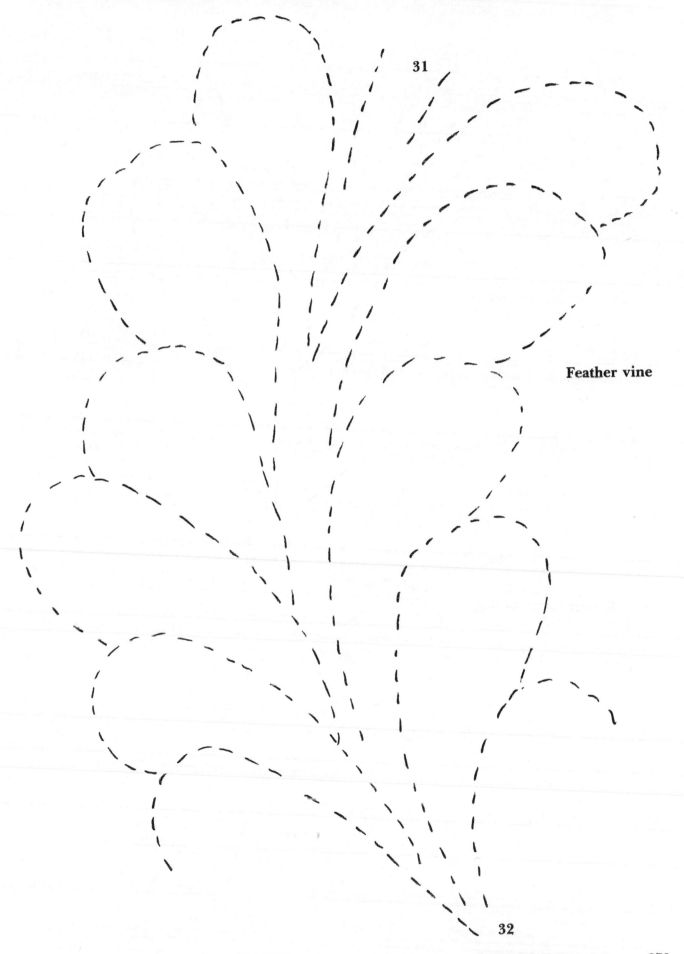

31

Feather vine

32

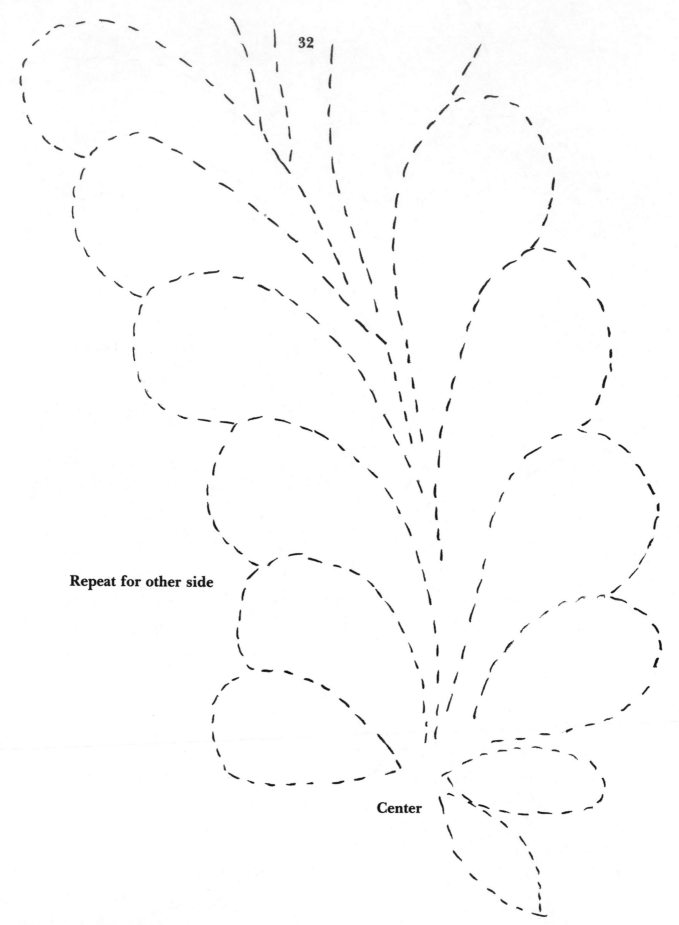

32

Repeat for other side

Center

**Floral motif for end
of feather vine**

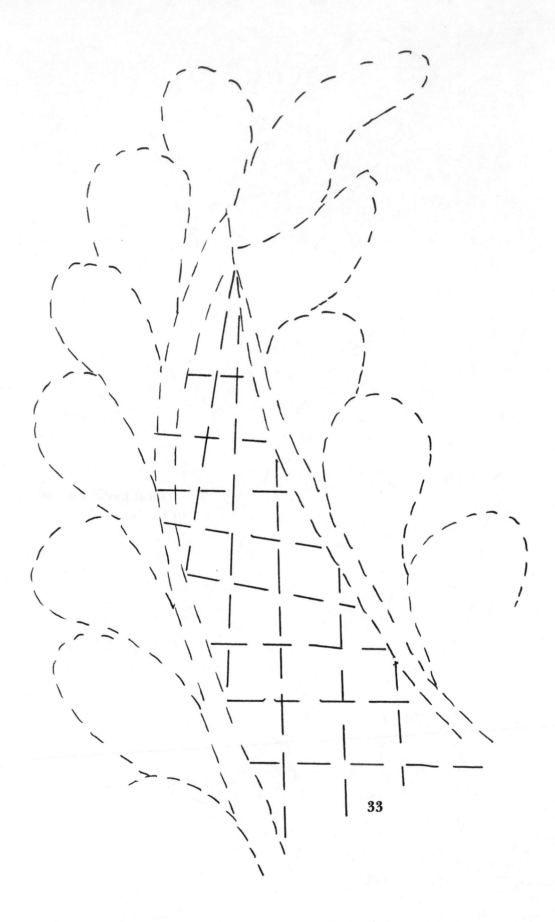

33

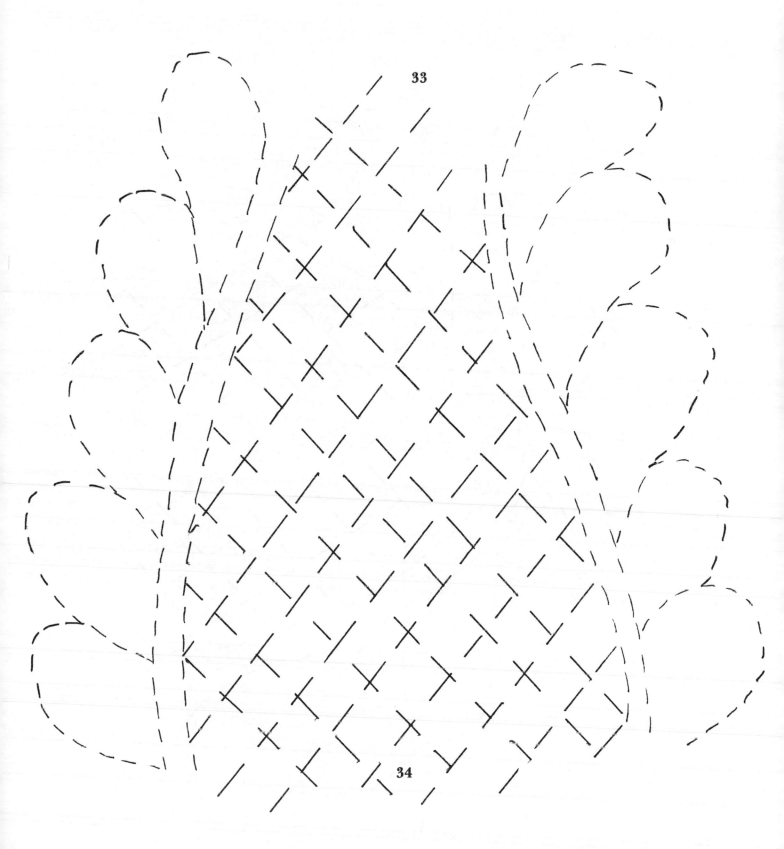

33

34

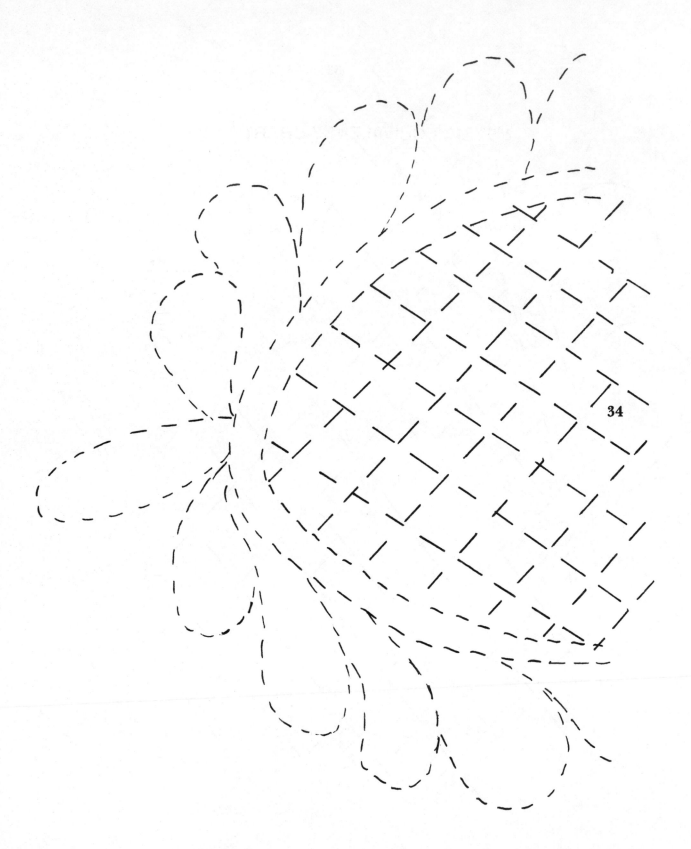

34

METRIC EQUIVALENCY CHART

MM—MILLIMETRES   CM—CENTIMETRES

INCHES TO MILLIMETRES AND CENTIMETRES

INCHES	MM	CM	INCHES	CM	INCHES	CM
⅛	3	0.3	9	22.9	30	76.2
¼	6	0.6	10	25.4	31	78.7
⅜	10	1.0	11	27.9	32	81.3
½	13	1.3	12	30.5	33	83.8
⅝	16	1.6	13	33.0	34	86.4
¾	19	1.9	14	35.6	35	88.9
⅞	22	2.2	15	38.1	36	91.4
1	25	2.5	16	40.6	37	94.0
1¼	32	3.2	17	43.2	38	96.5
1½	38	3.8	18	45.7	39	99.1
1¾	44	4.4	19	48.3	40	101.6
2	51	5.1	20	50.8	41	104.1
2½	64	6.4	21	53.3	42	106.7
3	76	7.6	22	55.9	43	109.2
3½	89	8.9	23	58.4	44	111.8
4	102	10.2	24	61.0	45	114.3
4½	114	11.4	25	63.5	46	116.8
5	127	12.7	26	66.0	47	119.4
6	152	15.2	27	68.6	48	121.9
7	178	17.8	28	71.1	49	124.5
8	203	20.3	29	73.7	50	127.0

YARDS TO METRES

YARDS	METRES	YARDS	METRES	YARDS	METRES	YARDS	METRES	YARDS	METRES
⅛	0.11	2⅛	1.94	4⅛	3.77	6⅛	5.60	8⅛	7.43
¼	0.23	2¼	2.06	4¼	3.89	6¼	5.72	8¼	7.54
⅜	0.34	2⅜	2.17	4⅜	4.00	6⅜	5.83	8⅜	7.66
½	0.46	2½	2.29	4½	4.11	6½	5.94	8½	7.77
⅝	0.57	2⅝	2.40	4⅝	4.23	6⅝	6.06	8⅝	7.89
¾	0.69	2¾	2.51	4¾	4.34	6¾	6.17	8¾	8.00
⅞	0.80	2⅞	2.63	4⅞	4.46	6⅞	6.29	8⅞	8.12
1	0.91	3	2.74	5	4.57	7	6.40	9	8.23
1⅛	1.03	3⅛	2.86	5⅛	4.69	7⅛	6.52	9⅛	8.34
1¼	1.14	3¼	2.97	5¼	4.80	7¼	6.63	9¼	8.46
1⅜	1.26	3⅜	3.09	5⅜	4.91	7⅜	6.74	9⅜	8.57
1½	1.37	3½	3.20	5½	5.03	7½	6.86	9½	8.69
1⅝	1.49	3⅝	3.31	5⅝	5.14	7⅝	6.97	9⅝	8.80
1¾	1.60	3¾	3.43	5¾	5.26	7¾	7.09	9¾	8.92
1⅞	1.71	3⅞	3.54	5⅞	5.37	7⅞	7.20	9⅞	9.03
2	1.83	4	3.66	6	5.49	8	7.32	10	9.14

Index